# LINUX FOR
# HACKERS

*3 Books in 1 – The #1 Hacking Course from Beginner to Advanced. Learn it Well & Fast.*

# TABLE OF CONTENTS

## LINUX: The Ultimate Beginner's Guide to Learning Linux Command Line Fast, with No Prior Experience

# LINUS: The #1 Crash Course For Beginners To Master Linux Operating System Quickly, With No Prior Experience

# LINUX FOR HACKERS: Unlocking Advanced Techniques

## in Hacking with Kali Linux

# LINUX

*The Ultimate Beginner's Guide to Learning Linux*

*Command Line Fast, with No Prior Experience*

## Mark Reed & CyberEdge Press

# INTRODUCTION

Linux is an open-source operating system developed and maintained by thousands of developers from all over the world. The Linux operating system is an alternative to commercialized operating systems such as Windows and Mac OS X. Despite the great design and third-party applications provided by both Windows and Mac to their user base, they still control what their users can do. Microsoft, for example, decides what firewall you should be using as a user, and Apple, despite providing high-grade hardware to its users, still restricts them from using third-party apps such as virtualization software, emulators, and graphic applications. On the other hand, Linux offers complete freedom to its users with its extensive code base that consists of over one million lines of code. Linux codebase is one of the most important contributions to open source software development.

Linux is an ambitious project with a large user base that is enthusiastic about computers. Although most Linux users are tech enthusiasts and people directly working in computer science fields, it can also be a tremendous day-to-day operating system for regular users, businesses, scientists, and gamers alike. For beginners and experienced system administrators who use Linux exclusively every day, this book provides information about Linux and its components in a simple, easy-to-understand way.

# Impact of Computers

We have changed the world by using computers because they offer us convenience, power, and simplicity. In the early days of computer innovation, we communicated with computers using complicated electronic devices such as punch cards and microprocessors. However, with time, programmers have found ways to make it easier for end-users to customize their computers to meet their wants and needs. With decades of technological and scientific progress, in 2021, we can now communicate with computers from a smartwatch to a telecommunications satellite that revolves around our planet in split seconds.

Operating systems have enabled humans to communicate with computers, allowing our technological expertise to advance rapidly. Operating systems provide end-users with a graphical user interface that will enable them to communicate with the computer's processor through an output device, such as a keyboard, mouse, or the hand we use for touch devices. Operating systems translate our instructions into machine language almost instantly, so the computers can understand them and return their results. Linux is one of these operating systems with a considerable demand in the IT industry and is required to run more than 90% of servers and high-level supercomputers with complex networking architecture.

Currently, Windows and Mac OS are among the most popular desktop operating systems worldwide, occupying a staggering 90% of the market. Linux accounts for only 10% of the market, but its rapid adoption by tech enthusiasts and programmers makes it an influential platform in the computer world. Aside from being one of the most popular operating systems in the public cloud, Linux is almost the best operating system for individuals wishing to make a career in the tech industry. Multinational companies such as Apple, Netflix, Amazon, and Facebook use Linux to secure and maintain their infrastructure.

This book aims to provide concise and clear information about Linux to help both novices and experienced programmers learn Linux and use it effectively.

# Linux and Its History

Linux began as a hobby project by its creator, Linus Torvalds, back in 1991. It has now grown to be one of the most significant open-source projects in the world. Linus Torvalds was a student at the University of Helsinki, and he was fascinated by systems programming. At first, he experimented with a few programming languages. Later, he began working on the Linux Kernel, which became the basis for hundreds of Linux distributions created by various open source communities. In addition to desktop operating systems, Linux is also compatible with embedded systems such as Aurdino, routers, televisions, and automobiles such as Tesla. Linux is also the basis for Android, the most popular mobile operating system today.

Linux Distros, like Debian, Arch, and Red Hat, are popular Linux packages that use the Linux kernel to develop their own operating systems. Linux code and software are all open source, so a novice can quickly learn how they are written and maintained by visiting their online repositories. There is no restriction on people using Linux and its repositories to make commercialized software. However, it is important that a freeware version of the Linux distro is made available for enthusiasts as a gesture to the community. For example, you can easily download Red Hat Linux into your local system, however if you want to install it on a dedicated server, then it is important that you have a working license for it.

# Why Was This Book Written?

To understand Linux and its advanced features, you must have sufficient networking, programming, and systems engineering knowledge. Many books on the market assume you are proficient in these three areas, making it very difficult for beginners with no experience to master Linux. This book is different from all those traditional books as it focuses on delivering the required information so that a beginner can understand it. Several real-life examples and scenarios are provided with layman explanations to help readers consume the data effectively.

Following these three rules will help you make sense of most of the information provided in this book:

1. Create Mind Maps or Short Snippets

Draw a mind map whenever you learn a new concept. You can use mind maps to learn new ideas in an engaging way.

2. Use the Passive Recall Method

You should remember the core concepts in a chapter or a section in your own words whenever you complete that section. You can gain a deeper understanding of the basics by passive recall. In addition, it is recommended to teach those concepts to someone unfamiliar with the subject. Explaining concepts to someone unfamiliar with the subject can strengthen your foundation. The famous scientist Richard Feynman has mentioned it several times to master any topic effortlessly.

3. Code Yourself

To learn any subject or a new skill, you have to do it on your own. Is it possible to learn guitar by watching videos on YouTube rather than playing it? In short, no. The same holds true for programming or anything related to computers. It would be best if you got your hands on it before you can comprehend it. Start playing with Linux on your desktop or laptop based on the inputs provided in this book. There is no other method of learning about Linux effectively.

Please answer these questions in your notebook or using a text editor before diving into the world of Linux. Look at them only after you finish the book. These questions can serve as a reflection on what you have learned from the book:

- What is your favorite operating system and why?

- Why are you hooked on Linux?

- Have you ever tried any Linux distro?

- What are you hoping to achieve by the end of this book?

- Are you aware of basic networking concepts?

- Did you ever have any experience working with terminals?

- Web vs. Desktop programming? What will you choose from both of these?

- Why do you think Linux can be an excellent fit for your requirements?

- Will you be able to adapt to the Linux ecosystem for your daily use completely?

- Why do you feel Linux is a better operating system than Windows and Mac OS?

If you are learning Linux, don't worry about these questions. You'll get the hang of it by the end of the book. Before embarking on your new Linux journey, I want to tell you that as a programmer with more than ten years of experience, programming is not easy and can be highly frustrating at times. Most of the time, you will be clearing errors caused by simple errors. However, all your frustration and disappointment will disappear once you see your final product. To be a great Linux sysadmin or programmer, you need to be curious about what is happening in the background and find ways to handle any problems. You need to look for hints, so begin now!

# CHAPTER 1

## Introduction to Linux

By popularizing open-source software and technology, Linux made an important contribution to the computer world. Starting as a pet project in 1991, it has spread to almost every area of computing since then. Linux is used by everybody from multinational companies to high school students creating silly Arduino projects. In today's world, Linux has become a critical component of the internet and many of its applications.

In spite of Linux's popularity in the technological sphere, it is still difficult for a novice to grasp its basics quickly. Windows and macOS, the other two most popular operating systems globally, occupy more than 90% of computers as the default operating systems. It is mainly due to people's inability to comprehend Linux's capabilities that it is not used as a daily driver. With the introduction of user-friendly operating systems such as Manjaro, Linux Mint, and SUSE Linux in the past few years, Linux has been gaining users rapidly.

For both newcomers and experienced programmers, learning about Linux's philosophy and how it is maintained can be an eye-opening experience.

# What Is Linux?

Linux is an open-source operating system that provides its users with efficiency and excellence. Unlike Windows or macOS, it makes it easy for users to communicate with computer hardware as well as embedded systems, such as databases and servers. Linux has a special component known as the kernel that processes all instructions. The Linux ecosystem relies on software built around the kernel, and therefore it has become a vital component.

Although Linux provides many additional advantages for system administrators and technology enthusiasts, it is also important to know what similar features it has to Windows and macOS.

# Characteristics of Linux

1. **It Can Detect any Hardware**

   Linux is designed so it can understand even before booting what hardware it's being asked to run on. Linux system kernels analyze different hardware components such as RAM, GPU, Sound card, Trackpad, Keyboard, Processor, and motherboard to provide the best possible user experience. Open-source developers who maintain Linux repositories have written and will be writing code for supporting different processors. The process of detecting and installing drivers for all hardware devices takes place almost instantly, making it easy for an end-user to install Linux locally without having to spend a lot of time troubleshooting. Servers and databases can also be detected by hardware detection.

2. **Efficient Process Management System**

   Operating systems need to check the processes running in the design and find a way to maintain them without crashing the computer. Effective process management is fundamental for any operating system. Programs are prioritized by Linux programmers based on their importance and the amount of processing power they consume. Third-party libraries are used by many Linux distros in order to automatically end background processes without affecting users. As a user, you can adjust your settings to free up processing power for resource-hungry graphical software.

### 3. Efficient Memory Management

Managing your memory resources efficiently requires the ability to leverage the power of RAM, which Linux provides. You can get the most out of your hardware using Linux. Many versions of Windows and macOS limit the hardware capabilities in order to extend the life of the computer. On the other hand, Linux makes the most out of them without reducing their efficiency. As a Linux programmer, your software needs to be capable of managing memory efficiently.

### 4. Interfaces

Linux includes a variety of interfaces that make it easy to interact with its components. Nowadays, graphical user interfaces are an essential component of operating systems. Linux provides a vast range of desktop interfaces such as KDE and XFCE to enhance its users' experience while using the operating system. The terminal is the most important of all the interfaces, as it allows users to interact effectively with the Linux kernel through the shell medium.

### 5. User Authentication

Linux systems provide complex authentication procedures for creating user accounts and groups. Creating user groups with various limitations and privileges is as easy as clicking a button when you first start using Linux. Linux administrators can easily provide access and revoke it, unlike Windows and Mac systems, where many settings need to be changed. It is for this reason that hosting providers and database management services use Linux as their daily driver for serving their clients. Access to sensitive files such as passwords and hash files is restricted through user authentication.

### 6. Development Tools

Linux is a complete development environment that provides access to separate libraries from various programming languages. As Linux binaries are open-source and its documentation is straightforward, it is easier for programmers to design for Linux than Windows or macOS. Additionally, there are many open source tools like IDEs for creating Linux applications. Working with Linux is quite liberating, especially for programmers.

Windows and Mac both require their developers to use an IDE developed by their own development teams. Creating Mac applications is only possible with Xcode, a software designed by Apple. Xcode does have its own merits, but it also includes a lot of laborious procedures and kills a lot of developers' productive time. Because Apple prohibits the use of other IDEs, you are forced to use Xcode. This philosophy is not supported by Linux. Any development tools, regardless of what binaries they use, if they are compiled and can pass instructions to the Linux kernel, can be deployed to a Linux system.

# Linux and Its Capabilities

In addition to these essential characteristics, Linux also provides advanced functionalities for its users. As Linux is primarily a professional system, you must understand its capabilities completely before learning about it.

1. **System Virtualisation**

   Virtualization is the greatest innovation in computing. With virtualization, you can run any operating system inside one operating system without worrying about additional resources. As an operating system designed for remote and isolated environments such as databases, Linux can be used with any virtualization platform. Linux systems provide excellent virtualization capabilities, which are utilized by many servers. In the past decade, software such as Docker has expanded the capabilities of Linux virtualization. By using virtualization, you can run different versions of Linux without worrying about data loss or damage.

2. **Clustering**

   Using clustering, computer scientists and administrators can run multiple systems as a single system. Each system can be called a node and can be configured in Linux. Additionally, cluster nodes can be configured to provide different services. Clustering is a complex operation and requires hardware optimization, which is only possible with the Linux kernel.

3. **Optimised Computing**

   To perform experiments and make decisions in experiments, supercomputers and scientific computers need optimized calculations. The Linux operating system and its prioritization capabilities can help computer scientists achieve optimized computing standards.

4. **Cloud Computing**

   The cloud is the latest industrial standard for managing and utilizing data. Only a few Linux distributions are designed specifically to work with cloud computing architectures at incredible speeds. Linux's virtualization capabilities can also be used to interact efficiently with cloud computing hardware. With their software capabilities, Linux programs are able to control a network of hosts and guest machines.

5. **Storage**

   It is one of the advanced features of Linux to work with network storage systems of any format. Linux can be linked with advanced storage systems such as Fibre Channel and Info Band for storing data and applications efficiently.

6. **Forensic Device**

   Linux distributions such as Bodhi Linux can be used as live software and interact with system resources without requiring authentication. Forensic experts primarily rely on Linux systems to find any backups or files when a cyberattack occurs.

## Linux and Open Source

In spite of the fact that all the functionalities listed above can be achieved on Windows and macOS systems with customization and software installation, professionals continue to rely on Linux due to its open-source nature. Microsoft Windows and Apple MacOS are proprietary operating systems developed to create products and generate revenue for computer companies. The proprietary operating systems all limit the resources available to developers, making it difficult for wannabe developers to build applications using their inbuilt libraries. Open Source systems, on the other hand, make their libraries publicly accessible and accept suggestions for changes to those libraries from all over the world.

The open-source nature of these systems also makes it easy for security enthusiasts to find and patch vulnerabilities. The problem with proprietary operating systems is that they are difficult to analyze, so it requires a much longer time to fix vulnerabilities that can be devastating. In 2016, the ransomware virus that used a Windows vulnerability destroyed thousands of businesses and their data. As Linux and its supporting operating systems are regularly patched and updated, these problems can be limited.

Companies will also be able to worry less about licensing paperwork in the future if they utilize open source software. A constant monitoring of proprietary software for Windows and macOS operating systems makes your logging information available to them. By contrast, the Linux operating system prevents individuals from accessing sensitive information effectively.

With open-source operating systems and software, the world can benefit from innovation. Despite the overwhelming dominance of Windows and MacOS in the financial industry, Linux remains the driving force behind their success. When we use operating systems that are open source, we strive for other operating systems to become responsible. Linux resources and documentation are usually available on the Internet, which allows new developers to experiment with various embedded systems with ease. Artificial intelligence, such as robotics, is developing with the aid of open-source Linux software and kernel diagnostic tools.

## Linux Distributions

Due to Linux distributions, Linux has become a global phenomenon in the computer science industry. Linux distributions normally include the Linux kernel and a set of applications relevant to the philosophy, purpose, and target audience of the distribution. With a single installation file, these components can all be installed locally. Each Linux distribution is designed for a specific purpose. Linux distributions, for example, are exclusively developed for computer scientists who experiment with technologies such as artificial intelligence and machine learning. NASA and other private institutes use Linux core knowledge to create distributions that suit their needs. Linux distributions can be created by anyone in a short period of time. It is challenging, however, to maintain sophisticated features that improve the Linux user experience. As a result, there is a lot of competition from different vendors and groups in the Linux space.

By installing all applications from their official websites or using package managers, Linux distributions are designed to reduce the amount of automated work you may have to do. When using package managers to install applications, conflicts can arise due to dependencies. Many users rely on Linux distributions to streamline this process. It takes a lot of effort to understand the purpose of the different types of Linux distributions.

Ubuntu Linux is the most popular Linux distribution. Due to its popularity, it is preinstalled on several laptops and desktops manufactured by companies like HP, Dell, and Lenovo. While Ubuntu Linux is the most popular alternative to Windows for regular users, many other Linux distributions are favored by computer enthusiasts and programmers involved in many fields. We can gain a better understanding of the Linux ecosystem by understanding the different core philosophies of these distributions.

1. **Debian**

   Having survived various hurdles over the past thirty years, Debian is the most popular and oldest Linux distribution. It is the most widely supported Linux distribution worldwide. The Debian system is the foundation for distributions like Ubuntu and Knoppix. Debian-based systems are popular due to their package installer, apt-get, which seamlessly installs dependencies and software for users. Despite this, Debian is criticized for not being able to run on old systems and on computers with inferior hardware. Debian users also complain about buggy interfaces and poor graphical card integration.

2. **Arch Linux**

   For programmers who are interested in learning about how Linux works, Arch Linux is considered a bible. Linux systems based on the Arch architecture use Pacman as a package manager, which allows users to keep software dependencies from conflicting. Arch Linux is used by Linux distributions such as Manjaro and Endeavour. It is equally important to keep in mind that Arch Linux can run well on old hardware or when connected to embedded devices like Arduino.

### 3. Red Hat Linux

Commercial enterprises use Red Hat Linux extensively for server and database management. The Fedora distribution is the child software of Red Hat Linux. Red Hat Linux can only be installed if a working license is purchased, but Fedora Linux can be installed on any computer. Fedora comes with a Red Hat package manager. Red Hat Linux provides hundreds of tools that can help system and database administrators to perform their jobs more efficiently. For companies with operating licenses for their products, Red Hat Linux also offers paid support.

### 4. Knoppix

Knoppix is an operating system based on Debian that can run on a USB or CD, but not as a traditional operating system. Knoppix was designed primarily to be used as a live CD for live exploits and penetration testing. Knoppix is also widely used to recover abruptly crashed systems. As soon as your live version ends, all the files you have downloaded or installed will be deleted. However, many programmers create persistent USBs for Knoppix to save data on the USB rather than on the computer's hard disk.

### 5. Ubuntu

Ubuntu is the most popular Linux distribution available in desktop, server, and core editions. Despite the fact that each has its own purpose, Ubuntu engineers have developed the core version to serve them best. Future technologies such as robotics and the internet of things are extensively using it. Ubuntu, however, is criticized for having a lot of bloatware pre-installed. Despite the ease of installation of this software, we recommend downloading the lite version for best results.

### 6. Linspire

Ubuntu is the freeware version of Debian, while Linspire is the commercial version. Linspire comes with preinstalled applications tailored to your needs. It has great optimization features to work with any hardware. Linspire Live, the live version of Linspire, is also quite popular with forensic enthusiasts. As Inspire is a commercial product, all its source code is protected, encrypted, and cannot be accessed. Linspire engineering has come under fire from Linux enthusiasts for violating the spirit of freedom that open-source software offers.

7. **Gentoo**

A unique feature of Gentoo is that it gives its users complete control over the Linux kernel. The code is compiled locally, so you will get the best performance possible based on your hardware configuration. Gentoo is also called an operating system that provides powerful customization abilities to the end-user. Using Gentoo also means you need to handle the installation procedure yourself. The interface asks you to choose everything according to your preferences.

While installing Gentoo Linux, some programmers customize the Linux kernel according to their preferences. Gentoo offers a number of configurations that other distributions cannot, but it is considered to be less supported by the community due to its wide array of options. Gentoo Linux is a serious platform, so make sure you are patient enough to fix any errors that may occur as you interact with it.

8. **Slackware**

It is one of the oldest Linux legacy distributions still being maintained by its wonderful developer community. In contrast to other Linux distributions, Slackware emphasizes simplicity and stability. It's also the only Linux distribution that pays more attention to the Unix roots of Linux. Considering that it is a legacy distribution, it is impossible to find solutions to dependencies on your graphics cards or processors. A lot of functions in Slackware Linux are based on shell scripts and text.

# Linux Kernel Numbering System

A version number is provided for every Linux distribution in order to provide greater transparency and efficient prepackaged distribution. According to the pre-packaged distribution you selected while downloading, version numbers may differ.

In order to avoid confusion for developers, all Linux distributions use the Linux kernel numbering system.

*It follows the structure as shown below:*

1. x. y

Here, 1 is the direct version of the Linux distribution, x signifies whether it is a stable version or a beta version, and y signifies the patch level. Usually, it is a beta version if the 'x' is an odd number, and a stable version if the 'x' is an even number.

For example, if the version number is 6.3.2, it is the 6th updated version of a Linux distribution and a beta version with the second patch. Beta versions are software releases exclusively for developers to test operating systems and report any bugs before the stable release. Testing beta versions is an integral part of software development.

## Linux Distribution Components

Almost all Linux distributions come with pre-installed packages, libraries, and applications that enhance the performance of Linux systems. Before diving deeper into the Linux ecosystem, it's important to learn about some of the popular software that comes preinstalled with your Linux distribution.

We now discuss the essential software that every Linux distribution needs for everyday usage and troubleshooting. Different distributions use different methodologies and use cases to install software.

## GNU

Open-source software has become increasingly popular in industries due to GNU. The GNU project played a critical role in the development of UNIX-based operating systems in 1984. The GNU project has successfully created tens of applications with the help of thousands of developers. With the exception of the Linux kernel, the GNU project has developed tools for almost all domains of the Linux ecosystem. In addition to being open source, GNU software provides a general public license for easy sharing between various Linux distributions.

There are different command line principles you need to understand in order to use the GNU project's software. Almost all of the software is designed to work exclusively with the terminal instead of the standard GUI interface. Linux has been shaped by GNU software over the years and has a significant impact on the ecosystem. The development of any new Linux software is loosely based on one or more GNU software projects. Because the source code is all available, it is easy to learn Linux programming from this software.

Knowing some of the more popular GNU software can help you better understand Linux's capabilities:

1. **Autoconf**

   As part of the process of developing software for Linux systems, this GNU software package is used to configure different packages. More than a hundred vendors and thousands of additional pieces of hardware equipment are supported by Autoconf. The Autoconf software consists mainly of hundreds of bash scripts that can automate the process of configuring these hardware devices. Linux developers must expand their support to different devices and embedded systems.

2. **Bash**

   Most Linux distributions come with the command-line interpreter Bash. The ability to automate different tasks in a Linux system relies heavily on bash scripting. Through bash, the programmer can provide instructions to both the hardware and the software. A bash command-line interface is a shell program and thus inherits all the qualities of a shell program.

3. **Binutils**

   Linux consists of binary files and libraries that programmers must use explicitly to interact with the Linux kernel. Otherwise, the software will run slowly or even become unresponsive. Binutils is GNU software designed for working with binary files of all types.

4. **Diff**

   It is an exclusive GNU tool for finding differences between two files of a similar format. If you wish, you can mark differences with lines while reading them and delete them or modify them via the software.

5. **ed**

ed is a popular basic text editor that was developed by the GNU project. Linux distros such as Red Hat Linux and Gentoo are shipping with ed as their default text editor.

6. **GCC**

Compilers are the most popular Linux software from the GNU software team. Even though the GNU project has created compilers for many programming languages, C and C++ compilers are famous with Linux users. GNU C and C++ compilers are easy to understand while using and provide reduced run time even for complex applications due to their optimization capabilities. It is shipped along with a GDB debugger to debug already written applications.

7. **GIMP**

GIMP is a graphic manipulation software that is an alternative to the famous Adobe Photoshop on Linux systems. With GIMP, you can perform different kinds of image manipulation techniques with ease.

8. **GNOME**

GNOME is one of the popular desktop graphical interface packages that is shipped with many Linux distributions. It was initially developed as freeware software for the GNU software team. Since then, it has grown into a separate project, with hundreds of enthusiastic developers trying to make it better. Today, GNOME is the most popular GUI interface for all Linux systems. Even though it is not as smooth as XFCE, it, however, provides many customization capabilities.

9. **Gnumeric & LibreOffice**

Linux users complain that there is no excellent office software available. However, it is not true. There are many office products such as Gnumeriuc and LibreOffice, which can be used to create text documents, sheets, and slides with many customization options.

### 10. Gzip

Gzip is an archiving software that can help users to create or decompress zip files. Linux users often use formats such as .tar to compress files. Even Linux essential command line tools provide an easy way to compress tar files but not for zip files. Fzip solves this problem with ease. It's similar to WinRAR but uses faster algorithms to process data.

# Opportunities With Linux

If you plan to become a computer professional, Linux is the best operating system to experiment with. Almost all companies and organizations use Linux to maintain their resources, and hence there are thousands of jobs available for both freshers and professionals. Linux is not only the future but also the present. Because Linux software is open-source, many Fortune companies recommend it to their clients. Anyone can take advantage of the prowess of Linux to build a successful career regardless of their field. You only need to understand the basics of Linux, the necessary software, and the philosophy of Linux.

*Here are some career opportunities:*

### 1. System Administrator

With the foundation of the Linux system, you can apply for system administrator jobs where your job will be to monitor users in the system and solve if any problem occurs. System administrators also decide when to turn on or off the systems based on the organization's requirements.

### 2. Penetration Testers

All organizations need to increase their security to avoid any fatal attacks on their databases and servers. Companies hire penetration testers with Linux knowledge to help them secure their systems. Penetration testers mainly need to understand Linux networking and dictionary attack tools to secure systems.

### 3. Linux Programmers

Linux programmers are hired to create software that can be directly interacted with the Linux kernel. Linux programmers need to be thorough about different distros, dependencies, packaged software, and licensing details to create new software. Commercially, you often need to write software Ubuntu and Debian systems as they are more popular with the tech industry.

### 4. Forensic Specialists

There is also a lot of scope for being hired as a forensic specialist if you are thorough with the Linux basics. To be proficient at forensics, you need to be aware of Linux live USB functionalities and how to use these live software to recover files that are either deleted or accessed by attackers. Kali Linux is probably the best Linux distro for forensic specialists. However, you can use any other distro such as Bodhi Linux to recover files from all operating systems.

### 5. Database Administrators

Almost all databases use relational query languages such as SQL to store data effectively. While it is possible to access this database using a Windows system, many hosting providers depend on Linux to effectively manage these databases. As a database administrator, you need to rely on file management and manipulation commands to achieve more with your database data.

### 6. Server Maintenance

All multinational companies and organizations rely on high-end servers to manage their websites and process requests given by the end-user. All these servers need to be encrypted and regularly updated not to fall prey to open vulnerabilities. For better career opportunities in this field, all server maintenance professionals need to be proficient with Red Hat Linux.

### 7. Data Scientists

All data scientists depend on Python and tools such as Scipy to write data science models. However, all these software can easily be deployed in a Linux system, and engineers looking forward to making a career in data science need to be well aware of all Linux foundation topics described in this book.

8. **Cloud Computing Specialists**

   With the growing amount of data organizations are handling these days, using a cloud system is a more portable and intelligent decision. Most cloud computing tools rely completely on Linux systems, and hence a cloud computing specialist needs to have thorough knowledge about Linux basics.

Apart from these career opportunities, Linux acts as a great daily driver for people who love customizing their databases and using an operating system with no bloatware.

With enough introduction to Linux, you are now all set to install Linux on your system.

# CHAPTER 2

## Linux Installation

The majority of computers on the market come preinstalled with Windows, with the exception of Apple computers that come preinstalled with Mac OS. Only less than 5% of manufacturing companies preinstall Ubuntu distributions while shipping them to users. To install Linux on your computer, you need to follow the same steps regardless of the Linux distro you choose. You can also dual boot your Linux system with windows or macOS with the exception of the latest Apple silicon chips, where Apple has restricted users to only use macOS as their only primary OS. Throughout this chapter, the user will learn about how to install Linux, how to install it as a dual boot system, and how to install it as a virtual machine for added security and for people using the newest Apple silicon chips.

### Installing Linux as a Fresh System

Remember that all your pre installed or saved files in your windows or macOS system will be erased whenever you do a fresh installation. To not regret it later, make a complete backup of your system or transfer all your files to your external hard disk:

1. **Know about your computer's hardware**

   The foremost thing a Linux enthusiast should know is about the hardware features of his computer. Use a terminal or windows control panel to list your processor, RAM, whether you are using an HDD or SSD, GPU, and similar details. It is better to write all of them on paper as it helps to check the internet quickly if you face any errors while installing Linux. All Linux distros also have specific hardware requirements that need to be satisfied for you to install them on your computer. For example, Manjaro, a famous Arch-based Linux distribution, requires at least 4GB Ram to perform with better consistency as a daily driver.

2. **Download the ISO files**

Once you have noted down your system hardware details, it is now time to download your famous Linux distribution. Every Linux distro has its website. Search in google to find the official website, or you can use websites like distrowatch.com to download iso files of all popular Linux distributions. However, it is highly recommended to download from the official website for better safety. You can also verify using the md5 hash file that is present in the official Linux distro website to check the authenticity of the file.

Linux distribution usually comes with different desktop environments such as XFCE, GNOME, and KDE. All the popular Linux distros provide links to all these desktop environments on their official website. Please choose one of them and download it into your local HDD or SSD.

3. **Make live USB**

Once you have downloaded the ISO of the file, you should now make a live USB from it. You can use software such as Rufus to make a live USB from the ISO file.

*Procedure to follow:*

1. Run the Rufus software after inserting the USB into your computer. Make sure that the USB is 3.0 instead of 2.0 for faster results.

2. Rufus interface provides you an option to select the ISO file from your local system. You can either select from your downloads folder or drag the file to the Rufus interface to insert it.

3. Select whether your system has UEFI or legacy BIOS. To check what BIOS your computer supports, check your manufacturer's website or the manual you received when you brought your computer. Usually, to enter the BIOS menu, you need to

enter the ESC button repeatedly while booting up. Once you enter the BIOS menu, it will be listed whether your PC manufacturer has used UEFI or Legacy BIOS.

And that's it. Enter the Start button in Rufus, and the software will do the rest of the work for you. It usually takes at least ten minutes to create a live USB from your ISO file. So, don't panic or close the windows if the progress bar is moving very slow.

If you want to use the Linux system exclusively to create your Linux live USB, you can use the dd command all Linux distributions support. To work with the dd command effortlessly, you need first to copy the location of your ISO file.

## Making Linux Live USB Using dd Command

Find the name of the USB you will use for installing a Linux distro using the lsblk command.

*Linux Command:*

```
$ lsblk
```

The above commands will present you with a result in a similar way below.

*Output:*

```
sdb 7:45 1 63.4G 0 disk
```

The USB can now be further observed to be divided into two partitions.

All the Linux OS data will be sent to the first partition, and the second partition acts as a boot loader for your bootable USB to detect BIOS systems.

Before installing the OS using the dd command, you need to unmount the OS data partition.

*Linux Command:*

```
sudo dd bs = 4M if={enter the path} of=path of the usb conv=fdatasync
status=progress
```

*Example:*

```
sudo dd bs=4M if=/Downloads/arch.iso of=/dev/sda1 conv=fdatasync
status=progress
```

*Output:*

```
making live usb ….. 15%
```

Once you click the Enter button in the terminal, the Linux iso file will be installed into the USB, making it bootable for installation or live forensic purposes.

Before learning how to boot into the Linux USB, it is essential to know a little about creating a dual boot system for using a Linux system along with windows or mac. While there are many arguments that dual booting Linux with another operating system can slow down, it has been debunked many times already that dual booting doesn't decrease the efficiency of software or hardware resources. The only exception will be the boot time that will be affected, as you will get an option to choose where you want to boot into.

However, before deciding to dual boot your system, follow these three essential rules:

1. Make a complete backup of your Windows files. There are chances of your data being deleted or corrupted.

2. Get spare Windows Live USB for repairing any damage that may occur because of a dual boot system.

3. Make sure that you have a Windows recovery disk for reinstalling it immediately without any hassle.

Once you are clear with these terms, create a bootable USB using a tool such as Rufus or using the default dd command.

# Partitioning for Dual Boot

Partition is a computer technique that helps users divide their internal hard disks into multiple areas and use them for different purposes. To run Linux as a dual boot system, you need to create a new partition along with your existing partition.

*Steps in Windows:*

1. Go to the disk management utility in your control panel and select the disk you will use to install your Linux.

2. Make sure that you have shrunk the volume that you needed for Linux before executing this utility trick. Make sure that you have selected the exFAT partition for the Linux drive.

3. Once the partitions are created, reboot to make sure that the hard disk has shrieked.

*Steps in Mac:*

1. Go to disk utility in your applications and select the disk you want to make a partition for. Divide it using the GUI interface and select exfast as the default format for the disk.

2. Once it is done, make sure that you enter into recovery mode and clear the partitioned disk. As Mac systems often need fresh drives, cleaning them in recovery mode can be a great idea.

# Booting Into Linux Live USB

With bootable USB ready for various use cases such as fresh install or dual boot, it is now time to boot that USB for installing Linux in your system.

*Steps to be followed:*

1. Plug the USB into the port and power on the computer. When your manufacturer logo appears, either enter ESC or f12 repeatedly according to your manufacturer's rules. If you are using Mac, press the option key repeatedly once the Apple logo appears to boot into the device startup manager.

2. Once you enter into the boot menu, you can choose the USB drive and click enter into the live environment of the Linux distort. You can try the Linux distro you are going to install in this phase. You can even use the internet by connecting to an ethernet port. However, remember that you cannot save any files as a non-persistent device.

Many Linux enthusiasts also prefer using Live USB with persistent storage as their hard drive. To make your Live USB persistent, you need to add a persistence value for the disk during the USB disc with Rufus. To check whether or not your USB has become persistent, add a test folder and reboot. After reboot, if the folder still exists, then the persistence is activated.

# Installing Linux in a Virtual Machine

Apart from installing directly into the local machine, you can also experience Linux within a virtual machine of Windows or macOS systems. Several softwares such as Parallels, Virtualbox, VMware, and VMware fusion make this possible, with only a few steps to follow:

First of all, download the separate virtual box or VMware images from your Linux distress official website. While it is entirely possible to use the regular ISO files to install in a virtual machine, specific Virtual machine images can provide more processing speeds.

Remember that initially, for the virtualization software to work, your computer needs to support it. Unfortunately, not all low-end PCs work with this technology. To check whether or not your computer processors support virtualization capabilities, head over to your BIOS menu. Once you enter the BIOS menu, search for virtualization settings. If you can't find the virtualization settings panel, it is most likely that your computer doesn't support softwares such as VMware and Virtual Box.

After confirming your virtualization capabilities, install VMware or Virtual Box according to your requirements. If you are just starting with virtualization technology, then it is logical to use open source software such as virtual box. On the other hand, commercialized software such as VMware and parallels can help you achieve advanced capabilities while using Linux in your local system or servers using virtualization.

For this example, we will be discussing VMware workstation that can run in both Windows and macOS. The macOS version is named VMware fusion, whereas the Windows version is named VMware workstation.

1. Download the VMware software according to your system requirements. VMware workstation player is a free version that provides fewer features, whereas VMware workstation professional is a premium version that offers advanced virtualization tools for organizations.

2. Once the software is installed, you will be asked to install a keyboard driver necessary for virtualization to work. Accept and install it.

3. Make sure that the SHA 256 algorithm is verified for your downloaded Linux ISO. Installing corrupted or tampered OS can result in data theft or keylogging. So, make sure that you are downloading from official sources.

### Creating Virtual Machine

To install Linux in a VM, you need to configure your VM settings initially. Even though you can customize it further easily, we highly suggest using the below-mentioned settings for better initial customization of your Linux distro in a VM:

1. Click on the 'Create virtual machine 'button to select an iso from your files folder.

2. In the following interface, you need to select your guest operating system. In this instance for your required results, you need to choose Linux as the option and any version according to your Linux distro. For example, you can choose the Arch version if you are installing Manjaro Linux distro. Make sure to select the correct version of your distro after completing research.

3. In the next step, you need to provide the storage you are willing to use. Typically, it is better to create a 100 GB disk storage for Linux distros. You also need to select the RAM for your VM. Make sure to not exceed more than 60% of your current RAM for accessing the VM with a better speed. You can also select other settings such as processors, 3D graphics according to your hardware.

4. Once done with the customization, click Finish, and your VM will be created automatically on the left side of the Library.

Now power it on, and you will be booted into the standard Linux installation live booting interface that is common for all installation methods.

# Linux Installation

Now, irrespective of whether you are installing on the local machine or the virtual machine, as soon as you boot into the Linux installer, you will usually be asked to set a few default settings to install any Linux distro. While different distros use different settings, the below-mentioned steps are regular settings that one needs to be aware of.

Once you enter the live boot or power on a virtual machine, you will be welcomed with a desktop interface, where a file named " Try { Your distro name}" will be present. Click on it to kickstart the installation process:

1. At the first interface, you will be asked to enter the name and password of the Linux system.

2. The following interface asks you to partition your hard drive. If you are dual booting, then select the already partitioned drive and choose the option to erase the entire disk.

3. After the partition is completed, you will be asked to select details such as Time, Date, Network, and Keyboard setting.

4. Press the finish button, and the Linux operating system will get installed.

It usually takes a few hours to install Linux on your system entirely. So, be patient. Your computer may reboot several times during this installation procedure.

# Installing New Software

Before learning about several basic Linux concepts, a Linux enthusiast must understand how to install or update new software from a command-line interface.

Most popular Linux software provides offline installers with .deb and .rpm formats to install applications on Linux. You can double-click on the file installers to kickstart the software installation. Even though it is straightforward, it is essential to verify the file's authenticity, as a trojan can be easily bound in these installation files to gain access to the system.

## The Online Way

The online way is probably the most popular way to download or update software as all the package managers will pull the download files from their own servers instead of relying on third-party sources and mirror servers. Different Linux distros use different package managers, and hence there is a different way for installing new software in various Linux distros:

1. **Debian and Ubuntu**

   Both Debian and Ubuntu platforms come prebuilt with an advanced package manager known as apt-get. Apt depends on the Internet and its community curated public repositories to download and install the software.

   *Command:*

   ```
   apt-get install package_name
   ```

   Always replace the package name with your desired software name or the repository name. Please do research about the software you are downloading to know the exact package name.

   *Example:*

   apt-get VMware

   # This will download the VMware software from the apt d=repository

   You can also search with an apt manager using the below command.

   *Command:*

   ```
   apt-cache search google_chrome
   ```

   # This will search for the google chrome software from the apt manager

   If you are not comfortable with the command-line version of the apt package manager, you can use the synaptic package manager, which is a GUI version of the apt-get.

2. **Fedora**

   Fedora is a Linux distributor that offers simplicity to its users. All the software that needs to be installed in a fedora system will be packaged in .rpm format, a unique format designed to unencrypt the packages efficiently without corrupting the data.

   First of all, in your fedora system, head over to the section where you will find the Add/Remove software option. When you click on it, it will first scan all the packages present in the current system and provide their status on the left column. By the time the initial check is finished, you will understand the special privileges provided to different packages with the help of popup by the system.

   You can also reupload or install the packages already deleted by the system, as fedora stores those details in its cache memory.

To install new software, you need to use the update button, where you will have a text box to enter the package name of your choice. Once you have clicked the apply button, all the new packages will be synced to the Fedora local system and installed within a few minutes.

## 3. Arch systems

In the same way as Fedora, Arch systems use Pac-Man software package manager to install new software into your local system.

Pac-Man provides both GUI and CLI interfaces. Only distros like Manjaro have used GUI in their systems, while other distros like endeavor primarily depend on CLI to install new software.

*Command:*

```
Sudo Pacman -S packagename
```

Remember that you always need to run Pac-Man as a root user for successful installation of various software.

## 4. Xandros

Xandros is pre-installed with software known as Xandros networks that can be used to install or remove the software. As Xandros is primarily used in servers and databases, it is essential to update or change the software to patch vulnerabilities regularly and ensure that the data is safe.

Head over to Xandros network and press the plus symbol on the left side of the screen. Xandros provides an online interface to select the packages of your choice.

Remember that, as of now, there is no way to install third-party packages to the Xandros network as it deals with sensitive data installed in servers. So, you are out of luck if you are trying to install customized packages.

## 5. SUSE

SUSE Linux distribution consists of a tool called Yast to install new applications in its root folder. It can seamlessly be used to install, update or delete applications.

Head over to the system control center and search for Yast. Click it, and you will be able to access file and package information about every software installed in the Local Linux system.

Please select your desired package and accept the conditions to install it simultaneously in your connected systems in the Linux network.

Yast also is very good at checking dependencies. If it has any empty dependencies, it searches in its database to replace them with similar repositories so that your installation time will not increase.

## Troubleshooting When Installing on a Linux System

While installing Linux and using it is straightforward, almost all users are bound at one time to troubleshoot it for solving a problem they are facing. No matter what troubleshooting you are doing, don't forget to take tree present backups of your system data. To help you in this section, we have provided solutions for the five most popular errors that Linux users may face in the beginning days of their Linux career:

1. **Linux failed installation**

   There is nothing more frustrating than Linux installation errors, especially if you are a long-term Windows user trying to migrate to Linux. In these situations, most of the time, the problem of installation error is mainly due to the installation media itself. Make sure the USB or CD you are using is writable and is working. You can easily verify it using another system that runs Windows or Linux.

   For verification, Linux provides a checksum to verify that the official Linux image data and your downloaded one are the same. We always suggest you repeat the downloading, transferring, and running the file procedures all again after formatting the data to solve the issue.

2. **Linux system hanging**

   Like any other operating system, Linux is sometimes possible to hang or freeze because of high processing applications consuming its resources. Most of the time, Linux will hang while booting up due to being unable to read all the application logs or sudden power off that creates corrupted hard drives. Linux administrators always need to find the reason for the slow performance of the system by using a Live CD of the same distro.

To solve this problem while booting into the Linux system, press Ctrl + alt + del button. This will take you to a virtual console where you can start to read the log files and clear them to reboot the system like in normal instances. Sometimes, system hanging will also be because of hardware issues such as RAM and GPU problems.

### 3. Sluggish performance

Often Linux administrators had to troubleshoot the reason for the sluggish performance of the system. You can compare the slow performance with other systems near to you. If you are sure that your Linux system is underperforming, you need to start an entire system health checkup. All Linux distros provide GUI-based applications to start these system-based health checks quickly.

To troubleshoot this problem, at first, you need to analyze all of your installed applications and delete some of the applications that are consuming the largest cache or are running abundant background processes, which is affecting the system's overall performance. Reinstalling resource abundance systems or upgrading your hardware is the most probable solution for these kinds of problems.

To find the processes that are consuming more resources as you can use the top command.

*Command:*

```
sample@linux: top
```

This will list all the processes and let you understand which are taking more memory, overloading the CPU, and crunching system performance. Either delete them or reinstall to solve this problem and recheck using the top command.

### 4. GRUB errors

GRUB is the boot manager that Linux and its kernel use to initiate the first Linux system process. When you are trying to boot up to your system, the GRUB boot loader often appears and informs you of the errors that are stopping you from entering into your system. These errors mainly occur when your GRUB is not updated, corrupted, or accidentally deleted by other system processes and malware.

To solve most GRUB-based errors, you need to be aware of the Live USB functionality. Log in as a live user and download a new GRUB or replace it from your persistent USB. Using Gparted manager and or by clicking on the repair button will help you automatically fix this problem if you are connected to the internet.

5. **Weak system security**

Even though Linux is the best operating system out there for being secure, it can sometimes be affected by vulnerabilities because of reckless system management. When someone gets access to a vulnerable system, they can quickly get the passwords of outdated programs such as Apache, MySQL, and OpenSSL with few attacks.

To get rid of these kinds of attacks, a system administrator needs to update the system constantly.

# CHAPTER 3

# Linux System Administration

System administration is a challenging task since many components of the Linux system need to be constantly and consistently verified. Automating scripts, cleaning the trash files, or detecting malware can also help Linux administrators effectively maintain a computer system. It takes dedication for a sysadmin to establish a career in the industry. To be a system administrator, you need to be aware of different Linux core concepts and should have sufficient programming skills in languages such as Python and shell.

Irrespective of the experience, any Linux administrator needs to hold the same responsibilities and strictly follow the organization's guidelines. Different organizations use different guidelines to secure and maintain their Linux systems to achieve peak efficiency. Knowing the different tools required for system administration and various configuration files that can help individuals change the system's performance is crucial for making a career as a sysadmin.

## System Administration Tasks

All Linux enthusiasts need to be aware of the characteristics of a system administrator and the administrative processes they need to carry out to maintain the system:

1. **Manage User Accounts**

   Systems administrators' main task is to manage different types of users and groups in their network. Often they end up adding or removing users for various reasons. All the encrypted passwords of these accounts also need to be safely migrated to safe storage by the system administrator if it's an administrative network. Often, sysadmins need to recover passwords that are forgotten or delete accounts that no longer serve a purpose in their network without messing up with other users' data.

2. **Installing and Configuring Systems**

   All sysadmins are responsible for installing, configuring, customizing, and removing tools from the network. They often install tools such as docker to initialize virtualization services on their network. It is one of the regular tasks of a sysadmin to update whatever distribution of Linux they are using on a regular basis either automatically or manually to fix vulnerabilities as soon as possible. Many sysadmins also depend on Python automated scripts to update the systems automatically.

3. **Printer Management**

   Sysadmins are also responsible for managing all printing services in a network. In spite of the fact that it may not seem technical, a printer is often a device that is interconnected for the use of multiple users, and it is therefore essential to provide users with a prioritized queue that will enable them to use the services effectively. Whenever a print job fails or is ignored, system administrators must focus on queue monitoring.

4. **Installing New Hardware**

   A sysadmin is not entirely dependent on the software itself. Hardware is still the pioneer in computers because of its ability to maximize the performance of software. As a system administrator, you need to perform constant checks to make sure nothing is wrong with the installed hardware. All these checks should be performed after completely shutting down the systems. Any issues with the hardware devices need to be resolved as soon as possible by replacing them with new ones. Installation of drivers after replacing the hardware is also vital to peak the performance of these devices.

## 5. Software Installation

Sysadmins need to experiment with different applications and services in order to know if they are appropriate for that environment. You must learn how to archive using the Linux command line in order to install software, which is typically packaged in a .tar or .rar format. Installation of the software is always a learning process as different software provides different instructions.

A sysadmin should first thoroughly read the manual provided by software developers before installing them in the network. It is also solely for this reason that virtualization softwares such as VMware are developed. You can first create a trial operating system and experiment with the software in it. Once you are entirely aware of the procedure, installing them in your actual systems becomes easy. Be sure to take a backup of your sensitive files before installing any new software, as there is always the possibility of a malware attack.

## 6. Importance of Backups

Organizations rely on backups in order to protect themselves from complex and unreliable situations. Backups contain all the data associated with your hardware and can be used to go back to previous settings with ease. You must schedule some of your time as a sysadmin to monitor and create new automated backups. Currently, most sysadmins work with cloud networks, so experimenting with permanent data loss is imperative.

## 7. Automation

Automation is the most critical priority for sysadmins as there will be a lot of tasks to be taken care of. Automated tasks can be done with scripting languages such as Python and shell. Understanding Linux core binaries, kernel, and libraries is essential to creating automated tasks within Linux. Backups, updates, hash file checks, security verifications are some of the many tasks that may require automation.

## 8. System Performance Monitoring

It is a common phenomenon that systems become slow when there are a lot of processes running. As a sysadmin, you must constantly run parameters that help you decide which processes consume more memory and energy on your systems. Once you know the processes and are sure that they are not as important, then shutting them down or clearing their caches is considered a preferred option. System performance can also be analyzed by constantly performing checks and deleting any possible malware that may have reached the system. Hackers are always trying to mess up with the systems for their gains by sending trojans or spoofing techniques. So, make sure that all the running processes are encrypted and are not leaking out any sensitive information.

### 9. Shutting Down Systems

While booting up a Linux system is often straightforward, shutting down a system is not an easy task as you need to make sure that you are not interrupting any processes that are required to be run. Always use the shutdown command Linux provides instead of using the GUI shutdown button to turn off the computer.

### 10. Network Monitoring

A sysadmin should have efficient knowledge of complex networking concepts such as routing tables, packet injection, and network spoofing to ensure that the network data is secure. Analyzing network traffic using tools such as Wireshark is highly recommended.

Always make sure that all the systems in your network are connected to the network. Network problems may occur due to bad LAN wires or adapter driver issues. When there is a problem with the network, a troubleshooting procedure must be followed to determine whether it is a software or hardware issue. Since companies can't afford downtime for their services, you must ensure that the connection is always active.

### 11. Security

While a sysadmin can't possibly find vulnerabilities present in the system or network by using penetration testing techniques, he should make sure that the files are not corrupted due to remote or physical server attacks. Use log files to monitor the system regularly for potential abuse from attackers and to block their IP addresses.

While it may seem overwhelming after knowing a plethora of tasks that a sysadmin needs to perform, it is still a field with many potentials. These jobs are competitive because sysadmins are essential to organizations that rely on internet traffic. In order to help you gain a better understanding of what a sysadmin needs to do, we will now discuss processes such as booting using command-line examples.

# Linux Booting Process

Linux and all its distributions need to be first booted for their services to work on a web server or a relational database. As a sysadmin, all you have first to do is press the power button. Once you click it, the booting procedure will start, and the distribution installed on the hard drive will be processed within a few seconds. Sometimes, when there is an update or a check, it may take a few minutes to boot the Linux system. When Linux boots into the system, the first file that the kernel loads is called the 'init 'file. It acts as a genesis process for all your processes that follow further.

If you would like to check how the system is performing immediately after booting, enter the following command below in a terminal.

*Command:*

```
ps ax | more
```

*Output:*

```
PID TTY STAT TIME COMMAND

1 ? S 0:45 init
```

In the above result, PID 1 shows that it is the first process that has been initiated in the system. Understanding how init functions is crucial for a sysadmin. Whenever Linux refuses to boot or gets crashed immediately, you can analyze the init process logs to troubleshoot your system.

In addition, the init file determines which processes need to be launched immediately after booting a Linux system. A separate algorithm is used to prioritize which processes should be started immediately. The factors that influence this algorithm are mentioned below.

# System Administration Commands

A Linux administrator should always be aware of users in the network. Linux provides several default commands to track the users and the processes they are running efficiently. Even though other users cannot see other users in the system for privacy reasons, the root user can always observe all the processes and user information. However, remember the actual data will always be encrypted and cannot be read by the system administrator. As a Linux user, you should be concerned if your network data is unencrypted, since this makes it easier for a network monitoring tool such as Wireshark to observe your data:

**1. whoami**

You can find your system username with this command.

*Command:*

```
example@sample: whoami
```

*Output:*

```
example
```

Example is the name of the system from the output.

**2. who**

The who command will display a list of all the users logged into the system as well as the time of their login.

*Command:*

```
example@sample: who
```

*Output:*

```
example     12:23

Tom         08: 34

Sam         07:34
```

**3. w**

Information about all users in the system and the processes they are running is displayed with this Linux command.

*Command:*

```
example@sample: w
```

*Output:*

```
example     12:23:12     w
```

```
Tom          08: 34        gnome-session

Sam          07:34         firefox-browser
```

Using this system command, Linux administrators can keep track of all their users at all times.

**4. id**

Use this Linux command to find out your userid, groupid, and all the groups you belong to.

*Command:*

```
example@sample: id
```

*Output:*

```
uid = 23321 gid = 64722 groups = 100 (Linux admin) 300 = (sysadmin)
```

# Creating a User in Linux

As a Linux sysadmin, you constantly need to add or remove users from your system. Only the root user can be able to perform all these tasks initially. A root user, however, can extend these privileges to system administrator accounts. Linux provides both command line and GUI methods to add users.

### GUI User Manager

All Linux distros provide an easy way to add a user to your system from the settings option. Once you reach the setting option, look out for the details section and click on About. When you enter your password for the system, you will be able to add a new user to the system via the 'users' interface.

You need to enter the user name, password, and the type of account ( standard or administrator) to complete the procedure. The standard account doesn't have any special privileges, whereas the administrator can execute any command. Upon clicking the "Apply" button, a new user will be created with the entered name.

### Linux Commands

As a sysadmin, you can perform the same procedure in the shell environment using the below command:

*Syntax:*

```
user add options nameoftheuser
```

*Command:*

```
sudo user add dude
```

#This will create a new user named dude.

*Command:*

```
sudo passwd dude
```

#You can give a password to the new user.

*Command:*

```
Sudo useradd -m Home
```

# Creates a new user with a home directory

By specifying -d, you can write to a new directory instead of the default directory

command:

```
Sudo useradd -d Home .
```

## su

su is a Linux command that helps the present user to run commands as another user if the password is provided

*Command:*

```
su user1
Password:
```

*Output:*

```
user1@
```

#Login as user 1

*Command:*

```
su root
Password:
```

*Output:*

```
root@
# Login as root
```

If you are the root user, you need not enter the password for the user to become an existing user.

*Command:*

```
root@ su user2
user2@
```

# login as user2 without any authentication

Some Linux systems don't provide the password to the root user at first. To add a password for the root user, you need to access the sudoers file in the/etc/ folder and add your chosen password.

# User Management Commands

## 1. Userdel

With this command, a Linux system administrator can quickly delete a user from the system.

*Format:*

```
userdel -r <Name The User>
```

*Command:*

```
root@sample: userdel -r user1
```

## 2. User mod

Usermod is a Linux command that is used to modify the properties of an existing user.

For example, you can modify the name of an already existing user using the below command.

*Syntax:*

User mod -c < New name of the user> < Old name of the user>

*Example:*

usermod -c 'user2 'user1

# Passwords for Users

Passwords are essential for any user to access their system files. Linux provides an easy way to access all the passwords or create a new password on the local system using the passwd command.

## 1. Passwd

When you enter this command in the shell, the shell will ask you to enter the current password twice and the newly decided password twice.

*Command:*

```
passwd

Enter current password:

Enter new Linux password:

Reenter new Linux password:
```

Remember that you will not be able to see the password on the screen on all the Linux systems. You can't even see stars as you see in web forms.

Root users, however, need not enter the current password and can change the password of any user in the system instantly.

*Command:*

```
root@system: passwd

Enter new Linux password:

Reenter new Linux password:

Password changed successfully
```

## 2. Openssl

When you use the regular passwd command, it will be saved in an unencrypted form in the shadows file. If you want to save the password in an encrypted form, you need to use the OpenSSL command.

*Command:*

```
root@system: OpenSSL passwd samplepsswd
```

*Output:*

```
3hwehhe843he
```

You can use the salt option with open SSL to generate more distinct hashes for the same password.

*Command:*

```
root@system: OpenSSL passwd -salt 24 samplepsswd
```

*Output:*

```
24r23hdhdhdsqas4
```

Watch the result where the distinct hash is generated with an initial value of 24.

## Linux Groups

Groups are essential for organizations. A Linux system administrator needs to set permissions based on the group they belong to. While there are graphical interfaces to solve this problem, we recommend using terminal commands such as vi or vigr to manage groups effectively.

## *groupadd*

With this command you can add users to different groups immediately.

*Here is the Command:*

```
Groupadd < Name of the group>
```

*Example:*

```
Groupadd sample group
```

If you are a system administrator, you can check all the groups and the group users using the /etc/group folder.

If you are a regular user, then using the groups command, you can find all the groups that you are a part of.

*Command:*

```
sample@first: groups
```

```
Password:
```

#This will display all groups that the first belongs to

*Output:*

```
first sysadmin Linux system bash group
```

## groupmod

Groupmod is a Linux command that can be used to modify the details of an already created group. For example, you can change the name or the admin of the group.

*Command:*

```
groupmod -n <name of the old group> < name of the new group >
```

*Example:*

```
groupmod -n windows Linux
```

To head over whether or not the names of the groups have changed, you need to open the /etc/group file.

## groupdel

groupdel is a Linux system command that can permanently delete a particular group from the system.

*Command:*

```
groupdel < name of the group >
```

*Example:*

```
groupdel Linux
```

## gpasswd

With Gpasswd, you can easily change the control of a group from one user to another.

*Command:*

```
gpsswd -A <nameoftheuser> < name of the group >
```

*Example:*

```
gpasswd -A user1 sample group
```

The above command makes user1 the system administrator for the sample group.

It is also important to remember that the group admin need not be a member of the group. So, if you are a system administrator of your organization, you can maintain the groups without actually being a part of them.

File /etc/gshadow holds all the names of the group administrator.

# Basic System Administrator Commands

A system administrator manages the configuration of different users, upkeep them, and make reliable operations required for the Linux system's security and performance. Sysadmins also handle servers and need to manage them, remembering how much resources need to be allocated for a particular user or group. Not following these rules may result in a budget for the organization.

## 1. Linux uptime

As a system administrator, you often need to know how long a particular system is running. Even if there is one active user, it will reflect on our uptime command results.

*Command:*

```
Uptime
```

*Output:*

```
12:34:32 up 45 min , 7 users , load average: 9.4 , 0.5 . 7.8
```

Here the command displays details about the time it has been up, number of users, and load average simultaneously.

## 2. Linux service

Linux service is a Linux command designed to start, stop, or restart a daemon service from a shell script file. All the scripts related to services will be stored in the/etc/init.d directory.

To start a service, you need to use the following command.

*Command:*

```
Service name_of_script start
```

To stop a service, you need to use the following command.

*Command:*

```
Service name_of_script stop
```

To restart a service, you need to use the following command.

*Command:*

```
Service name_of_script restart
```

To see the status of a service, you need to use the following command.

*Command:*

```
Service name_of_script status
```

### 3. Nohup command

Usually, when we exit a process, it will end automatically. Many, however, will not end and show a popup to terminate the process. Nohup command automatically tries to complete these processes without worrying about the popups that may arise.

*Command:*

```
Nohup PID 32423 3534
```

This will end the process with the pop ups automatically.

### 4. PMap

The pump is a system command developed to report a memory map of one or many of the selected processes. To check memory maps, however, you need PID for the process.

*Syntax:*

```
pmap PID
```

*Example:*

```
pmap 3242
```

Output:

```
3242: su

3242: firefox

3242:download-manager
```

You can know the memory map of multiple processes using the below command.

*Command:*

```
pmap pid1 pid2 pid3 ….
```

*Example:*

```
pmap 4324 5432 4564
```

*Output:*

```
4324: su

5432: firefox

5432:download-manager

5432: su

4564: chrome

4564:vlc
```

Learning about the memory map of different processes can help you end the sub-processes consuming more memory and are not serving any purpose.

To display additional information about the memory map, you need to use the following command.

*Command:*

```
pmap -x 3232
```

To display additional information about the device and the memory map, you need to use the below command.

*Command:*

```
pmap -d 3232
```

## 5. Wget

Wget stands for web get. It typically downloads web pages locally into your system. It is the most popular non-interactive web downloader software in Linux. Wget can download web pages even when the user has sent them to the background, and hence it consumes less memory. Wget can download HTTP, HTTPS, and FTP protocol websites in the same structure as the original website.

To use wget, you first need to install it on your local system using the following command.

*Command:*

```
sudo apt-get install wget

pacman -S wget
```

You can also download the .rpm file or .deb file from their official website.

To download only one specific URL from the web, use the below command.

*Command:*

```
wget <Name of the url>
```

*Example:*

```
wget www. wikipedia.org/worldwar2
```

*Output:*

```
download completing ……..    100%

Total bytes downloaded …. 343k

download speed …..          54k/s

saved to                    /home/downloads
```

If you want to save the downloaded web file with a different name, use the below command.

*Command:*

```
wget -O <nameofthefile> <URL of the file>
```

*Example:*

```
wget -O sample www.wikipedia.or/cryptocurrencymining
```

The above URL will be saved with the provided name instead of the default name.

You can download the limit at which the software can download the files using the below command.

*Command:*

```
wget –limit-rate=<Number of limit><Enter the URL>
```

*Example:*

```
wget –limit-rate=200 www.wikipedia.org/cryptocurrencymining
```

This will make the file not increase the limit of 200k/s.

Sometimes, users decide to download huge files. However, it is impossible to download files all the time without shutting down their computer. To solve this problem, we can download partially using the below command.

*Command:*

```
wget -c < Enter the URL here>
```

*Example:*

```
wget -c www.google.com/doodles/all
```

This is a 4.5GB web page, and hence it is not reasonably possible for all the data at one go. So, Whenever you enter the above command, the wget software will resume the download process from its last progress.

To download multiple files, you need to enter all the files in a text file and call it using the below command.

*Command:*

```
wget -i < Name of the text file>
```

*sample.txt:*

www.google.com/mail

www.wikipedia.org/cryptocurrencymining

www.wikipedia.org/sat

www.amazon.com/prime

*Syntax:*

```
wget -i sample.txt
```

Now, the command will download all the four web pages in the order in the text file.

You can also try to download the entire website using the below command.

*Command:*

```
wget —mirror -p —convert-links -P ./home/sample www.wikipedia.org
```

However, remember that downloading a whole website into your local system needs a lot of memory. For example, the example website " Wikipedia" we used has more than 100TB of memory.

## 6. ftp

As a system administrator, you must easily understand different file transfer protocols to exchange files between two other servers.

FTP ( File Transfer Protocol) is the most popular transfer protocol that can even exchange directories over a wireless network or a LAN network. SFTP is the advanced version of FTP used by organizations to encrypt the data while transferring them.

To use all FTP commands, you need first to open it in the shell terminal.

*Command:*

```
FTP open
```

To connect to an FTP server with a hostname or IP address, you need to use the below command.

*Command:*

```
ftp ipaddress/ HostName
```

*Example:*

```
ftp open 45.23.12.1
```

To download a file from an FTP server into a local machine, enter the below command.

*Command:*

```
FTP get <Name of the file>
```

You can upload a file into an FTP server using the below command.

*Command:*

```
FTP put < Name of the file>
```

After entering all the file names in a text file and calling it in a shell terminal, you can upload multiple files.

Command:

```
ftp mput *.txt*
```

Once all your operations are completed, you need to close the FTP server.

Command:

```
ftp close
```

## 7. Free

The free command helps to provide information about the unused memory usage in a RAM and swap memory present.

*Syntax:*

```
free
```

*Output:*

```
Mem total used free cached

1922. 1876 323 1121. 212
```

You can also change the memory format to display in kb, MB, or Gb.

With the below command, you can know how much memory is being spent in a specific interval.

*Command:*

```
free -s < specific time interval>
```

## 8. Last

If you want to find the last logged-in time of a particular user or all the users in your network, then you can use the below command.

*syntax:*

```
last
```

*Output:*

```
user1 Sun Aug 12 21:34 logged in
```

From the above output, we can understand that user1 has logged into the Linux system at 21:34 on Aug 12. If the user has logged out, the output will show the last login time and how much time he had stayed in the system.

## 9. Shutdown

Shutdown is a special Linux system administrator command that brings down the system in a secure way. If the sysadmin enters the command, then all the users in the network will be notified about a system shutdown and will be provided time to end all their processes.

*Command:*

```
shutdown < Time for shut down>
```

*Example:*

```
shutdown 3
```

The system administrator user can input a message for all the users not to be confused about why the system was being shut down.

*Output:*

```
Broadcast message from Admin …….
```

The system is going to shut down in 3 minutes for maintenance.

If you want to, however, shut down the system immediately, then enter the below command.

*Syntax:*

shutdown now

With the below command, you can shut down the system and reboot it after a particular time.

*Syntax:*

```
shutdown -r < Time for reboot>
```

To print a message while shutting down the system, you can use the below command.

*Syntax:*

```
shutdown <time> < " message ">
```

*Example:*

```
shutdown 5 " This is the maintenance mode for the system "
```

If you want to stop the shutdown process, then enter the below command.

*Command:*

```
shutdown -c
```

## 10. Info

Not all Linux shell software will have man pages that are usually used to provide helpful information for the user. Some software uses undocumented files to display information as a document. To see these kinds of files, you need to use the info command.

*Syntax:*

```
info
```

*Output:*

```
… Display information…

Help file
```

## 11. Env

env is a unique system administrator command used to manipulate or add new environment variables for your system. Environment variables are required for running the software in a Linux system. While all softwares create their own environment variables when the software is installed, it is however required to change them.

*Syntax:*

```
env <change address> <software name>
```

## 12. Du

du is a Linux command that is used to describe disk usage. It will check all the information of files and directories within the system almost instantly.

*syntax:*

```
du
```

## 13. shred

Usually, in Linux, when we delete a file using the del command or the standard GUI interface, it becomes easy to recover them with recovery software such as Disk Drill. However, sometimes sysadmins need to delete files in a way that they cannot be recovered.

To destroy the recovery process, the shred tool divides the data multiple times, shreds it, and overwrites the data by destroying it.

*syntax:*

```
shred < enter the file name>
```

If you want to watch the shredding progress on the terminal, you can enter the below command.

*Command:*

```
shred -u -v < enter the file name>
```

You can apply shred functionality on an entire drive using the below command.

*Command:*

```
shred < enter the device name >
```

*Example:*

```
shred /dev/sda2
```

## 14. Mount

Mount is a Linux command that needs to be used to connect an external device to your local Linux system. Linux directly doesn't allow external devices to connect to your local systems for safety. When you mount a device, all the files and directories in the external file system will be available to the users.

External devices such as pen drives, USBs, wifi adapters, and hard drives all need to use the mount option to make them work with Linux.

*Syntax:*

```
mount -t type < Name of the device> < Name of the directory>
```

Immediately the mounted file will be added to the /etc/fstab file.

To list all the current mounted file systems to your Linux system, enter the below command.

*Command:*

```
mount
```

You can also use the umount command to detach an external file system that has been attached to the device.

Command:

```
umount -t type < Name of the device > < Name of the directory>
```

When you select the unmount option, the file will be deleted from the /etc/fstab file.

## 15. Route

The route is a Linux sysadmin command used to display the op routing table available for the system.

If you have a router, you need to use this command to understand how your network packets are traveled and their destination. Wireless enthusiasts mainly use the route to find any vulnerabilities in the system.

Conversely, wireless hackers also use route to trace any packets that the administrator uses to access the system.

*syntax:*

```
route
```

*Output:*

```
Kernel IP routing table

Destination Gateway Flags

122.23.2.1 10.22.1.1. UG
```

You can add a default gateway to make sure that all network packets pass through it.

*Command:*

```
route add default gw < enter the IP address here>
```

To look at the routing cache information related to the Linux system, use the following command.

*Command:*

```
route -Cn
```

## 16. Man

The man is a short-term command for looking at the reference pages for software installed in Linux. All software developers use the man command to provide required information to the user. The user needs to select one of the many arguments to understand details about different sections related to software.

*Syntax:*

```
man [ select the option [ select the keyword ]
```

*For example:*

```
man ls
```

*Output:*

```
Name

ls. - list directory contents

Description
```

This command will list all the files in a particular directory.

When you entered a system Linux command, it displayed all the details about using the man command. If the information is more than the shell interface, you need to enter ctrl f to enter into the whole screen to move the details of the text as you feel like.

Usually, the man page is divided into three sections. The first section is the command's name, the second section provides details about the arguments that can be used with this command, and the third section is a description that includes info about what functions this command can function.

To display all the man topics for a particular software or tool, enter the below command.

*Command:*

        man -a ifconfig

If you want to search for a keyword in many available keywords, then enter the following command.

*Command:*

        man -k config

# Advanced Sysadmin Commands

Now we will discuss some of the default Linux commands that help Linux sysadmins be perfect at what they do and increase their productivity drastically.

### 1. Find

Find command helps Linux users to find particular files or directories based on different parameters such as size, user ownership, and permission.

To find files by name, you need to use the below command.

*Command:*

        find -name "enter the file name or format."

*For example:*

        find -name ".txt."

This will display all the text names in all directories in your shell terminal.

To find new files other than the attached file, then you need to use the below command.

*Command:*

```
find -newer sample1.txt
```

All files newer than the sample1.txt of the same file format will be displayed on the shell terminal.

To find a file and immediately delete it, you can use the below command.

*Command:*

```
find -name sample.txt -delete
```

Once the file is found, it will be deleted automatically. Make sure before executing this terminal because the data will be gone forever.

If you want to find a directory from your file system, you need to use the below command.

*Command:*

```
find type -depth -name Downloads
```

This takes some time as the shell command needs to go through many directories and subdirectories to find it. If this is a hidden folder, you need to enter the password for opening the directory and the associated files.

You can find the files associated with specified permissions using the below command.

*Command:*

```
find <Enter the name of the directory> -perm 777
```

## 2. Locate

Locate is the database version of the find command. As a Linux administration, you often need to search databases and locate easy to use relational database patterns on the command line itself.

*Syntax:*

```
locate [enter the option enter the pattern ]
```

## 3. Cal

Cal is a special Linux command used to display the calendar along with the current date highlighted on the shell terminal.

*Syntax:*

```
cal
```

You can see the calendar of any month of the previous or future year using the below command.

*Command:*

```
cal <month> <year>
```

## 4. Sleep

Sleep is a pretty normal feature in all operating systems. It lets all functions pause for a few minutes or hours until you decide to start again. You can apply these sleep features to a shell terminal using the below command.

*Syntax:*

```
sleep time

sleep [ details about minutes or seconds or hours ]
```

Command:

```
sleep 34

sleep m
```

# Here m stands for minutes. Enter h for hours and s for seconds

To exit from sleep mode, all you need to enter is ctrl+c.

## 5. Time

Time is a display command that provides the user with an estimated time for how long a process can run. If the software you are trying to run doesn't offer verbose mode, the command will display how much time a process is running.

*Syntax:*

    time ls

This command will display the time for all the processes that are running in a directory.

## 6. zcat

zcat is an inbuilt Linux command that can help users access files present inside a zipped file. You may need to enter the password for the zipped file if it is encrypted.

*syntax:*

    zcat < Name of the file>

*Example:*

    zcat sample

*Output:*

    opening zip file content….

    sample.img. /343k

    sample.mp3 / 3232k

    sample.mp4 / 34222k

## 7. df

Linux df command is a special one that provides details about disk space used in the file system. It gives the number of blocks used and the number of blocks available for a user when the said file system is mounted.

*syntax:*

    df <file name>

*Example:*

    df -a sda1

This will provide disk space for the external device in bytes instantly.

## 8. $date

This command provides an easy way to display the current date and time of the Linux system.

*Command:*

```
[sam @ testsystem ] $ date
```

*Example:*

```
[sam @ testsystem ] $ 12232021 111234
```

# CHAPTER 4

## Linux Security

While being the most secure operating system, Linux is still prone to attacks from intelligent hackers and crackers. No matter how safe the Linux kernel is, if it is connected to a network, then there is a chance that a hacker can access it using known or unknown vulnerabilities in the system or the services the system operates. As Linux exists mainly in a work environment directly linked to servers, databases, and the cloud, security becomes more crucial than ever. To master Linux, a programmer should be aware of various secure techniques that penetration testers and security analysts recommend companies and individuals follow to decrease the chances of their Linux system stopping getting hacked. However, remember that no method can guarantee you 100% security as hackers often use themselves as bait to manipulate people to crack systems.

It is also important to remain anonymous as an organization or individual as a massive chunk of data is often exchanged. Linux provides easy access to the Onion network, Proxy servers, and VPN to make tracking your identity a problematic task.

# Why Is There a Chance of Getting Hacked?

As most of the organizations rely on Linux to maintain their servers and databases, there are high chances of attackers trying to monitor your network traffic and find sensitive information that can help them gain access as a system administrator. Attackers often use system access to misuse services or most of the time for stealing information such as credit card numbers and account credentials. Even companies like Google and Facebook with high levels of security have faced problems with hackers in recent years. Hacking provides unwanted privileges to the attacker and can affect your organisation's reputation as most of the individuals are worried about their privacy on the internet.

# Password Security

All passwords of both Linux and Unix systems are stored in a particular file in the system known as a passwd file. Anyone in your system can get immediate access to your passwd file, but it is almost impossible to guess your password from it as it is highly encrypted. Whenever a user logs in to the system, the boot procedure will check your encrypted file with your entered password and allow you to enter your system only if there is a match.

All password cracking software specially designed to exploit Linux systems uses the same method to gain access to their target system. For cracking the systems, hackers use dictionaries of popular words that people can use as passwords. Some hackers also create custom dictionaries according to the target user for faster results.

To make this hack happen, the hacker should first gain access to the Linux system. This can be achieved by using vulnerabilities that may present in your network services, such as FTP or SMTP that handles your mail. Once they get access to the system, they will copy the file into their servers and match the password encryption from their potential dictionary attacks. Tools such as Hydra and John the ripper are popular ones that use this strategy to gain access to compromised Linux systems.

In the early 2000s, Linux systems were heavily exploited due to their weak password security measures. It also became complicated to maintain user groups with passed files because there are chances of people using the same passwords, making it easy for attackers to access the system. As hackers also started to crack hashes of the passwords with high processing hardware, the usage of passwd files to access system privileges became a controversy in the Linux community. To counter these problems, however, the Linux system has been updated with the functionality of shadow passwords for more secure authentication support.

## *Shadow Passwords*

Shadow password is a unique system file that stores Linux files and is available only for root users to restrict users in the network from exploiting the system. All the user passwords will be held in an encrypted form in the location /etc/shadow.

The shadow password file provides more security to the system by using a complex hashing algorithm to add more randomness to the encrypted password. When a hacker gains access to the shadow file, he needs to crack the hashes and crack the hashing algorithm along with all passwords of the users in the network to gain access to the Linux system. The hashing algorithm is represented using a key or salt with an encoded password that matches the system's root password.

Shadow file also has a specific format to make sure that everything matches precisely, even if someone spoofs the system network traffic by any chance.

Shadow file format:

1. Username - The name of the root system

2. Password - This is the encrypted password that is formed because of the hashing algorithm

3. Last password change of the root user

4. Expiration date of the password

5. Minimum time to change the password

6. Maximum time for a password to expire

7. Custom fields that the user can set for additional authentication measures

It is also important to remember that when you use select shadow files in your Linux system to save your authentication details, someone who has access to the passwd file can still look at all the users in the network from it. The only change is the encrypted passwords will not appear in the passwd file.

To make users change the passwords regularly, shadow files allow -M to initiate password change once the time expires.

*Command:*

> change -M 30 root

Here, 30 is the number of days for which the expiration will occur.

# VPN, Proxies, and TOR in Linux

Many recommend using Linux because it provides security that no other operating systems provide. However, the hard fact is many hackers also depend on Linux machines to exploit vulnerabilities and hence it is quite important that you know few features in Linux systems for securing your systems efficiently.

### 1. Use proxies

Proxies replace your system IP address and ports with another for helping you to access restricted content and to transfer information without being traced. Proxies act as a mediator and make it difficult for anyone on the Internet to track your activity. We recommend using Socks5 proxies for better security to your linux system.

To run a proxy chain in a linux machine, enter the below command.

*Command:*

```
root@server: proxychains
```

Once the proxychains interface is open, enter the below command on the shell terminal.

*Syntax:*

```
proxychains IP/PORT
```

*Example:*

```
proxychains 192.32.23.22/8080
```

### 2. Use VPN

VPN is a software that provides easier access to thousands of proxy servers for their users. Virtual private networks can help industries manage their authentication to their servers only when the users are logged in using a specific server. TOR is a popular VPN software that can help you access the internet with improved anonymity. TOR service can also make you access websites that are in the dark web using the .Onion links. When you use a VPN there is no chance of your ISP provider creating logs for your activity.

To install TOR in your linux system enter the below command

*Command:*

```
sudo apt-get TOR
```

Once TOR is installed, use the below command to start a TOR service and route all your traffic through one of their servers.

*Command:*

```
sudo start service TOR
```

### 3. Use Encrypted Mail

It is important to make sure that you are only using encrypted mail servers for accessing or sending information over the internet. Use services like proton mail instead of Gmail, if you are a system administrator.

# Network Monitoring in Linux

Even after following strict measures to secure root and user passwords, hackers can still access them by sniffing your user network traffic or using social engineering techniques to make the system administrator wholly or partially reveal their passwords. To counterattack these potential threats, it is crucial to constantly monitor your Linux system files and sensitive folders related to the root user.

All computers are connected to a network in the form of the Internet. In organizations, all the computers are connected through a private network to exchange information with each other. As a system administrator, you must learn some of the networking command-line tools present in Linux to easily monitor the network traffic whenever there is an emergency. Most of the time, you will be troubleshooting various default errors.

## 1. ifconfig

Ifconfig is fully abbreviated as interface configurator. ifconfig can be used by system administrators to perform specific tasks such as initializing an interface or assigning an IP address.

Initially, enter the ifconfig command to display all the output related to networks connected to the system.

*Command:*

```
ifconfig
```

*Output:*

```
etho — Information about it

WLAN - Information about it
```

You can select a specific interface to get more details about, as shown in the below command.

*Command:*

```
ifconfig wlan
```

To assign an IP address and gateway to an interface, you can use the below command.

Command:

```
ifconfig wlan0 < Enter the ip address > netmask < enter the gateway address>
```

You can enable a wireless or wired network as a system administrator using the below ifconfig option.

Command:

```
ifup wlan0
```

Similarly, you can disable a wireless or wired network as a system administrator using the below ifconfig option.

```
ifdown wlan0
```

## 2. Telnet

Telnet is a Linux command used to create a remote connection from the Linux system using the TCP/ IP protocol that provides a better transaction limit for the user. However, remember that all the data is unencrypted and can be easily spoofed by using applications such as Wireshark.

It is also essential for the system administrator to install the telnetd package for creating a TCP/IP connection.

*Command:*

```
sudo apt install telnetd /Downloads
```

Once the software is installed, it is time to use either the Ip address or the hostname to start a connection.

*Syntax:*

```
telnet nameofthehost/Ip address
```

*Example:*

```
telnet testuser
```

When you enter the below command, the system will automatically make a TCP/IP connection with the testuser.

To test whether or not a TCP/IP connection has been established, you can use the below command.

*Command:*

```
systemctl status telnetd
```

You can also do all these tasks by opening a new telnet shell terminal with the below command.

*Command:*

```
telnet >
```

Once all your commands are entered, you need to log out from the telnet terminal to end the remote connection.

*Syntax:*

```
> logout
```

## 3. SSH

SSh is a secure protocol used by Linux systems to connect to a remote server for performing both simple and advanced tasks without getting your IP address traced. All the data is encrypted using the SSH256 algorithm making it easy to run complicated commands such as tunneling, forwarding on a Linux server.

To work with SSH, you need to install clients such as OpenSSH in your local system.

*Command:*

```
sudo apt install OpenSSH-client
```

To connect to an ssh based system, use the below syntax.

*Command:*

```
ssh nameoftheuser@host [ can be both hostname and IP address ]
```

*For example:*

```
ssh testuser@192.23.2.1
```

In the above command, ssh says the shell terminal to create a secured encrypted connection, the user name is our address, and the host is the computer we are trying to connect with. With SSH, we can easily communicate with private networks and remote networks.

To check whether or not a secured connection has been made, use the below command.

*Command:*

```
sudo service ssh status
```

This will provide all the information about the network server details.

All encrypted connections need a safe key generated by the user to log in and access the data quickly.

*Here is the command:*

```
ssh-keygen
```

This will generate both private and public key files for the user. Ensure to save the private key file and upload the public key file for immediate access to the encrypted connection.

*Some of the encryption techniques used by SSH:*

- Hashing

  Hashing is a computer algorithm used to generate a cryptographic key based on the data being sent. If a part of data is manipulated, the connection will not accept as it doesn't have the same fingerprint as generated. Hashing makes it difficult for anyone to read others' data without a correct hashing algorithm.

- Symmetrical encryption

  Symmetrical encryption is a special encryption algorithm that uses only a single key for both encryption and decryption. Even though many say that it is unsecured, it is still used by many local Linux systems to communicate data easily. It is recommended to be used when the data is exchanged between private networks.

- Asymmetric encryption

  Asymmetric encryption is an advanced encryption algorithm that uses private and public keys to make a secure connection. SSH, most of the time, uses Asymmetric encryption to make a connection.

## 1. Mail

Linux provides an easy way to send emails with the mail command using secured protocols such as SMTP and telnet.

To use the mail command, you need to download the below package into a Linux system.

*Command:*

```
sudo apt install mailutils
```

When you try to install mailutils, a popup will rise in the shell terminal as it is a package that modifies the system extensions. Select that you are ok with the changes by pressing the "yes" button to install the package completely.

Once the package is installed, enter the below command to select mail using the mailutils command-line interface.

*Command:*

```
mail -s " Enter the subject here " < Enter the recipient address
here>

    < Enter the mail data from here>
```

You can also add attachments using the below command.

*Command:*

```
mail -s " Enter the subject here " < Enter the recipient address
here>

    < Enter the mail data from here>

    a /path/downloads/1.img
```

If you want the received mails for your address, you need to enter the mail command below.

*Syntax:*

```
mail
```

*Output:*

```
You have 23 new messages
```

## 2. Traceroute

Traceroute is a network troubleshooting utility tool that provides information about the number of hops and packets that have been transferred to reach a particular destination. To load a webpage, for example, you need to know how many packets are being sent. The traceroute command Linux system administrators to diagnose network issues quickly.

*Here is the syntax:*

traceroute hostname

*Example:*

traceroute www.google.com

This will display the gateway address, hops, and all the packets that need to travel to display the web page on the shell terminal.

You can also produce the same results but by using the IPV6 protocol using the below syntax.

*Example:*

```
traceroute6 www.google.com
```

### 3. Tracepath

tracepath is similar to the traceroute command but with root privileges. The only reason why few system administrators prefer using tracepath instead of traceroute is only when the network is weak.

*Syntax:*

```
tracepath www.google.com
```

### 4. Ping

Linux administrators use the ping command to check if the connection is still available. It will send a few packets to the server and check whether the network hosts are active. While troubleshooting network issues, ping is the first tool you need to use as a system administrator.

*Syntax:*

```
ping < Destination name>
```

*Example:*

```
ping www.google.com
```

*Output:*

```
Sending packets … 1 2 3

connection established

www.google.com - 4 packets - 192.223.21.12
```

You can limit the number of packets that you wish to send using the below command.

*Command:*

ping - c 25 www.facebook.com

You can check whether the host has an IPV4 or IPV6 using the below commands.

*Command:*

ping 4 www.twitter.com

# 4 represents the IPV4 protocol

*Command:*

ping 6 www.wikipedia.org

# 6 represents the IPV6 protocol

## 5. Netstat

Netstat is a network utility command used to describe different statistics related to both wired and wireless networks connected to the Linux system. This command can provide some statistics for the user by routing tables, several open sockets, and ports and types of connection ( both TCP and UDP).

To use this command, you need first to install it in your system using the below command.

*Command:*

sudo apt install net-tools

To display an introduction about the netstat tool and start on your terminal, use the below syntax.

*Syntax:*

netstat

To display all the existing connections and details about them, enter the below command.

*Command:*

netstat -a

Enter the below command to display only TCP connections but not the UDP connections to your Linux network.

*Command:*

netstat -at

Enter the below command to display only UDP connections but not the TCP connection to your Linux network.

*Command:*

    netsat -au

To display the connections that are listening to ports right now, use the below command.

*Command:*

    netstat -tnl

It is sometimes logical to check the network statistics for a particular user or a process when performing your network checks. Netstat provides commands for making this possible for sysadmin.

*Command:*

    sudo netstat -nlpt

Now, a new interface will open, enter either UID or PID to provide results.

To display all the network statistics for the Linux system, enter the below command.

*Command:*

    netstat -s

## 6. ss

ss is an additional Linux tool that provides advanced network monitoring statistics that are not provided by the netstat command. It is primarily famous for the kernel userspace details it provides for every network interface in the system.

*Syntax:*

    ss

To use TCP ports, use the below command.

*Command:*

    ss -lt

To use UDP ports, use the below command.

*Command:*

```
ss -lu
```

## 7. Dig

DNS name servers are essential for any website to work. They act as a phonebook for IP addresses to replace them with domain names. For example, it is tough to remember 192.32.32.12, the official Google IP address, to enter everything, but it is easy to remember www.google.com and join in the address book.

While a web address is entered, A DNS lookup is performed first. Linux provides a command called dig to get the domain information quickly.

To install the dig command, you need first to download a package with the below syntax.

*Command:*

sudo apt-get install dnsutils

Once you get it installed, use the below command format to check dns lookups for any of your favorite websites.

*Syntax:*

dig < Enter the domain name >

*For example:*

dig www.youtube.com

*Output:*

youtube.com 8080 US A 193.23.23.12

Query time: 1.1s

You can also trace the DNS path using the below command.

*Command:*

dig www.youtube.com +trace

If you want to perform batch queries for multiple domain names, you need to enter all of them in a text file using the cat command first, as shown below.

*Shell Command:*

cat > sample.txt

google.com

youtube.com

wikipedia.org

facebook.com

twitter.com

Now, you can query the text file using the below command.

*Command:*

dig -f sample.txt +short

Using short will display only the DNS address of the domain names, as shown below.

*Command:*

193.23.12.11

197.23.12.11

187.23.12.45

121.21.23.11

186.32.34.12

### 8. nslookup

To look up DNS-related queries, you can also use another Linux command known as nslookup.

*Syntax:*

nslookup www.twitter.com

## 9. Route

All Linux systems have a routing table to route packets to their destination. To look at the Linux system's routing table, enter the below command.

*Syntax:*

```
route
```

You can display all the IP addresses present in the routing table using the below command.

*Syntax:*

```
route -n
```

You can change your default gateway address to your Linux system using the below command.

*Command:*

```
route add default gw < enter the IP address here>
```

## 10. Host

To display the domain's IP address, you need to use the host command in the shell terminal. Remember that sometimes IP addresses and DNS lookup can be the same. But most of the time, they are different.

*Syntax:*

```
host www.twitter.com
```

You can only get the IPV4 address using the below command.

*Command:*

```
host -4 www.twitter.com
```

You can only get the IPV6 address using the below command.

*Command:*

```
host -6 www.twitter.com
```

You can also display the cname records of the domain name using the below command.

*Command:*

```
host -t cname www.twitter.com
```

You can display any domain name's TTL ( Time to Live) information using the below command.

*Command:*

```
host -v -t a www.twitter.com
```

## 11. Arp

All Linux systems have an ARP table to deal with network emergencies. arp command can be called using the below syntax.

*Syntax:*

```
arp
```

## 12. Whois

Whois is a special Linux command used to display valid n record information related to a website for the user. Sometimes you can also get complete details about the site owner. However, nowadays, many hosting services are providing anonymous features for the site owner.

*Syntax:*

```
whois www.twitter.com
```

*Output:*

```
Domain Name: www. twitter.com

Registrar: Twitter INC

whois server: whois.publicdomainregistry.com

Name server: NS1.Twitter.com

Status: Secure SSL clienttransferprohibited

Updated Date: 21-oct-2021

Creation Date: 12-08-2007

Expiration Date: 30-01-2099
```

# CHAPTER 5

## Linux Foundation Topics

Linux is the only operating system that is used in smartphones to complex server environments. It can be installed everywhere, from your old local computer to isolated environments in space stations. Linux is an operating system that supports modern environments. Learning about the foundations of Linux can help you drive faster on your journey to master Linux systems with perfection.

Once you have installed Linux on your system, your system will be rebooted, and the system will welcome you with a login screen. Enter your password to enter the world of infinite possibilities. Linux is an operating system that can be tinkered with according to the user's wishes. While the end-user can change its User Interface, software installation, and overall experience according to their desire, the core kernel that processes the user's instructions to the system hardware is the same for all the Linux distros. Understanding the basics we mention in this chapter is an essential prerequisite for any Linux enthusiast.

To help readers quickly grab the information, we divided the core topics essential for a Linux programmer into four pyramid blocks. All these blocks are told sequentially to help a beginner grasp the necessary topics for Linux mastery. Open your Linux system in a virtual machine and mess with it to get a feel for Linux. We recommend using Linux Mint for this chapter as it uses a basic version of the Linux kernel.

### First Block - Linux Shell Environment

Graphical user interfaces ( GUIs) were invented not more than fifty years ago. Before developing graphical user interfaces, computer users always relied on the terminal to enter commands into an operating system. For example, the Unix system's core functionalities are driven mainly by a shell to intercept instructions from the users. Modern Linux distributions ship with a shell interface, and many programmers depend on it more than the regular graphical user interfaces.

Shell is invincible and can help you perform any task without worrying about complex graphical user interfaces that may consume your memory and resources. The shell allows you to run scripts from languages such as Bash and Python to run different programs, compile or debug them, and perform various kinds of operations that the operating system is capable of. Even though it is true that the shell is not as user-friendly as GUIs, the shell is efficient and serves its purpose for developers and Linux system administrators. Many Linux distributions such as red hat Linux also force users to run programs only on terminals for security reasons.

To help you understand more about shell and its complicated features, we will discuss bash shell. Bash is abbreviated as Bourne Again shell and is the most popular shell environment in Linux distributions. There are many other shell versions of bash, but the dash used by Unbuntu distributions is probably the most popular of all. As a beginner, instead of relying on different shell versions, we suggest you depend entirely on bash and consider it standard while interacting with system resources or software developed for the shell environment.

## What Shell Interface Can Perform?

Using a shell interface, you can control any Linux distribution, even from remote locations. It becomes easy to log in to your servers, databases, or even home networks with just a few commands with a shell interface. If you are away from your computer, you can also use an Android or iOS app on your smartphone to control your servers using ssh interface. Shell interfaces can also be high-speed compared to GUI interfaces due to their lower graphic requirements. For example, suppose you try to make a dictionary attack using GUI software. In that case, it usually takes a few hours, whereas if you perform the same dictionary attack from a terminal, then it can be completed within twenty minutes. Shell commands are pretty easy to remember once you get used to them.

Many get overwhelmed with the Linux shell environment as there are potentially thousands of commands that a Linux administrator needs to master to perfect themselves for any troubleshooting issues. It is just a misconception that you need to remember all these commands to become perfect at Linux programming or management. Programming or Linux administration asks you to find logic when there is a problem but not remember solutions for the issues. By gathering and linking the commands for the Linux systems, you can perform even complex operations efficiently. Many programmers combine conditionals, loops, and advanced programming structures with Linux systems using a shell interface.

Shell programs have potentially infinite use cases. You can make backups, perform scheduling tasks or constantly update your chosen software with a few commands in a shell terminal using bash. Shell is essentially a command-line interpreter that sends instructions from the end-user to the Linux kernel. In Microsoft Windows, DOS acts as a replacement for a shell interface. Dos, however, is very limited by its features. On the other hand, the shell interface is versatile and powerful.

## Shell Prompt

Arch Linux is a popular Linux distribution that is considered challenging by many Linux enthusiasts as it doesn't come with a graphical user interface. So, when you try to boot into an Arch Linux system using the bootable USB for the first time, you will be welcomed with a shell prompt. Typically, every Linux distribution boots into a shell prompt, but all the Linux distributions have a preinstalled graphical interface. It will be overridden and stay in the background.

Once you start following instructions provided by the Arch Linux command-line interface, you will be asked to create an account and password. Immediately when your user account is created, a $ sign will appear on the terminal. It typically means that the system has accepted you as a regular user and provides your own set of system files and home folders.

A shell interface can also be used to log in as a root user instead of a regular user for special privileges. After entering your password and consent, your shell interface $ sign will be replaced with a # sign when you log in as a root user. When you are a root user in a shell interface, you can perform any operation, even the ones that can destroy all your system files permanently to lock you out from your system forever. So, it is recommended to log on as a root user only when you know what you are doing.

In a shell interface, along with your user name, the system name will also be shown.

*Example:*

```
[sam @ testsystem ] $
```

From the above example, it is evident that the shell interface is being accessed by sam in the test system environment as a regular user.

*Example:*

```
[sam @ testsystem ] #
```

From the second example, it can be understood that the shell interface is being accessed by sam in the test system as a root user.

The prompts that we have provided can be customized according to our convenience. Programmers develop much software as hobby projects to beautify the syntax that is entered in the shell interface. Beautiful, is an excellent open-source tool available for Debian-based systems that does the same thing seamlessly.

At first, typing in a shell interface can seem strange as you often make mistakes and end up understanding them. Sometimes a few errors can make you break your head for hours until you learn how to clear them. Shell interface and bash scripting can both be learned only through practice. Once you hit an enter button in an interface, the process will be started and executed immediately. Hence, you need to be completely aware of bash programming to create feasible software running on these systems.

## Running Commands

As a Linux enthusiast, you must understand some of the basic commands that we will mention now in this chapter. Open a terminal in your Linux distribution and type the commands that we provide in the coming chapters. Observe the results and understand explicitly what the command is doing to make it remember better. All commands provided in this book are basic commands that need to be remembered by heart if you are serious about making a career with Linux.

## Block - 2: File Management

Linux file management is one of the most important topics that a system administrator needs to manage Linux efficiently. As in Linux, everything is either a file or a process; we need to make sure that all file operations are known.

Files are also case-sensitive in Linux. For example, dope.txt and Dope.txt are two different files. All regular files such as programs and executables will have standard white color in a Linux system, whereas directory files will be blue.

### 1. file

First of all, to know the file type you are dealing with, enter the below command.

*Command:*

```
file doc.txt
```

The result will provide details about text file format and what it can be used for. Every third-party application creates a new file type that helps its users quickly develop files related to the application.

### 2. Touch

Touch is a special file command that is used to create new empty files irrespective of the type. If the user specifies a class, a new empty file will be created for that particular format.

*Syntax:*

```
touch < enter the file name>
```

*Example:*

```
touch sample1
```

You can create two empty files at the same time using the below command.

*Command:*

```
touch sample1 sample2
```

### 3. rm

rm is a Linux file management command that is used to delete files or directories. Using the rm command will make the file get deleted permanently. Unlike GUI, where there will be a trash option to recover your files, rm will not provide that option. Many Linux distros use complex algorithms to make the deleted files unrecoverable.

*syntax:*

    rm < Name of the file>

*Example:*

    rm sample1.txt

## 4.  cp

cp is a Linux command that is used to copy a file or directory into another directory.

*Syntax:*

cp < previous file name> < new file name>

*Example:*

    cp sample1 sample2

If you use the above command, then the file will be copied to the same destination.

If you want to copy a file to a different destination, then use the below command structure.

*Command:*

    cp sample1 /home/Downloads

## 5.  mv

Mv is a Linux command that can move one file or directory from one location to another.

*Command:*

    mv sample1 /home/downloads

If you don't specify the location, then this command will not work.

## 6.  Rename

Even though you can use the mv command to rename files, it is not recommended as a good practice for system administrators. Linux enthusiasts should use the 'rename 'command to rename files and directories instead of the more popular mv command.

*Syntax:*

```
rename 's/nameofoldfile/nameofnewfile/ '*.docx*
```

You must mention that file type at the end of the command because there are chances of correctly finding the file if there are two file types with the same name.

**7. install**

install is a special Linux file system command used to copy particular files from one directory to another. When using the cp command to another directory, some files such as man pages cannot be reproduced. To solve this problem, Linux administrators should use the install command.

*Command:*

```
sudo install example.txt sample.txt downloads
```

All the man page files or make files present in your folder will be copied to the /Downloads folder.

## *File Manipulation Commands*

While the above commands have helped us change the file's destination, the commands that we are going to discuss now will help us manipulate the file contents.

**1. open**

To manipulate any file, you need first to open it. While there are many ways, the most popular one among Linux users is by using the cat command.

*Command:*

```
cat <name of the file>
```

This will print all the details present in the file on the shell terminal.

If the file content is more than one page, it becomes easy to see it one go. For these purposes, where you have to determine what the file consists of, it is more logical to use fewer commands where only one page will be shown at one time.

*Command:*

```
less sample.txt
```

If the file content is large, the command will adjust the terminal window according to the height and width provided.

*Command:*

```
more text.txt
```

If you want to view the content present in the files using line numbers, you should use the nl command.

*Command:*

```
nl sample.txt
```

## 2. Head

Head is a special Linux command that is used to display only the first ten lines present. You can, however, change the default value from 10 to any number you want.

*syntax:*

```
head < name of the file>
```

You can also open two files with the default ten lines each by using the below command.

*Command:*

```
head sample1.pdf sample2.pdf
```

You can directly specify how many lines you want to display using the below command.

*Command:*

```
head -20 sample1.txt
```

## 3. Tail

System administrators mainly use the tail command to read the errors that have occurred in the files. With the tail command, a system administrator can look at the last ten lines of a file by default. Both head and tail commands are often used to compare two files.

*syntax:*

```
tail < Name of the file>
```

*Example:*

```
tail sample.txt
```

*Output:*

```
1

2

3

4

5

6

7

8

9

10
```

You can specify the number of lines you want the tail command to display using the below command.

*Command:*

```
tail -n <enter number> < enter the file name>
```

*Example:*

```
tail -n 20 sample1.txt
```

You can display multiple files at the same time using the below command.

*Command:*

```
tail sample1.txt sample2.txt
```

## 4. Cat

Cat is one of the versatile Linux commands which can be used for different purposes.

Mostly, Linux users use the cat command to display the content present in them.

*Example:*

```
cat sample1.txt
```

It supports more than 40 file types that can be displayed on the shell terminal. If necessary, it will open software that will display or run the file selected.

To create a file using the cat command, you can use the > symbol.

*Command:*

```
cat > <name of the file>
```

*For example:*

```
cat sample.txt
```

When you click the enter, you will be taken to an empty shell to enter your code or text. Once completed, you need to enter ctrl+d to save your file.

You can also use the cat command to append details to an already existing file. This can be achieved using the >> command.

*Syntax:*

```
cat >> ( name of the file )
```

*Example:*

```
cat >> sample1.txt
```

Once the file opens, add your code or text and save it using the ctrl + d button. Once the file is saved, the entered new data will be appended to sample1.txt.

We can also use the cat command to copy content from one file to another file using the below command.

*Command:*

```
cat ( name of the old file) > ( name of the new file)
```

*Example:*

cat sample1.txt > sample2.txt

You can also use the cat command to easily concatenate contents into two files to a single new file.

*Here is an example:*

```
cat sample1 sample2 sample3 > sum
```

All the content in three files, sample1, sample2, and sample3, will be shifted to sum.

If you want to display line numbers for any file using the cat command, you can follow the below one.

*Command:*

```
cat -n < Name of the file>
```

## 5. Tac

This is a special Linux command that does everything cat does but in reverse order.

*syntax:*

```
tac < name of the file>
```

You can also use the tac command to separate the content using a prefixed string or symbol.

*Syntax:*

```
tac < name of the file> —separator " String you want to use "
```

# Linux Directories

Every Linux user has his own home directory where all his individual and system files will be saved. The home directory is the first directory that is processed when the user logins to a system. The /home directory is also the standard subdirectory of the root directory. Remember that all the directory notations will use forward-slash (/) to represent the path of directories.

Linux users usually use a GUI-based file manager to look at the Linux system's home directory quickly. To use the Command line to open the home directory, use the below command.

*Command:*

```
cd /home
```

## 1. cd

Cd common is a Linux system command that can be used to change the current working directory.

*Syntax:*

```
cd < Name of the directory>
```

While working as a Linux administrator, you often need to change your working directory. With cd, you can quickly move to a directory from anywhere.

*The command for changing to home directory:*

```
cd ~
```

The above command will take you to the home directory directly.

*The command for changing to the root directory:*

```
cd /
```

The above command will take you to your root directory. If you are a root user, then this will take up to the absolute path of Linux.

Users can also enter the absolute path to move to the location they desire seamlessly.

*Command:*

```
cd /root/ download/ firstdownloaded

cd -
```

Linux also provides an easy way to the previous directory that you have dealt your operations with.

*Command:*

```
cd * *
```

This command can help you to reach the parent directory easily.

## 2. ls

Ls is the list command in Linux that lists out all the files irrespective of what format they are in a directory.

*Syntax:*

```
ls
```

If you want to list out hidden files too, you can use the below command.

*Command:*

```
ls -a
```

If you want to list out files between a prefixed size, you need to use the below command.

*Command:*

```
ls -l —block-size = [ size of the block ]
```

Usually, the size will be described in M, which represents a Megabyte.

If you want to directly display all files in the home directory of the Linux user system, then you can use the command.

*Command:*

```
ls ~ ~
```

### 3. Mkdir

As a Linux user, you often need to create your directories. While it is easy to create a folder or directory using the GUI interface in the file manager of your choice, using mkdir is preferable for Linux system administrators.

*Command:*

```
mkdir < name of the directory>

mkdir sampledirectory
```

You can verify whether or not the directory is created using the ls command.

*Command:*

```
ls
```

It is also possible to create multiple directories at the same time using the below command.

*Command:*

```
mkdir <directory 1 > < directory 2 > < directory 3>
```

### 4. rmdir

This is the Linux system command that can be used to delete a directory. However, remember that the rmdir cannot delete the subdirectories that are present. The directory need not contain any other subdirectories for this command to work.

*Command:*

```
rmdir <name of the directory>
```

To delete all the subdirectories from a directory and all the data associated with them, you need to use the following Linux system command.

*Command:*

```
rmdir -p home/downloads
```

### 5. Rename folder

Rename is not a system command, and hence it first needs to be downloaded for being used.

*Command:*

```
sudo apt install rename
```

Once the software is installed, you can rename a directory using the following command.

*Command:*

```
rename <expression> rename
```

In this command, the expression can be used to rename one or more directories based on the conditions provided. For example, you can make all lowercase directory names into upper case directory names.

# File Permissions in Linux

As discussed before, Linux provides both user accounts and administrative accounts, which can be added to a group. To understand the complexity of a Linux system, you need to be aware of the file permissions that Linux provides for its users.

The below command will display all the users and their current process for the system administrator.

*Command:*

```
ls -lh
```

Based on these results, the sysadmin will check the progress of a task or find out if there is any suspicious activity in the network.

## Chown

As there will be many files in a system, the user who creates the file is known as the owner of that file. Linux provides a way to restrict this file to other users and allows the original owner to share the ownership with users in the system using the chown command.

*Syntax:*

```
chown <user name of the new owner> <file name>
```

*Example:*

```
chown testuser1 map.img
```

You can also provide access to an entire group, as shown below.

Command:

```
chown testgroup1 map.img
```

Now, all the users in testgroup1 will access the file and modify it according to their wishes. Remember that the original user can only provide readable permissions sometimes without giving the power to edit it. To understand these types of commands, you need to have a good idea about file permissions.

All the files in a Linux system usually have three types of permissions.

1. Read (r) - This file permission will allow the user to read it but not modify or delete it.

2. write (w) - This file permission will allow the user to edit, modify, or delete it. However, remember that you also need permissions of that particular directory to rename or delete it. If not, then you can only edit the content.

3. Execute (x) - This file permission provides you a way to execute the program apart from writing, modifying, deleting, and renaming it. With executable permissions, you can control how the file operates.

## chmod

To set file permissions easily, Linux provides a command known as chmod. You can select all three permissions, namely read, write and execute, using the chmod command. The permissions are set using the flags associated with each file.

*syntax:*

chmod options permission <name of the file>

*Example:*

```
chmod 777 sample
```

777 is the number for providing executive permissions to the file.

## *Block - 3: Process Management*

Process management is an essential task for a Linux user to run as many crucial programs as they can on computers RAM. All processes have a typical lifecycle and get terminated on their own or sometimes when the user ends manually. A system administrator often needs to schedule processes or complete them because of system handling or to provide memory resources for the more resource-hungry graphical applications.

In these instances, it is essential to kill these processes manually. Knowing about details such as PID and signal can make this process easy.

### 1. Top

This is a Linux system command that lists all the running processes in the system now. It provided different details such as PID, time, and CPU usage for all the processes.

*Syntax:*

```
top
```

*Output:*

> Tasks: 43 total, 2 running, 40 sleeping, 0 stopped, 1 zombie
>
> PID. User. %CPU. % Mem Time. Command

We can browse all the processes listed by using the up and down button in the terminal. You can also easily filter all these processes by CPU and memory usage.

Apart from the top command, you can also use the ps command to display the process information for a particular user. When you are a sysadmin, you can look out the running processes for just one user instead of everyone using the ps command.

*Command:*

```
ps aux | grep user1
```

The above command will display the process only related to user1.

## 2. Kill

Killing a process can be done by various commands provided. However, you need to remember that if you are a regular user, you can kill only the processes that belong to you but not another user. On the other hand, if you are a root user, you can kill all the processes of all users or one specific process of a user with just a PID.

Linux systems use signals whenever it kills a process. SIGTERM is a signal that ends a process after automatically saving all their procedures gracefully. SIGKILL, however, is another signal that is designed to kill the process forcefully. SKILL comes in handy, especially when you are dealing with suspicious malware that affects your systems.

To use the kill command in the shell terminal, all you need is the PID of a process. To find the PID for your desired process, use either the top or ps command.

*Command:*

```
kill 5473
```

This command will end the running process irrespective of whether it is a background or foreground process.

If the process is not ending for some reason, then use the below command.

*Command:*

    kill -SIGKILL 5473

You can also use the top command to kill processes as it is an interactive shell interface.

First, enter the command top to list all the processes. Now when you are sure that the shell is running, enter k to activate the kill interface. Once activated, you have to find the PID from the processes and enter it to kill the process.

Killing processes can also be done using a GUI interface known as the system monitor. Find your processes and left-click on them to find an option to kill the process. Once done, close the window.

## 3. killall

Killall is a special Linux command that can be used to kill a process and all its sub-processes by entering the process name along with it.

*Command:*

```
killall chrome
```

If you want to end all the processes forcefully, they use the command.

*Command:*

```
killall -SIGKILL chrome
```

If you are a system administrator and need to end the process of another user, then you need to use sudo as shown below.

*Command:*

```
sudo killall chrome
```

## 4. pkill

Not all the time will we be able to end a process with a name. In some instances, you will be unable to find a process and kill it because many other processes run with the same name. For these kinds of processes to kill them, use the pkill command.

*Command:*

```
pkill chrome
```

It will then close all the processes with the name chrome or a string matching chrome.

**5. xkill**

xkill is a special Linux system command that is used to kill an X server client.

*Command:*

```
xkill { name of the server }
```

You can also enter the PID of the X server.

Command:

xkill PID

## *Block -4: Logging System*

Log Files provide an easy way to understand what has happened inside a system for a period of time. Proprietary operating systems such as Windows and macOS don't provide access to system log files unless you are an administrator of the system. Linux is an exception here because it provides an easy way to read log files for all the users in the network. If you are a root user, then you can edit or replace log files according to your requirements.

Log files can help system administrators to constantly track different processes, users and groups that exist in their system. While troubleshooting errors, all linux administrators will first find a log file for the hardware or software associated with that problem. All the logs in Linux are usually saved according to the rules given in the daemon syslogd.

syslogd makes sure that once the system is logged in by a user to create log files according to the users activity. You can also create encrypted log files using your own set of hashing algorithms. However, always make sure that you remember your password for the syslogd file to recover all the log files without any encryption.

*File format for logs:*

Rules

Enter rules here

End of the log file

You can prioritize where and how log files need to be created using the rsyslog file present in a linux system.

# Working with Text Files

Text files are an integral part of all operating systems, and knowing how to use them effectively is an essential skill for a Linux enthusiast. Linux is an immediate predecessor for Linux systems that store data exclusively in text files instead of the different formats we use nowadays. As Linux still inherits some of the qualities of Unix systems, it is still essential to understand the various functionalities of text files. In Unix systems, all system configuration and database management was done by searching and editing simple text files. Even though Linux has adopted supporting various new formats with time, text files are still an excellent way for programmers to interact with system binaries without messing up other essential files in the root source.

GUI interfaces also have many restrictions that can be a headache, especially during troubleshooting any errors. Manual text file configurations such as XML and HTML have become pioneer mediums to get the most out of the Linux environment. There will be no GUI, especially in server environments, making it mandatory for system administrators to configure text files to make any system changes.

Even though it can be a slow way to interact with core Linux, you can speed up this process by learning shortcuts or default commands that can save a lot of your time.

## *How to Edit Text Files?*

To edit text files, you need to install a text editor. Many third-party text editors are developed exclusively for Linux systems. When talking about text editors, understand that we are not talking about GUI-based text editors such as gediit, which ships with GNOME-based systems. Text editors we are mentioning now are exclusively used in the command terminal. While there is much terminal-based text editor software, the most popular ones are vi and emacs.

### Using VI for Your Text Editing Purpose

The vi editor is case sensitive, and hence while opening or creating any file, you need to make sure that you are using the correct case-sensitive letter.

Creating a file using vi editor is straightforward. Enter the below syntax with your desired name.

*Command:*

```
vi < Enter the file name >
```

*For example:*

```
vi sample
```

You can also use the path to create a file in a specific directory, as shown below.

*Command:*

```
vi /Home/Downloads/Example/first.txt
```

Once the file is created, you will enter into the command mode to enter your content. However, remember that you cannot enter any text in the command mode. To add text, you need to enter the insert mode by pressing i. Enter anything you want in the insert mode and when you are done, enter the ESC key to return to the command mode again.

To save and quit the text file you have written, you need to use:wq command in the command mode.

# CHAPTER 6

# Linux Programming

Programming is engaging, complex, and intuitive. In addition to sysadmins looking forward to a career in Linux administration and server development, anyone who wants to create or maintain software needs to be able to give instructions to computers, and programming is the only way to do that. Linux is a powerful operating system designed to help programmers create new software that can help thousands of people worldwide. With Linux, you can develop applications for any other operating system, servers, databases, and even high-performance satellites. There are Linux tools for every programming language you can think of in the programming world. Despite the fact that some operating systems, such as Ubuntu, include pre-installed compilers and debuggers for popular programming languages, it is often necessary to install them manually.

Most popular Linux distributions come with the GNU software development kit. The GNU software development kit consists of tools that can compile both C and C++ code. All these tools will provide an easy way to debug your code without the need for additional IDEs. The following sections in this chapter will introduce you to the basics of programming in Linux and about its shell scripting capabilities.

# What Is Programming?

Programming is essentially the task of writing computer programs. Computer programs consist of step-by-step instructions, also known as algorithms, to solve a particular problem. For example, an image manipulation program such as Adobe Photoshop solves the problem of designers editing their photos, and software such as Final Cut Pro solves the problem of editing videos. Every software has a purpose that it is destined to do. To solve this problem, computers need to be provided with inputs that they can understand and use these inputs to solve the problem in real-world situations.

A program sends all instructions to a central processing unit, which consists of a microprocessor which can interpret machine language and execute your instructions sequentially so that it can give back results. The speed with which the computers can run these instructions is based on their processing power. All the executions the computer makes usually are stored in Random Access Memory (RAM) and are directly responsible for the runtime execution of programs.

Here is an example of a real-life program called VLC, which is a media player.

1. Installation

   First, you need to install the software that is written and compiled by a set of programs. Different software requires different requirements. For example, the software VLC needs Java to run. So, we first installed Java on our machine. If Java is not installed, then the software will not start.

2. Program Execution

   The primary focus of VLC is to play media files of different formats. So, whenever you run a file format that the program supports, the program will start executing in RAM. The program opens the software, will analyze the file, sync the audio with video, and will play to you.

3. Program Termination

   Once you terminate the program, the program will be taken away from the RAM, and all the background services that the program is running will end. All the saved information by the program will usually be kept in the hard drive before the program's termination.

The above example should have provided you with an excellent overview of how programs work. To write these kinds of complex programs, you need to learn different programming languages. Every programming language has a specific purpose. For example, C is a programming language that is designed to communicate with hardware kernels. In contrast, Java is a programming language designed to make it easy for enterprises to work with a large codebase.

*When does the operating system come into the picture?*

While programs are combined to form software, operating systems are designed to run these programs. Not all software can be run in all operating systems. Final Cut Pro is a great exclusive software that only runs in Mac systems. Ultimately, the programmer decides to make it available for different platforms as it takes a lot of time to develop programs for different operating systems and environments.

Operating systems act as an intermediary between the software and the hardware. Operating systems make it easy for developers to create software. They provide specific libraries that the programmers can use to invoke different features such as networking, optimization, and input/output control.

In Linux, shells are the command processors that programmers need to learn to create programs for Linux systems. A shell can usually be started using a terminal or sometimes can even be started in the background by other processes. The desktop environment such as GNOME, XFCE, or KDE , that a Linux user uses to run GUI-based applications is typically a shell-based interface with more complex features.

# Tools for Computer Programming

To write programs and combine them to form software, you need to use different tools. Linux provides one or many of these tools for the programmer using it primarily as a development environment to create new software.

1. A text editing program

   All the program code needs to be written using a text editor for it to be compiled. All your program instructions need to be written in a sequential order in the text program for the shell to execute it.

2. Code compiler

   Any high-level programming language needs a compiler to find whether or not your syntax is the incorrect format supported by the programming languages. Linux is preinstalled with GNU C and C++ compilers for helping programmers write working programs.

3. **Software building**

   Once the programmers write the program using the logic, they need to insert them into a package to ship it into different Linux distros efficiently. Software building is usually a complex process and requires many libraries to be integrated for every component to function correctly. Linux provides various GNU tools to solve this problem.

4. **Debugging**

   Debugging is a significant part of software development. Even though programmers create software, they are bound to deal with bugs once the software is written entirely. All the bugs need to be found and rewritten so that the end-user doesn't face the problem anymore. GNU debuggers that come along with Linux are essential for software development.

5. Version control

   As a programmer, one uses tens of libraries for adding different components to their software. Version control helps programmers automatically update the libraries used in the software and make changes to the code so that the application doesn't crash abruptly. Linux comes by default with revision and concurred version control systems to rewrite your software whenever required efficiently.

# Using the GNU C Compiler

GNU C compiler is one of the most popular Linux tools because it can help developers create software for three languages - C, C+, and Objective C. To compile any program of these languages, you need to enter GCC in the command line interpreter.

GNU C compiler provides an easy way to port a program written in ANSI C to Linux. Usually, it takes a lot of customization and code rewriting to make it compatible with Linux. Still, the GNU C compiler does the job within a few minutes because of its unique auto-detect features. With GCC, it also becomes easy to connect to files together with an executable file.

To start compiling a C file using the GNU C compiler, you need to use the following command.

*Command:*

GCC name_of_the_program

# GNU Make

When you create new software, you need to write rules to understand what libraries and components it can use to build the software step-by-step. GNU make is typically a build software that is created by the GNU project for this purpose. It works efficiently and helps programmers write their compilation scripts without depending too much on automated softwares to make it for them. GNU Make, however, is hated by many other developers because it makes the job challenging and counterproductive for them. Irrespective of which group you belong to, GNU Make is an essential GNU software that you need to be aware of.

All programmers first write their code in a source file and use Makefile to write their rules. You can customize make files to delete execute files, object files or rename them automatically.

*A makefile usually consists of rules in the below-mentioned format:*

Target …: { Target Variables or requirements here}

requirements …: { Specific requirements for file needs to be written here}

Rules

…

{ Specific rules that need to be followed should be written here}

…

# GDB Debugger

GDB debugger is a portable debugger that runs in almost all Linux distros and supports C, C+, ADA, and GO languages. GDB provides an easy way to alter the execution of programs by providing a way to change internal variables and call functions quickly. These functionalities help programmers to check the software with different values and find why the software is crashing at various instances.

GDB also provides remote debugging for embedded systems. GDB is primarily a command life-based software, but many third-party developers have developed frontend GUI software for the GDB debugger. Lazarus, Eclipse, and Xcode are some IDE that easily links GDB to the workflow.

Command to debug a program:

GDB program

# Shell Scripting

We have already discussed extensively about a specific type of shell script tool called bash in the previous chapters. As a Linux programmer, you also need to ensure that you have a sufficient understanding of other shell scripts such as C shell, Korn shell, and GNU shell. Shell scripting helps Linux administrators and system engineers effectively control the processor instructions sent into the Linux kernel. Shell takes input from the users, translates them, and makes sure that the kernel understands the language. It follows an order of execution based on the order they are written.

Shell is fundamentally a programming language that is developed to run on a Linux terminal. While most Linux shell commands are essential, they can also become complex when the time is right. It consists of standard programming components such as variables, control structures, and loops for executing the commands sequentially.

*Here is an example shell script:*

```
# !/bin/sh

# Author: testcode

# The bash script starts from here, and this is a comment

echo "What is your city name?"

read CITY

echo "Hello, you belong to $CITY"
```

Output:

```
$./test.sh

What is your city name?

New York

Hello, you belong to new york

$
```

The above program is provided for you to understand basically how a shell program works. All the components that are essential for writing effective shellcode are mentioned now in this section. Don't forget to open your terminal in a Linux system and experiment with the code while learning new topics from this section.

# Understanding Shell Prompt

Shell Prompt has different features and can help you type commands. If a $ sign appears, then it means that the prompt has been initialized. The shell reads your instructions if they are appropriate, and when completed, you can press the enter key to make them run.

## Comments

Comments are common in any scripting language. They help programmers to understand the commands or provide information about different packages. A '# 'sign always precedes a comment. Comments are an excellent practice to help other people understand what logic you are applying to make the program solve a problem. As Linux users use mostly open-source software, writing code with clear comments is appreciated by the community.

*Example:*

```
#!/bin/csh

# Author: Learning Linux easily
```

Before starting other shell scripting basics, we recommend you open a simple text editor such as vi on the left side of your monitor and the regular command-line interpreter on the right side. Carefully follow the instructions, enter them on the left side, and wait for them to execute on the right side. This setup can help you learn shell programming effectively.

Remember that shell script is similar to other high-level programming languages and consists of regular programming components such as variables, functions, and control structures no matter how complex the script gets.

```
# Starting a shell file
```

All shell files consist of .sh as the extension type.

Here is a command to open a shell file with the nano editor

*Command:*

```
$ nano sample. sh
```

Here is a command to open a shell file with the vi editor

*Command:*

```
$ vi sample.sh
```

Depending on the editor you are using, you may need to change the command. Please refer to --man option of your editor for default commands for open-shell scripts.

Also, it is essential to remember that you can directly execute the shell file that has been just written.

*For example, when you execute a shell file:*

```
./sample
```

*Output:*

```
Permission denied
```

The reason is, to execute a shell file in Linux, you need to first provide execution privileges to it. To provide execution privileges, you can use the chmod command.

*Command:*

```
chmod 777 example.sh
```

*Command:*

```
./example.sh
```

This time, the file will be executed successfully.

You can also use chmod +x for providing permission files for executing.

*Command:*

```
chmod +x example.sh
```

## Shebang Line

No matter what type of shell script file you are working on, you need first to provide the complete source of the shell interpreter for the terminal. If not, all the shell statements will not be executed.

For the regular shell, the below-mentioned code is the shebang

*Code:*

```
#!/bin/sh
```

However, remember the interpreter source will change according to the shell type you are using.

For example, shebang for the C-shell is

*Code:*

```
#!/bin/csh
```

## Echo and Read

For any programming language, taking input from the user and displaying output to the user is essential. For example, let us assume that you are using a calculator app on your smartphone, the numbers you enter are the input. After performing mathematical calculations, the result the calculator app gives for you is the output. Shell scripting uses echo and read for achieving these.

*Example:*

```
#!/bin/csh

# Author: Learning Linux easily

# This is a script to explain input and output in the shell
```

```
echo "What is your name?"

read NAME

echo "Hello, How are you doing $NAME ? "
```

1. When you execute the above example, the below set of chain reactions will occur in a shell.

2. The shell will first check for the computer interpreter source and will move to the following line as it checks out correctly.

3. As there are comments followed by a # line in the following line, the interpreter will ignore these lines until they reach the 4th line.

4. In the 4th line, the shell interpreter will find the 'echo 'in-built function used for output by the Shell language. It will print whatever is there in between the quotes onto the computer screen.

*Here for example:*

```
What is your name?
```

The command will reach the following line, where it faces the read command used by the shell to take input from the user and store it into a variable called NAME. The command will move further only when the user gives input.

*Here for example:*

```
Obama
```

Once the user has entered an input called Obama to the shell interface, the interpreter will move to the following line where it sees an echo statement again with a call to variable value in the quotes. It will then the already provided input by the user to that echo statement and will end the program execution successfully.

*Here for example:*

```
Hello, How are you doing, Obama?
```

## Understanding Variables

In the example mentioned above, the user input is stored in a variable and is called in then by the echo statement. If you are confused, how a shell program could have done that, it is because of a programming feature known as a variable.

A variable is nothing more than a pointer to the actual data that you are representing.

*For example:*

```
read NAME
```

In this command, the input provided, whatever it may be, the user will be stored in the NAME variable. It provides a location, and it will print whatever value is there in it when you call it. You can create both static and dynamic variables, depending on your program purpose. You can assign and delete variables composed of different values belonging to other data types, such as text, number, and boolean.

Variables are usually of three types in shell programming.

### 1. Local Variables

A variable that is present in the current instance of the shell is known as a local variable. So, for example, if your shell starts a new program, then a local variable cannot be accessed because it can only be available to the instant shell terminal that created it. Local variables are usually used for programs that need encrypted conditions, such as network monitoring databases and servers in Linux systems.

### 2. Environment Variables

A variable that can be used by all the child processes that is started by the shell is known as an environment variable. For example, suppose a server software is called antivirus software. In that case, all the variables used by the server can be checked by the antivirus if the variables in the server are environment variables. Many softwares are functional only because of the environment variables as they often need to interact with different programming components or child processes to function correctly.

### 3. Shell Variables

A shell variable is a special kind of variable that can be used to make a variable work as both local and environment variables according to different preset conditions. Shell variables are more logical and need more code to make them effective in real-world applications.

## *How to Define Variables?*

Defining any variable needs to have a specific format, as shown below.

*Format:*

```
variable_name=variable_value
```

Remember that you don't need to use a semicolon, and there should be no spaces before and after the = symbol. In other high-level programming languages such as Java or Python, you can use spaces for better readability. This also helps us understand that Shell programming language focuses more on efficiency than the program's readability. This may seem difficult for new beginners, but once you get the hang of the messiness of the code, you will be able to execute and write further instructions at a much faster pace, especially when you are dealing with regular expressions.

*Example:*

```
#!/bin/sh
NAME = " Name of the Employee "
echo $NAME
```

When you provide execution permissions to it and execute it the output will be displayed.

*Output:*

```
Name of the Employee
```

## *Read-Only Variables*

All variables can usually be modified by another instruction. However, it is not logical to replace a variable all the time, especially when you are dealing with a sensitive problem. Shell programming provides a readonly command to use to solve this problem whenever the programmer doesn't want the variable to be replaced.

*Example:*

```
#!/bin/sh

NAME = " Name of the Employee "

readonly NAME

NAME = " Sam"

echo $NAME
```

When you provide execution to it and execute it.

*Output:*

```
Error: NAME is a read only variable
```

## *Unsetting Variables*

Unsetting Variables is a shell technique where the already present values in a variable will be deleted when it is used. Programmers often use unsetting variables to clear memory space once their role is completed in program execution. However, remember that unsetting variables are recommended only when dealing with complex programs that require more than average computer resources.

Example:

```
#!/bin/sh

NAME = " Name of the Employee "

unset NAME

echo $NAME
```

When you provide execution to it and execute it.

Output:

```
----
```

An empty space will be shown, representing that the variable value has been deleted and is hence now a null variable.

## *Special Variables*

Special variables in the shell script are reserved for specific functions. All of these use special Unix variables and help programmers interact with parameters in programming effectively.

Remember that all the special variables will be followed by the symbol '$'.

The first special variable will be the '$ 'itself when invoked, which gives the PID of the current shell.

*For example:*

```
$echo $$
```

*Output:*

```
46727
```

The above $ has shown 46727 as the PID.

**1. $0**

This is a special variable that provides the file name of the file when you execute it.

First of all, let us create a shell with the name experiment

*Command:*

```
$ vi experiment.sh
```

*Example:*

```
#!/bin/sh
# File created with a name as experiment.sh
echo " File Name: $0"
```

*Run it as:*

```
$ ./experiment.sh
```

*Output:*

```
File Name: ./experiment.sh
```

## 2. $n

This special variable invokes the parameters depending on how it is written on the script or inputted by the user. Remember that here 'n 'is the position of the argument.

*Example:*

```
#!/bin/sh

# File created with a name as experiment.sh

echo " First parameter: $1"

echo " Second parameter: $2"
```

*Run it as:*

```
$ ./experiment.sh USA UK
```

*Output:*

```
First parameter: USA

Second parameter: UK
```

## 3. $#

This special parameter provides the number of arguments that are given for the shell script.

*Example:*

```
#!/bin/sh

# File created with a name as experiment.sh

echo " All parameters number: $#"
```

Run it as:

```
$ ./experiment.sh USA UK USSR
```

Output:

All parameters number: 3

As the parameters provided are three, i.e., USA, UK, and USSR, it has been given as the output.

**4. $!**

This special variable provides the Process ID of the last background command that has been executed in the shell.

*For example:*

```
$echo $!
```

*Output:*

```
47738
```

The above $ has shown 47738 as the background PID.

**5. $?**

$? is a special variable that outputs the exit status of the previous command that has been executed in the shell. This special variable will output 0 if the last command was unsuccessful. On the other hand, if the previous command does not execute properly, it will output 1.

*Example:*

```
$ ./experiment.sh Sam Tom

All parameters number: 2

$echo $?

0

$
```

As the previous command has been successful, the exit status has been printed as 0.

# Arrays in Shell Scripting

Variables store single data elements, and hence for most real-world applications, single data elements are not efficient. To use elements with multiple sets of data, Arrays can be used. You can use indexed and associative arrays to store and manipulate them efficiently.

*How to declare an array?*

You must declare an array before actually using it in the program.

*Command to declare a indexed array:*

```
array_name_ index = value
```

For example, City 0 creates the first element in the city array, whereas City 2 creates the third element in the city array.

To access array values, the programmers need to use the ${ array_name_ index format. }

Here, an index is the position of the element in the array. Remember that the index always starts with 0 instead of 1.

*Example program:*

```
/#!/bin/sh
```

Example program for An array

```
City [0 ]

City [1 ]

City[ 2]

City [3]

City [4]

Echo " First city: $ {City [0] }

Echo " Second city: $ {City [0] }

Echo " Third city: $ {City [0] }

Echo " Fourth city: $ {City [0] }

Echo " Fifth city: $ {City [0] }
```

*Run it as:*

```
$ ./city.sh
```

*Output:*

```
First city: New York
```

```
Second city: London

Third city: Istanbul

Fourth city: Paris

Fifth City: Delhi
```

If you want to access all the elements in an array, you need to use * or @. *

Command:

```
${array_name_ *}
```

Example:

```
$city[] *
```

# Operators in the Shell Programming Language

In any programming language, to combine statements and form expressions, operators are used. All these operators can be divided into three categories.

## *Arithmetic Operators*

Operators that can perform normal mathematical operations such as addition and subtraction are called arithmetic operators.

1. +

This operator is used to add two operands in a shell script

*For example:*

```
variable1+variable2
```

2. -

This operator is used to subtract two operands in a shell script

*For example:*

```
variable1-variable2
```

3.  *

This operator is used to multiply two operands in a shell script

*For example:*

```
variable1*variable2
```

4.  /

This operator is used to divide two operands in a shell script

*For example:*

```
variable1/variable2
```

5.  %

This operator is used to find remained for two operands in a shell script

*For example:*

```
variable1%variable2
```

6.  ++

This operator is used to increase the value of the operand by 1

*For example:*

```
variable1++variable2
```

7.  --

This operator is used to decrease the value of operand by 2

*For example:*

```
variable1--variable2
```

## *Relational Operators*

Operators which can be used to define the relationship between two operands are known as relational operators. The relational operator will provide a true or false boolean value for a particular relation.

1.  ==

This operator is used to check whether or not the two operands are equal.

  2.  !=

This operator is used to check whether or not the two operands are not equal.

  3.  <

This operator is used to check whether the first operand is less than the second operand.

  4.  >

This operator is used to check whether the first operand is greater than the second operator

*Example program:*

```
#!/bin/bash

#reading data from the user

read -p 'Enter first number: ' first

read -p 'Enter second number: ' second

if(( $first==$second ))

then

    echo first is equal to second.

else

    echo first is not equal to second.

fi

if(( $first!=$second ))

then

    echo first is not equal to second.

else

    echo first is equal to second.

fi
```

```
if(( $first<$second ))

then

    echo first is less than second.

else

    echo first is not less than second.

fi

if(( $first<=$second ))

then

    echo first is less than or equal to second.

else

    echo first is not less than or equal to second.

fi

if(( $first>$second ))

then

    echo first is greater than second.

else

    echo first is not greater than second.

fi

if(( $first>=$second ))

then

    echo first is greater than or equal to second.

else

    echo first is not greater than or equal to second.

fi
```

## Logical Operator

These operators are also known as boolean operators as they depend on logical operations.

**1. &&**

A logical and is operator is used to determine whether or not the two operands are true. If both statements are true, then the output will be true. If either one of them or both are false, then the output will be false.

**2. ||**

A logical or is a binary operator which returns false when only if both of them are false. It will print true if either one of them is true.

**3. !**

This is a special unary operator that will say opposite to the statement relation. For example, if the statement is true, then it will return false.

*Program Code:*

```
#!/bin/bash

#reading data from the user

read -p 'Enter first: ' first

read -p 'Enter second: ' second

if(($first == "true" & $second == "true" ))

then

        echo Both are true.

else

        echo Both are not true.

fi

if(($first == "true" || $second == "true" ))

then
```

```
      echo At Least one of them is true.
else
      echo None of them is true.
fi
if(( ! $first == "true" ))
then
      echo "first" was initially false.
else
      echo "first" was initially true.
fi
```

## Conditional Statements

While working with programming languages such as shell, you need to write programming statements to help people decide. And when the user makes a decision, then only that part will be executed. These are called conditional statements and help programmers to run only what is necessary.

*Syntax:*

```
if ( expression)
then
statement 1 executes
else
statement 2 executes
fi
# The conditional statement ends
```

*Example program:*

```
#Initializing two variables
first=20
seco d=20
if [ $first == $second ]
then
      #If they are equal then print this
      echo "first is equal to second"
else
      #else print this
      echo "first is not equal to second"
fi
```

## Switch Statement

A switch statement is the advanced form of a conditional statement that can execute everything related to a block if it is selected.

*Program Code:*

```
BIKE ="harley davidson"
#Pass the variable in string
case "$BIKE" in
      #case 1 "Hero"
      echo "Headquarters -Newyork, USA" ;;
      #case 2 " Duke"
      echo "Headquarters - Bhagdad, Iraq" ;;
      #case 3 "Vintage"
```

```
echo "Headquarters - Paris,France";
```

## Looping Statements

Loops help to repeat the same condition again and again until the condition is satisfied by the compiler. Looping statements help users to create complex applications. break and continue are some of the statements that can alter the flow of the loop statements.

*Program Code:*

```
#Start of for loop

for first in 7 14 21 28 35 42 49 54 63 70

do

# if first is equal to 42 break the loop

if [ $first == 42 ]

then

        break

fi

# Print the value

echo " $first"

done
```

*Output:*

```
7

14

21

28

35

42
```

Break and continue are the statements that can either break or skip the loops whenever they are encountered.

## Regular Expressions

Regular expressions are a particular branch of programming that helps describe several sequences of characters that can be used to quickly find solutions for a computing problem or perform an operating system task.

Many Unix uses regular expressions, and Linux commands such as sed, ed, grep, and awk for performing tasks. Knowing about some of these Unix commands and how they can maximize your shell programming effectiveness is necessary. All the regular expression-based scripts are executed using sed or awk, stream editors designed exclusively for this purpose. Regular expressions can be used in different programming languages, from Shell to Java and Python.

Linux uses two regular expression engines known as basic regular expression engines and extended regular expression engines. Most of the basic applications understand BRE rules, whereas complex applications need to be written with the help of the ERE engine provided by Linux.

## *Special Characters*

Regular expressions use some special characters that a developer cannot use in his script file.

.,*,$,{,},+,?,(,) are some of these special characters in Linux shell scripting. If you want to use these special characters in the Linux script, you can use a backslash to escape the character by the compiler.

Anchor character

1. <

This is used to locate the beginning line of the text in any file.

2. $

$ on the other hand, is used to check the end of a line.

3. .

You can use dot character to check everything of the new line, except for the new line

4.  *

An asterisk is used to describe an expression if it exists for zero or more times.

5.  ?

The question mark can be used only if the matching pattern exists before it once or none.

6.  ()

It means the text should exist at least once before this

7.  {}

Curly braces use a pattern to determine how many times the pattern should exist in the text

## Shell Functions

A function is a reusable code with a logical approach to a problem. A function can be used anywhere in a program with parameters if it is accessible. You can call these functions using shell commands as effectively as possible.

*Program Code:*

```
#!/bin/sh
hello() {
echo -n "Hello, "
echo $1 $2
}
```

*This is how the output of the script looks:*

Hello, John Smith

# Advanced Shell Programming Commands

Bash shell uses more than 50 special commands to help programmers create more efficient scripts.

## 1. filename(arguments)

This special command lets you replace your shell name with a filename and use arguments to perform regular expression statements. This can also be replaced as the source which provides details about that particular shell file.

*Command:*

```
experiment @ shell: source
```

## 2. declare

This special command is used to declare variables. When you use this special command, the variable's value cannot be changed by any local shell process.

*Command:*

```
experiment@ shell: declare var1=32
```

## 3. local

This particular command helps to create a local variable that users can use for that shell process only. Once the process is ended, the local variable will be destroyed automatically.

*Command:*

```
experiment@shell: local var1=32
```

## 4. return

This is a special command that is used to exit a shell with a return value. The programmer can adjust the return value according to their requirements.

# CHAPTER 7

# Cloud Computing With Linux

Reliable abundant Data are the basic building blocks for any organization that wants to develop its vision, products, and services. Until a few decades ago, data storage was entirely dependent on wired connections, which required a great deal of infrastructure and security to maintain. With the advent of cloud computing, organizations have been able to migrate all their existing data into a more secure and easily optimized cloud technology. As Cloud technology gained popularity, startups began to develop more robust applications to migrate, backup, and encrypt the data present in the cloud. Because most of these applications utilize the Linux platform, the demand for Linux engineers with experience in cloud computing technology has grown dramatically over the years. Beginners need to understand some of the key cloud computing tools and how to use them effectively with Linux.

## What Is Cloud Computing?

A cloud computing environment allows organizations to pool and share resources across a secured network. Compared to hardwired infrastructure, clouds utilize fewer resources to support applications and workloads. These technologies require software and hardware that is known as cloud computing. Around 80% of IT organizations will rely directly on cloud computing and its technologies by the end of 2025. Computer analysts expect cloud computing to occupy all computing streams and organizations by 2035.

# Different Types of Clouds

Cloud computing can generally be classified into three types.

1.  **Public Cloud**

    The public cloud is a computing infrastructure that allows all data storage and running applications to be accessible for clients via the Internet. Your cloud space will usually be shared with other organizations, and hence limitations arise when your data starts to increase rapidly. For example, if you create a WordPress website, your data will be stored in a public cloud belonging to WordPress and many others. Public cloud hosting is cheaper, but security is a concern.

2.  **Private Cloud**

    Private clouds are cloud computing infrastructures in which all the data storage is solely dedicated to an organization. For example, popular social networking websites such as Facebook and Twitter use private cloud infrastructure to ensure that the data they are collecting will be held safe. Private clouds can be customized based on your requirements and, therefore, offer more security and efficiency.

3.  **Hybrid Cloud**

    A hybrid is a cloud computing architecture that utilizes both public and private cloud infrastructure. Hybrid clouds are a rarity in today's competitive environment because they are quite complex to manage. With hybrid clouds, your organization will benefit from improved compatibility and integration.

## Understanding Basic Cloud Technology

A cloud system can be set up with just three computers with today's technology. Rather than using the standard hardware components for logging into Linux systems, a virtual machine is used to start a cloud. All data in the cloud can be accessed through Linux software, which is truly open source.

1. **Virtual Machine Monitors**

   Virtual machine monitors are also known as hypervisors that can help administrators run operating systems on virtual machines. To maximize the capabilities of your cloud technology, ten Linux operating systems can be installed on a single hypervisor. To install Linux in hypervisors, you need to have a kernel installed. Famous Linux distros used for cloud computing are Linux distros such as Redhat Linux and Fedora. If you want to run multiple Linux distributions simultaneously, you can also use the Xen project instead of a virtual machine.

2. **Cloud Storage**

   The reason for the popularity of cloud storage is due to the demand for the production of hardware. Every website, application, service, or mobile app needs data to improve their services. Hypervisors in the cloud can store data, and there is also a chance that the data can be shared between these hypervisors.

3. **Cloud Configuration**

   When working with a cloud computing system, it is essential to remember that all the configurations should be pre-installed. Otherwise, it becomes difficult for the system administrator. You can use shell scripting to master the cloud systems.

*To start a cloud, you need to follow four simple steps:*

1. Install Linux on one of the host computers and open one or more virtual machines according to your requirements.

2. Make sure that you have entered your native architecture features in all these operating systems

3. When you are set, log in to the system and run a virtual machine using a hypervisor.

4. When the hypervisor is running, move the data to another virtual machine.

## *Cloud Emerging Technologies*

Several details related to the emerging technologies should be understood in order to maintain a cloud computing system.

1. **KVM**

   Kernel virtualization module is a particular Linux driver that provides the ability for cloud systems to interact with the operating system.

2. **Virtual Machine Manager**

   In order to manage your cloud effectively, you need a tool that can handle all virtual machines. Virtual machine manager provides features to configure them easily.

3. **QEMU Processor Emulator**

   QEMU is virtualization software that spoofs the software to believe that the operating systems are being run on hardware instead of the cloud. Every time QEMU is run, it launches a shell.

4. **Virtualisation Viewer**

   Virtualization viewer is a command console that helps programmers easily debug any errors that may occur while running the virtual machine. A libvirt daemon also allows us to manage viral machines.

# Essential Software in Linux for Cloud Computing

Cloud computing is dominated by open-source software. For private enterprises, it is quite challenging to create software for different types of servers on the computer network. All cloud computing services such as SaaS ( Software as a Service), PaaS ( Platform as a Service), and IaaS ( Infrastructure as a Service) depend on virtualization software to make a real machine.

To master the efficiency of the cloud for your organization, you need dedicated services in addition to open-source software.

1. **OwnCloud**

   Owncloud is a dropbox alternative for Linux users. It provides real-time sync features for more than twenty famous Linux distros with a dedicated sync and share server for your organization. Owncloud provides remote server access for modifying databases that run on MySQL, Orale, and MariaDB.

It provides advanced functionalities that can help run applications that depend on encryption, music streaming, and online document viewing. Owncloud also provides an automatic trash feature for all its users.

## 2. NextCloud

NextCloud is also an alternative to Dropbox but is used by enterprises with large-size file uploads. Files as large as a few Terabytes can be uploaded with strong security and synchronization features.

## 3. Cozy

Cozy is a synchronization tool available for cloud services. It provides many functions and an efficient app engine to help Linux system administrators involved with cloud computing tasks. Cozy also provides easy GIT collaboration for all its users.

## 4. XigmaNAS

XigmaNAS is open-source software that provides a customizable storage option for all data in a computer network. It uses software RAID to control how data should be shared. It offers different features such as FTP, NFS, and RSYNC. It can also be used to manage SSL certificates.

# CONCLUSION

First of all congratulations for completing the main chapters of the book. Linux is tough to learn, but with the help of our detailed explanation with various command line code, we hope that you have learned complex Linux topics effortlessly. As a programmer it is important that you improve some traits and follow some tips that are recommended by successful programmers . These traits can help you to approach programming and linux system management in a more positive way.

## 1. Use Github

Github is an online repository that can help you to store your code remotely to easily work with your team members or to share your code as open source software. As most of the linux software is shared via Github to the rest of the world, it is important that you know how to work with it. Learn the basics for easier version control, making commits and for downloading dependencies. Github provides both free and professional versions for all of its users. With the free version, all your code will be made public. Whereas, with the professional version, all your code will be private only for your team.

## 2. Use Q&A Boards

To create meaningful software, you need to clear many errors. Errors are frustrating and sometimes are tough to clear, even when you work hard. The programming community is wonderful as you can talk to other programmers about the problem you are facing and find a way to solve the problem. Websites such as stackoverflow are great resources for all programmers. Be a part of these communities and try to help other programmers and sometimes when you really need help, you will get from others.

### 3. Increase Productivity and Be Consistent

To write better programs you need to be strong at both system design and programming skills. All programmers need to focus on their productivity to write more lines of code. Use tools such as pomodoro time to do focused work, instead of falling prey to procrastination. Consistent learning is also important for improving your programming and algorithm skills.

### 4. Clear Errors

There is nothing better than clearing an error for a programmer. Clear errors and understand why they occured. This approach can help you to clear bugs way before they occur. Using advanced programming structures such as exceptions can help you to create efficient code.

### 5. Learn Automation

For any programmer, it is important that he creates an automated environment where most of his tasks will be completed without actually doing them. Mostly, system administrators should find ways to automate reminders for completing the work without any delays. Improve your Python skills as it is the most recommended scripting language for system administrators.

### 6. Never Stop Learning

Programming is a never ending knowledge zone. To be proficient in the field you need to believe in continuous knowledge. Follow forums, newsletters and magazines related to Linux for knowing what is happening in the industry. Be curious regarding emerging technologies and learn them. Following Linux influencers on Twitter can also be a great way to keep updated with the latest technologies.

### 7. Try Different Distros

As a Linux user, you have many options in front of you about what distro you may need to run. While it is fine to use only one of your comfortable distros, we however recommend you to try different Linux distros for understanding different environments. For example, with Arch Linux you can understand the complexity of dependency management. On the other hand, with debian variants you will be able to understand more about programming with embedded systems. Every Linux distro has a different story to tell for you. So, don't miss out.

## 8. Learn Basic Mathematics

We can't stress out how important mathematics is while solving logical problems in programming. As Linux programming involves a lot of interaction with the Linux kernel, it is important that you have a solid foundation with mathematical topics such as Linear Algebra, Calculus and Matrices for writing better programs. Computational Thinking is always essential for writing complex software.

Linux is a great operating system that will change your life and increase career opportunities. We are happy to have been provided an opportunity to discuss Linux and its functionalities in this book for you. Never stop learning. All the best!

# REFERENCES

*An introduction to Linux basics.* (n.d.). DigitalOcean.
https://www.digitalocean.com/community/tutorials/an-introduction-to-linux-basics

Blum, R., & Dee-Ann Leblanc. (2009). *Linux for dummies.* Wiley.

Barrett, D. J., Silverman, R. E., & Byrnes, R. G. (2003). *Linux security cookbook.* O'Reilly.

*Introducing Linux distros: Choose the right Linux distribution for your needs.* (2016). Apress, New
York, New York.

Dalheimer, M. K., & Welsh, M. (2006). *Running Linux.* O'Reilly.

*The Linux command line for beginners.* (n.d.). Ubuntu. https://ubuntu.com/tutorials/command-line-for-
beginners#1-overview

*35 Linux basic commands every user should know (Cheat sheet).* (2019, May 28). Hostinger Tutorials.
https://www.hostinger.in/tutorials/linux-commands

Wale Soyinka. (2012). *Linux administration: A beginners guide.* McGraw-Hill Osborne Media.

Wells, N. (2003). *Guide to Linux installation and administration.* Thomson/Course Technology, C.

# LINUX

---

*The #1 Crash Course For Beginners To Master Linux Operating System Quickly, With No Prior Experience*

## Mark Reed & CyberEdge Press

---

# INTRODUCTION

You have probably heard Linux mentioned somewhere. However, you might not have given it much thought since most people think that it is too difficult and only meant for computer gurus or enthusiasts who want to explore their machine more. However, this is far from the truth. Linux is a simple system that takes a different approach to how an operating system should work.

Let's say you own a vehicle; you don't really have to know everything about combustion engines to understand that they make the car move or know the principles of hydraulics to understand what's wrong when stepping on the brake pedal does nothing to slow down the car. Just like the combustion engine, an operating system handles the inner workings of your computer and ensures that everything runs smoothly. Sometimes things go wrong; in many cases you have a helpline number you can call when problems arise, and they get dealt with. If your car breaks down, you can call any breakdown car service to assist you. The same applies to computers.

Still, even if you get help and the problem is solved, such as with a broken-down car or crashed computer, many people don't understand the explanation given as to why the problem occurred in the first place. If they understood this information, it would help them deal with this issue if it recurred.

Having fundamental knowledge about the principles of an operating system and how it works gives you an upper hand and places you in a better position to understand and deal with problems as they arise. Also, if you know something or someone, you tend to have a better attitude and relationship with them. Just like with a car, if you hear weird noises every time you apply the brake, you know that you need to check on the brake pads and see if they need to be replaced. For computers, this is what Linux does. It gives you an all-access pass into the inner workings of your computer and other systems so you have a better understanding of your equipment. With the many advances in hardware design and performance, computers nowadays can process more data. With Linux, you can harness this computing power to the fullest.

Linux is a fantastic technology and the basis of many systems that we use today. It has grown from the hobby of one man to a worldwide sensation. With its vast applications, it pays to know more about Linux, and even you can become a pro at it.

This book is intended for anyone looking to learn more about Linux or as a reference guide for advanced users. It has examples and exercises to help you get a better understanding of the Linux system and to try things out on your own. It is structured to comprehensively teach you about Linux even if you are a beginner and provide you with the requisite skill set you require to take advantage of the versatility of this system. Having that in mind, let's take a look at what you will be learning in this book.

In chapter one, we will look at installing and setting up your operating system. You will learn about the various distributions of the Linux OS and how to select the right one for you. You will also learn about preparing your computer, installing software, setting up the system, upgrading, and more. At the close of the chapter, you will have enough knowledge to know which system to install and set up. In the second chapter, we will examine the desktop environments and dive deeper into the setup process. The third chapter is about system interaction. We will discuss how the Linux system interacts with various files, hardware, and even other system components. Chapter four takes a look at system administration and everything it entails. The fifth chapter is on security. It explains how you can secure your system since Linux is open-source, what the threats are, and how to deal with them. We will also delve into network security, and you will learn how to set up firewalls and how to protect yourself from hackers. Chapter six covers networking in Linux and all it entails. The final section is on cloud computing and how Linux has impacted this sector. At the end of every chapter, there will be some exercises you can do to help you internalize the theoretical concepts taught.

# CHAPTER 1

## Installation and Setting Up Your System

Before getting into what Linux is, you must understand what an operating system is. It is common to find users who have no clue what an operating system is or what operating system they are using. When you turn on your computer, you see a screen where you can write, draw, surf the web, play music, watch videos, and more. Ever asked yourself what makes the computer hardware, such as the mouse, screen, or keyboard, work the way it does? How does your computer processor know that you want to play a video file?

The operating system is responsible for how your computer works and acts as an interface between you and your computer. These systems are basically managers that are in charge of computer system resources. These resources include RAM, ROM, the monitor, the hard disk, or any connected devices. The operating system has management functions that determine who gets to access data from the hard disk, what appears on the screen next when you select a file, or how much memory a program gets.

There are many operating systems available, such as Windows, Mac OS, iOS, and Linux. Some of these systems are proprietary such as Windows, while others like Linux are open-source. What this means is that with open-source tools, you can examine and analyze the source code and make any modifications you want. This high level of customization sets Linux apart from other operating systems because you have complete control over what you want your computer to do.

In the beginning, Linux developers concentrated more on the networking and service aspects of the system. This made it a favorite among hobbyists but kept it from penetrating the desktop market. Many people still think that Linux is complicated because everything is done in text mode. However, the Linux community has worked hard to turn this system into one that can be used on a workstation as well as on midrange and high-end servers.

Today Linux is readily available either online or from local retailers. Users can now even purchase computers that come with a pre-installed Linux distribution. In the early days, you had to be an expert or have a solid background in computing to use Linux, but companies such as RedHat, Mandriva, and SuSE arose to provide versions of Linux that can be used by the masses. They integrated many components, such as graphic user interfaces (GUIs) developed by the Linux community to ease program and service management. With the addition of these user-friendly interfaces and MS Office-compatible programs such as word processors, Linux is quickly becoming an acceptable choice for everyday home or office use. Its application spans further than just being a workstation or a server OS. It also runs on gadgets such as phones, tablets, or even smartwatches. This makes Linux the only OS that interacts with such a wide range of hardware.

In this section, we'll take a look at how to select and install Linux onto your computer. We will also get into how to set up the system, troubleshoot, and even update or upgrade to a new Linux version.

## Selecting a Linux Distribution

As mentioned above, it was pretty hard to use Linux in the beginning. Many people chose not to learn it because even though documentation on every aspect of the system existed, the explanations were too technical for newbies to understand, thus discouraging them from learning the system. This realization pushed the Linux community to make changes to the accessibility of the system and make it more appealing to more non-techy people.

This paved the way for the development of Linux distributions which did not require that you have an in-depth knowledge of Linux to use them or have the system comply with your commands.

Nowadays, you can log in and start all the applications you want without having to type a single command and still have the ability to access the system core if need be. This system allows new users to get accustomed to the system instead of being forced to learn things the hard way.

So what is a Linux distribution? Linux distributions are the many operating systems created by various programmers, organizations, or companies that are individually tailored to suit their needs. They combine the Linux kernel and other software such as the GNU core utilities, graphical servers, a desktop environment, programs, and more. Each distribution has a different combination of these elements as they are built for a specific purpose to meet the needs of its intended users.

More and more Linux distributions are now being made for desktop users who are generally considered to be the least likely to know how a system works. The developers are working to create beautiful desktops or at least make them look like your former Windows or Mac workstation and compatible programs. There are a lot of sites with screenshots that can show you how your computer will look once you install Linux. Most of these distros can be downloaded for free and burned onto a CD or USB or installed in any machine you want. Here are some of the most popular Linux distributions:

- Linux Mint

- Manjaro

- Debian

- Ubuntu

- RedHat Enterprise

- Fedora

- CentOS

- Opensuse

There are many Linux distributions available, meaning that you are sure to find one that suits your needs, and you don't have to be an expert to get a suitable version. However, this also makes selecting a Linux distribution an overwhelming task. So how do you choose one?

The distro you will use will depend on how you answer the following questions: How excellent are your computer skills? Do you favor a modern or a regulation desktop interface? Are you using Linux for a server or desktop? For someone with reasonably basic computer skills, you will want to stick to the more newbie-friendly distributions such as Linux Mint, Ubuntu, etc. However, if your skillset ranges further than this average range, you can go for distros such as Fedora or Debian. If you have mastered computers and system administration, you can pick Gentoo or take on a challenge and build your own Linux distribution from scratch.

For a server-only distro, you have to choose if you need to have a desktop interface, or you want to use command lines only. Command-line only server distributions are not weighed down by graphics, but you will need to have a good understanding of the Linux command line. You can install a graphical user interface package in the server distro with the command line as well; for example, you can get Ubuntu-desktop by typing `sudo apt-get install ubuntu-desktop`. Also, while selecting a server distribution, do you want one that offers you everything you need when you download it, or do you want to adapt a desktop distro to serve your needs?

It is essential to consider your hardware when selecting a Linux distro. Since all distributions have similar basic packages based on the Linux kernel, what you should focus on is whether the distro you want will run on your hardware. For instance, LinuxPPC was made to run on Apple and other PowerPCs and does not work with x86 based devices. It can run on newer Mac computers, but you cannot use it on older machines because the technology is now obsolete.

## Hardware Checklist

You can install Linux on any computer; however, this also depends on the kind of Linux distribution you are installing and what you plan on using the computer for. Here are some basic requirements for any machine running a Linux distro.

1. **CPU**

   This is the brains of the computer, and it defines the speed at which your OS will run. Since Linux was initially designed to work on an Intel 386, it can pretty much run on any CPU. You can also run Linux on a Mac or even ARM-based machines such as Raspberry Pi. However, Linux distributions are popular on x64 (64 bit) intel or AMD PPC (G3-G5) and AMD processors, and today they are actively developed for these devices. The minimum requirements for a CPU are 2GHz Intel Pentium 4 or AMD K6 with a dual-processor. This will run the OS, but the desktop experience will be limited. If you can, get a computer with better or higher specifications.

2. **RAM (memory)**

   Most distros will require about 2 GB of RAM to run any graphical interfaces. However, if you want to utilize it for non-graphical based uses such as web page hosting, you can even run Linux with less than 10 MB of RAM. For better performance, the minimum RAM should 512 MB upwards.

3. **Hard Disk Drive**

   As with all things in Linux, it is possible to do it even in the smallest of setups. Certain distributions such as Puppy Linux can be run with a few hundred megabytes. However, for standard desktop installations, you will need about 20–40 GB of free space on your hard drive. This is enough space to let you explore the OS more. If you plan on converting your entire system to Linux, then the more space you have, the better. Newer Linux distros now support new drive technology such as RAID and SATA out the box, with enterprise-grade fiber channel disk arrays supported by Linux server distributions.

   Typically, Windows occupies 100% of the space on your computer, so to install Linux, you will have to repartition your hard disk and make some room. Newer distributions have made it even easier to partition your drive by making use of the free space on your HDD. If you are resizing your drive, try to give Linux as much space as you can. Don't forget to allocate some space for SWAP. SWAP is the area in which, if the RAM on your machine fills up, it will use this disk space instead. This is useful if you only have limited RAM, however on higher RAM specs, you probably won't need it. You can also set up your Linux OS on a separate hard drive if you have one. This way you don't mess around with system files as you are resizing partitions

4.  Video Cards or the Graphics Adaptor

Any graphics adaptor will work with Linux as long as your computer supports it. The minimum specification is having a standard graphics card capable of 1024 x 768 resolution. Ideally, a 3D accelerated graphics card with about 256 MB graphics RAM works well.

# Preparing for Installation

Once you have selected the distribution you want to install, you can download the .iso files for free from their respective websites, as well as a list of recommended system requirements for the distro. Despite what many think, installing Linux is very easy, as most versions have what is called a live distribution. This means that the OS will run from whichever device, either a CD/DVD, USB, or external drive, without making changes to your hard drive. This allows you to get full functionality without committing to an installation. Once you have gotten used to it, you can decide whether to install it or not by double-clicking on the install button and following the wizard prompts.

There are various ways you can install your Linux OS:

1.  Using a USB Stick

    You can install your desired Linux distro onto your computer via a bootable USB stick. After downloading the OS files onto your computer, download a universal USB installer to make your USB stick bootable. Then follow the prompts to install Linux onto the USB drive. After the operating system has been installed and configured, a small window will appear to let you know that your USB stick now ready.

2.  Using a CD-ROM

    Just like the USB drive, download the .iso files and burn them onto a CD, which you will then use to boot your computer in Linux.

**3.** Using Virtual Machine

This is a popular method of installing Linux. The virtual installation allows you to run your Linux OS in a machine with an existing operating system. For instance, you can have both Windows and Linux running on the same machine. Virtual machine software such as Oracle VM can install Linux distributions in the following easy steps. First, download and install a virtual box that suits your machine. Once the setup is done, download the operating system files and create a virtual machine to install the OS. Follow the prompts to set up the virtual machine where your Linux OS will reside. After you are done, you have the option to install the operating system or run it without installing it. There are additional steps in the installation process, such as setting up user accounts, which we'll examine later.

## Setting up the System

During installation, you configured some basics, such as selecting your preferred language, keyboard layout, and time zone. The next step prompted you to create a user name and password and also provide other login information such as your name and the computer's name to enable the installation of the Linux distro. This is the password you need to log into your account and perform any administrative tasks. In this pop-up box, you could also choose whether to let the system log you in automatically or require your password with every login. This step is vital if you plan on sharing your computer. It acts as an added layer of protection against any user making unsolicited changes.

After installation, your computer will reboot and display its desktop environment. At this point, you must perform a hardware check after the system restarts. Most of the hardware should work right out of the box with any Linux distro that has been installed, although you may be required to download additional drivers to get everything working well. This is because some hardware, such as graphics cards, require proprietary drivers to work. There is an open-source driver that will work with the card, but to get the most out of it you will have to obtain the drivers from the manufacturer.

# Command Line Interface

The Linux command line is a text interface that allows you to communicate with the computer, and it is solely based on textual input and output. A command is an instruction that is given to a computer instructing it on what to do. They are generally given by typing them in a command line and pressing enter. An all-text display mode, also known as the command-line interface, can consist of a console and a terminal window to display the command prompt. The command prompt or shell prompt is a short, automatically generated text message that appears at the beginning of the command line. It shows the user that the system is ready for the next command, data element, or other input and also helps the user to plan and execute the following operations.

On the default shell on Linux, the bash shell, the command prompt contains the username, computer name, and the name of the current directory. For example, if a user named *X* is working in a directory named *research* on a computer named *home*, the shell prompt would look like this: `[X@home research] $`

The terms command line, shell prompt, and command prompt are used interchangeably, especially when providing instructions on the commands being issued. For instance, an instruction might say, "Input the following at the command line," "Input the following at the shell prompt," or "Input the following at the command prompt."

There are two ways to obtain the shell prompt when using a GUI. Open the terminal window by clicking on the terminal window icon or menu item or switching from the graphical user interface to a console without closing any open programs, or press the CTRL, ALT, and F1 keys together, and the shell prompt will appear. After you are done, you can restore the GUI by pressing the ALT and F7 keys.

# Updating the System

Even though Linux has become more user-friendly, its systems are still fundamentally different from Windows or Mac, and it is best to understand these systems in order to use them well. There are two ways you can update your system in Linux, either using the command line or by using the update manager. You must understand that when updating Linux, every distro handles this process differently. This is because some distros are distinctly different down to the kind of files they use for their package management. For instance, Ubuntu and Debian use .deb, Fedora and SuSE use .rpm, etc. Another difference is whether during installation the distro is installed from source code or pre-compiled .bin or .package files.

Let us take Ubuntu, for instance, as an example of how you can update your Linux system. The Ubuntu distro uses two different tools to update the system, the apt-get command-line tool and the update manager, which is a GUI tool.

1. Using the Update Manager

   The update manager is nearly a completely automatic tool, which saves you the trouble of constantly monitoring your system to see if new updates are available. If updates are available, the update manager will pop up, depending on the urgency of the update. Security updates are set to appear daily and non-security updates weekly. You can also check for updates manually by clicking on the Administration sub-menu on the System menu and select the update manager. Once you open the manager, click on the Check button to see if there are new updates available.

   To update your system, check to see if the updates selected are the ones you want to install. By default, all updates are selected. Next, click on the Updates button, enter your superuser (sudo) password, and click OK. The system will automatically install the updates in the background, allowing you to continue with your work. Some updates such as kernel update require that you log out, log back in, or restart your machine. Once the updating is done, the update manager will pop up on the screen to report that your system is now up-to-date.

2. Using the Command-line Tool Apt-Get

   Ubuntu's package manager is called apt. It is a powerful tool that manages all your system packages via the command line. Using it to update your system does have one drawback: you have to check for updates continually. To use this method, open a terminal window and type *sudo apt-get upgrade*. You will be requested to input your password. Next, a list of the available upgrades will appear, and you can go over them. To accept all the updates, click on the Y key and hit enter. This will install the updates.

# Chapter Summary

In this chapter, we have learned:

- What Linux is and that an OS based on the Linux kernel or shell is called a distribution or distro

- There are numerous distributions available, some of which are designed to accomplish a sole purpose like running servers or act as network switches.

- Linux can be installed on your computer system via USB stick, CD-ROM, or virtual installation

- What the Linux command line is and how to interact with the OS using it.

- How to update your Linux OS.

# Exercises

Here are a few practical exercises for beginners.

**Exercise 1: Select a Linux distribution and install it on your PC**

Important tip: ensure that you read the information provided thoroughly to prevent causing any errors. Read every installation message carefully to make sure you install the OS successfully. Refer to the notes in this chapter if you need help.

**Exercise 2: Installing Operating System packages using the apt tool**

- Use the apt command-line tool to install the `clustalw` multiple alignment tool and the `clustalx` graphical user interface

- Take note of how many additional packages were required to satisfy the mandates for each tool

- Use the `clustalx` tool to align the rRNA sequences in `Align_Data/reference_sequences.txt`

- You can use the *apt-file* program to view which files have been installed by a specific package. Use this to view what was installed by the *clustalw* package

- Install apt-file with *apt install apt-file* (as root)

- Build the file cache with *apt-file update*

- List the files for clustalw with *apt-file list clustalw*

- Look at the directories the files are installed into

**Exercise 3: Installing Linux in a VM**

- Select a live Linux distro to install such as Ubuntu live and download its .iso image file

- Next set up a new VM and allocate some memory to it, (2GB) and on the hard disk (20GB)

- Add the ISO to the virtual DVD drive and start the step-by-step installation process until you successfully install the Linux distribution

# CHAPTER 2

## Desktop Environment

One of Linux's most distinctive features is its capacity for customization. You can adapt any aspect of the operating system to suit your specific needs, and this gives it a leg over other operating systems such as Windows or MacOS. For example, let's assume you want to install Ubuntu, which is a safe, user-friendly choice. However, there are about eight official different flavors of Ubuntu that behave and look different, and this mostly comes down to the type of desktop environment each is using.

Before you can fully understand what a desktop environment is accurately, let us expound a bit more on operating systems. All operating systems such as Windows, Linux, or MacOS have a kernel or shell which directly controls your computer hardware and translates any commands that are given by a piece of software into something that your equipment can understand. This way, it knows what to do when executing a command. The kernel also manages your hardware resources, such as memory management, for the various software you will be using intelligently.

So, in a nutshell, the kernel is the brain or the engine of the system, and it acts as a mediator between the software and hardware. However, this is not something beginners should worry about too much, as most of the interaction with the computer system will be via a graphical user interface. This is typically what a desktop environment is.

A desktop environment combines various components such as icons, menus, toolbars, and desktop widgets to provide a common GUI. They also include a set of integrated computer applications and utilities, but most importantly, they have their own windows manager, although it can be replaced with another compatible one. A computer user is free to configure their graphical user interface as they please, and desktop environments provide a simple way to accomplish this task.

Users are also free to mix and match applications from several environments. For instance, a GNOME user can run KDE applications such as the Konqueror web browser if they prefer it over GNOME's Epiphany web browser. However, one major drawback to using this mix and match approach is that many of these applications often rely heavily on the underlying libraries of their respective desktop environments (DE). This means that to install these applications, you will have to install a large number of dependencies, which can take up a lot of disk space. To avoid this, users can stick to using one desktop environment or choose alternatives that depend on fewer external libraries.

One advantage of using DE-provided applications in their native environments is that they tend to work better. Mixing and matching can result in visual discrepancies, such as having interfaces that use different icons or widgets than those installed, or imported elements not working as they should, which can cause confusion and result in the system behaving unexpectedly.

It is important to note that every environment is distinct in its nature and purpose. Deciding which DE to use will depend on your needs. Also, before installing a desktop environment, you need to install a functional X server because most environments support it. Although others also support Wayland as an alternative to X, many of these DE are still experimental. We shall take a more in-depth look into the X window system later on, but you can also visit X.org for more information.

# Types of Desktop Environments

Below are some examples of officially supported desktop environments available to Linux users.

1. GNOME

   This is a prevalent desktop environment among Linux users. It is free, open-source, simple yet powerful, and easy to use. It is so popular that other desktop environments referred to as "forks" were developed from it. These include Cinnamon, Unity, etc. It was designed to be highly customizable, thus giving Linux desktop users a pleasant computing experience. GNOME key features include a dashboard that shows an overview of all your activities, a system-wide search tool, powerful in-house applications, themes, extension support, and window snapping.

Its latest release, GNOME 3, showcases a modern, attractive user interface, and it also aims to provide better support for touch input devices. In addition, it now uses Metacity as its default window manager, and Nautilus comes as the default file manager with Google Drive integration. It supports desktop notifications using a convenient messaging system that you can turn on and off.

Some of the advantages of using this DE include its modern and touch-friendly user interface. You can also extend its functionalities by using GNOME shell extensions, and it is highly customizable. Some drawbacks include its hefty utilization of computer resources, such as the memory, compared to other alternatives because of its heavily graphical interface, and some of its extension management is unsatisfactory. Also, to customize this DE, you need a gnome-tweaking tool. Some of the major distros that use GNOME include Ubuntu GNOME, OpenSuSE, Debian, and Fedora.

2. KDE

This is another popular desktop environment — and the most highly customizable — because it is designed to give Linux users complete control over their desktop. KDE is more than a desktop environment. It is a collection of apps that include the DE. Where other environments require you to have a tweaking tool installed, for KDE it is all in the system settings. This allows you to personalize your desktop without using third-party tools, and you can even download widgets, wallpapers, and themes without using the web browser.

It offers a collection of basic applications you can use, and it is also compatible with other apps even if they were not developed using the KDE Development Platform. These built-in apps come bundled with a variety of essential features that are often absent in the alternative. KDE is an excellent choice whether you need a desktop environment that works out of the box or one that can be fully customized to suit your needs.

Some of its perks include being the most advanced, powerful, and feature-rich DE with a polished user interface. It also gives users a highly customizable and flexible experience with its wide range of applications and software compatibility. However, it does have some slightly heavy resource usage, and some components appear too complicated to use.

Its latest version, known as Plasma, is available in two variants: Plasma Desktop and Plasma Netbook. The Plasma 5 release includes features such as the Dolphin file manager and the Kwin windows manager. It has a converged shell with updated graphics stacks to enable smoother graphics performance. There are also workflow improvements made in the desktop notification area, modern launchers, and better support for high-density display (high DPI) and more minor features. Some distros that use KDE as their default include openSuSE and Kubuntu.

3. Xfce

The Xfce desktop environment truly embodies the traditional UNIX philosophy of modularity and reusability. It has several components that provide the full functionality one can expect of a modern DE while remaining relatively light. They are packaged separately, and you can select among the available packages to create your optimal working environment.

It is lightweight and easily adaptable to old hardware. It also has a modern, visually appealing look, and it is highly customizable. It comes installed with the Xfwm file manager and Thunar file manager. The user session manager handles logins, power management, etc. and you can set the background image, icons, widgets, and more through the desktop manager. It is, however, not touch-friendly, so it is not ideal for devices that have touch input. Manjaro Linux and Xubuntu use Xfce as the default desktop environment.

4. Cinnamon

Cinnamon was initially developed to be the default desktop environment for Linux Mint. It is a combination of several projects such as Cinnamon — a fork of the GNOME shell, Cinnamon screensaver, Cinnamon desktop, Cinnamon Menus, Cinnamon Settings Daemon, and more. Cinnamon has various customizable elements, such as panels, themes, and extensions. Since it is based on GNOME, it comes with several basic applications from GNOME. This DE also features the MDM display manager, Nemo file manager, Muffin window manager, Cinnamon session manager, Cinnamon translations, Blueberry — a Bluetooth configuration tool, and more.

Some of Cinnamon's perks include its sleek polished look, familiar interface, and customization capacity. Its small icons are not touch-friendly, thus it making it hard to use on touch devices.

## Desktop Environment Implementation

A system that offers a DE, a window manager, and applications written using a widget toolkit are accountable for most of what the user sees. The window manager supports the user's interactions with the DE, while the toolkit provides a developer with a library for applications that look and behave in a similar manner. A windowing system such a X or Wayland interfaces directly with the OS and libraries and provides the needed support for graphical hardware and input devices like keyboards.

The window manager operates on top of this windowing system, and while the latter provides window management functionality, it is still seen as part of the window manager. Applications designed to work with a particular manager in mind are made using a windowing toolkit, which is provided by the OS or window manager. This toolkit allows the applications to access widgets that let the user interact with the apps.

Some factors can influence a user's choice of DE; these include:

- The look and feel of the desktop environment. Some users are comfortable with a certain look or feel which they are familiar with. This is especially true for newbies or users who are transitioning from Windows or Mac to Linux. They might go for DE that has similar layouts to their previous operating systems.

- Flexibility and configurability. Experienced users may opt for DEs that are more configurable or customizable so that they can tune it to work how they want. For beginners, many prefer an easy-to-use environment that they can get used to quickly.

- Personal software preferences. Each DE comes with default software applications and a default way of how things are done. A new or casual user may want a graphic-rich interface, while a more experienced user may opt for a more straightforward interface or even user command-line interface tools.

# The X Window System

The X Window System is often referred to as the distributed, graphical method of working. It is an open-source, cross-platform, client-server, computer software program that provides a GUI in a distributed environment. It is distributed because you could run the display on a monitor in one location, even though the application is running on a computer somewhere else. The graphical aspect is brought in by the images and other graphics that are displayed on your screen. Despite how popular it is among UNIX users, it is not a UNIX product. It was developed in 1994 by the Massachusetts Institute of Technology (MIT) and Stanford University, and operates on a wide range of machines, even MS Windows-based versions. The X.Org Foundation is an open group that manages the development and standardization of X.

The X Window System, also known as simply X or X11, provides the basic framework for a GUI environment. At the base level, X uses the elements of the GUI on the user's screen and constructs methods for sending user interactions back to the software. Using application GUI development toolkits, an application developer can create an application interface. Because X has been designed to use a client/server model from the beginning, it is well suited for remote application use as well, letting you work from your computer directly with an application running on another computer. X is also hardware-independent, meaning you can run MS applications on a UNIX workstation. Some of its features include network transparency, customizable graphical capability, and the ability to link to different networks.

# X Architecture

We already know that X was designed using client-server architecture, the X.Org server, and the X terminal. Here the applications themselves are the clients because they communicate with the server, issue requests, and also receive information from other servers. The X server, however, retains exclusive control of the display and service requests from the clients. Applications only need know how to talk to the server and not bother with the actual graphics display device. The advantages of utilizing this model are pretty clear here. At the fundamental level, an application (client) can tell the server to execute specific instructions such as "draw a circle."

This would be no different from using a graphics library to write the application; however, X goes a step further. It does not require the application to be on the same computer as the server. This is because the protocols used to communicate between the client and server can work over a network or even on any inter-process communication mechanism that provides a reliable octet-stream. The preferable way to do this is by using TCP/IP protocols. Here is an example to better illustrate how powerful the X system is: you can run a processor-intensive application on your Dell computer, run a database monitor on a Solaris server while using an email application on a small BSD mail server, and use a visualization program on another server to display all this information on your Linux workstation.

It is clear that the X server is handling the graphics display. Since it runs on the actual computer or device the user is using, it's the server's responsibility to interact with the user. This means reading the input devices and relaying this information to the client so it can react appropriately. X also has a library named Xlib that handles all low-level client-server communications. The client has to use functions contained in the library to get tasks done.

## The Client/Server Relationship

X is based off a client-server architecture and is activated as a combination of the server and client programs. Here the terms "client" and "server" are used to refer to local and remote devices. Below are more client-server terminologies.

- X server – this refers to a program run on a local host that is connected to the user's display and input devices

- X client – refers to a program that runs on a remote host and processes data while communicating with the X server

- Application server – a program that also runs on a remote host that processes data and communicates with application clients

- Application client – a program run on a local host that is connected to the user's display and input devices

Modern X servers have the MIT shared memory extension and can talk with their local clients using local shared memory. This negates the need for network-transparent Xlib inter-process communication and enables the system to render larger images.

The X windowing system works like all client-server models where the X server contains several resources that it provides to the client. As stated earlier, the server and the client programs don't have to be on the same machine because X is included in the TCP/IP protocol. And since X is more of a protocol than a program, computers can still communicate even if they have different architectures. For instance, a digital OSF/I server can service a Linux and AIX client as well as either client system providing services to the OSF/I server. Similar to other network applications, a single machine can serve as a client or server.

The server interfaces between the application and the hardware, so when you input data through an input device, it is responsible for relaying this data to the application. This is referred to as an event. When a user presses a key, it causes an event that the application must react to. For example, if you click on a particular menu item, this event is relayed to the client application, which responds by requesting the server to show the pull-down menu. The server then passes this info onto the hardware, which shows the menu on a screen. A product of this separation of functionality is that one client could display info on several servers.

To start any process, an X server has to be running somewhere either on the same machine or network as the client. Some systems have a graphic login that starts automatically on booting in the desktop environment. Alternatively, the system can begin through the `startx` shell script. The command reads the `.xinitrc` and `.xserverrc` files in the home directory and treats them similarly to how the shell would manage the `.cshrc` and the `.kshrc` files. This is where applications such as the terminal window and the window manager are initiated.

# Configuring the X Window System

In the early days of the X windowing system, configuring a display meant that you had to have an intensive knowledge of the display's capabilities and the ability to express data about the resolution, position, color depth, font, and more. Since the arrival of the Video Electronics Standards Association (VESA) and display data channel (DDC) protocols, which allow a display to communicate these capabilities into a graphics card and then to the computer, configuration became more automatic. Configuring your hardware devices has also become a lot easier; you plug them in and start using them.

However, as with everything in Linux, there is an underlying configuration that you can use. In fact, the X.org implementation of X gets this information from several sources, the main one being the xorg.conf file. It also includes the files from the `xorg.conf.d` directory, which is located in `/etc/X11`. You can add additional configurations from the command line, desktop environment variables, auto-detection, or restoration defaults. However, you do not have to worry too much as most distros come with a configuration tool that configures X for you, or at least presents it in a less complex way.

Also, the Xorg setting command can automatically detect devices, so this negates the need for advanced editing. You might need to edit the directory if your hardware or equipment does not show up. Be extremely careful, as making any changes in the server can cause your machine to not load or even damage your monitor. There is also the possibility of permanently damaging your computer that accompanies editing any system file.

# Hardware and X

We know that the X server controls the input and output devices, and since new hardware is being developed every day, we cannot be very specific about hardware compatibility. To help, here are some generalities.

- As a rule of thumb, if the device uses a commonplace protocol such as PS/1 or PS/2, it should be well supported. However, if it is still new tech, the chances are that it might not be supported yet.

- For monitors – Linux doesn't have to be compatible with any specific monitor because this is the job of the video card. As long as your graphics card works with the monitor, then it should work.

- For video cards – the X server is determined by the chipset, and naturally, a lot of them are supported. However, revisions and newer cards might not be supported yet. Newer cards are now coming with better support and optimization, and some even have advanced features such as multi-headed displays, 3D, TV-out, DRI, and more. You have to research well to find out if the card is supported. A full list of supported cards can be found online. Also note that open-source drivers are developed incrementally, such that a card may work well for basic display function, but specialized features come later on in the development cycle. However, proprietary driver development differs.

- Keyboards – any keyboard should work.

- Mice and other pointing devices – most of these devices should be supported, including PS/2, bus, serial, USB, optical, and infra-red devices. Multi-button and wheeled mice are supported via the IMPS/2 or other specific protocols. However, they may need extra configuration for some applications.

You can check the hardware compatibility list on your distro's website to see what works with your release.

# X Resources

Virtually all X clients are customizable. You can set how a client looks, its size, placement, background and border color or pattern, whether or not the window has a scroll bar, and more. Some applications even let users redefine the keystrokes or pointer actions used to control the program. Most traditional UNIX programs relied on command-line options to enable users to alter how they worked. Although X applications support command-line options, this does not apply to all their features. There would be too many customizable features in a program to set them all via the command line. X has an alternative to customizing an application through the command line. The X server can store several configuration values for applications, so they are readily available when needed. If the application supports it, these defaults will be used whenever the program runs. These are known as resources, and they define a user's preference on a per-application basis for colors, screen placement, and other attributes. This makes application customization even easier.

Program components are named hierarchically, with each element identified by a class and instance name. The topmost level shows the class and instance name of the app itself. The class name of an application is often the same as the program name; however, the first letter is capitalized, such as Emacs. For programs beginning with X, the second letter is also capitalized, such as XTerm. Each definition specifies an instance with the corresponding resources and values. Under this, in the hierarchy, are the many attributes that comprise the definable aspects of an application.

These resource variables can be Boolean such as `scrollBar: False` or have a numeric or string value such as `borderwidth: 4` or `foreground: green`. In applications written using the X toolkit or other object-oriented systems, resources can be linked with separate elements or widgets in a program. There is a syntax that allows for independent control over a class of elements and a singular instance of the element. For example, for a hypothetical program called *xclient:*

```
xclient*Buttons.foreground: yellow

xclient*help.foreground: green
```

The first resource specification changes the foreground color of all buttons (in the Buttons class) in the application to yellow. The second one changes the foreground color of the help button (an instance of the Buttons class) to green.

Resource values can be set as program defaults in several ways, such as including resource files in your home directory or through the X resource database (xrdb) program. Xrdb stores resources directly in the server, making them available to all clients regardless of the machine the client is running on. Placing resources in files lets you customize multiple resources at once without the restrictions encountered when using the command line. Other than having a primary resource file (named `.Xdefaults` or `.Xresources`) in your home directory that sets application defaults, you can create system-wide resource files to set program defaults. Additionally, you can create resource files to set resources for the local workstation, networked machines, or for one or more specialized machines such as servers

The resource manager sets routines that automatically read and process resource files in a certain order. The arrangement for resource specifications and the rules of precedence by which the resource manager processes them are meant to give you the most flexibility in setting resources with the minimum amount of text input. You can specify a resource that affects a single feature of a single application such as the green help button in the earlier example or define a resource variable that controls a function of multiple elements within many programs with a single line. Take note that command-line options often take precedence over other resource settings. So you can set up the files to control how the application will work normally and use the command line to specify the changes you require for an instance of the application.

## Resource Naming Order

The basic syntax of a resource file is quite simple. Each client recognizes specific resource variables that can be assigned values that are documented in its reference page. Most clients are designed to utilize the X toolkit, which provides a standard set of elements or widgets like menus, dialog boxes, command buttons, etc. The naming syntax of certain resources parallels the element's hierarchy that is built into X toolkit programs. In a resource definition file, the most basic line you can have comprises the client name followed by an asterisk or a period and the name of the variable. A colon and space separate the client and variable names from the actual value of the resource variable.

```
For instance: xterm*scrollBar: True
```

If the client's name is absent, the variable will apply to all instances of the client. If it is specified as a global variable and a client-specific variable, the latter takes precedence for that client. However, you should note that if the client's name is omitted, the line should begin with an asterisk.

```
For example: *scrollTtyOutput: False
```

```
*scrollKey: True
```

Also, take care not to omit the colon at the end of the resource specification because the resource manager provides no error messages. If there is an error in the specification, such as a syntax error or a misspelling, it is ignored, and the value you set will not take effect. You can use the exclamation mark (!) at the beginning of the line to include a comment in the file or comment on one of the specifications. If the last character is a backslash (\), the definition is assumed to continue on the next line.

```
For example: xterm*VT100.translations: #override \

<Key>BackSpace: string(0x7F) \n\

<Key>Insert: string(0x1b) string("[2~")\n\

<Key>Delete: string(0x1b) string("[3~")\n\

<Key>Home: string(0x1b) string("[1~")\n\

<Key>End: string(0x1b) string("[4~")\n\

<Key>Page_Up: string(0x1b) string("[5~")\n\

<Key>Page_Down: string(0x1b) string("[6~")\n\

<KeyPress>Prior : scroll-back(1,page)\n\

<KeyPress>Next : scroll-forw(1,page)
```

## Toolkit Client Resource Syntax

As stated earlier, X toolkit apps are made of widgets, and there can be a widget inside a widget; for instance, a drop-down menu in a dialog box. The syntax of resource specifications for these toolkit applications matches the levels of the widget hierarchy. You should think of a resource specification having the following format:

```
object.subobject[.subobject. . .].attribute: value
```

Where the object refers to the client program or a specific instance of it. The subobjects refer to the levels of widget hierarchy, the attribute is a feature of the last subobject, and the value is the actual setting of the resource. The value of a resource is clear from the resource name or the description of the variable in the reference pages. For instance, resources such as *background* take color specifications, *geometry* takes a geometry string, *font* takes a font name, etc. Logical values like those taken by *scrollBar* can be specified as either *yes* or *no, on* or *off*, or *True* or *False*

# Tight and Loose Bindings

How components of a resource specification are linked is referred to as binding, and it can be done in two ways. The first is by a tight binding, which is indicated by a dot (.), or secondly by a loose binding, shown by an asterisk (*). A tight binding means that the elements on either side must be next to each other in the hierarchy. A loose binding, on the other hand — signaled by an asterisk, which is a wild character — shows that there are several levels between the two elements. You have to be very familiar with widget hierarchy to specify tight bindings, and it is not uncommon for them to be used incorrectly.

Take, for instance, this resource specification request.

```
xterm.scrollBar: True
```

This specification ignores the widget hierarchy of *xterm*, where the VT102 window, Tektronix window, and menu are all widgets. Here is the correct syntax:

```
xterm.vt100.scrollBar: True
```

A simpler alternative is to use the asterisk instead of deciphering the widget hierarchy.

```
xterm*scrollBar: True
```

If the program supports multiple widget levels, you can use a mix of asterisks and periods. However, using an asterisk is still recommended because it allows developers the freedom to add or remove levels in the hierarchy as they produce new releases of a program.

# Classes and Instances

Every resource specification component is associated with a class, and different widget attributes can belong to the same class too. Let's say, for instance, in *xterm*, the text (*Foreground*), text cursor, and pointer color are all defined as instances of the *Foreground* class. You can, therefore, set the value of all three individuals or via a single command, as shown below:

```
xterm*foreground: limegreen

xterm*cursorColor: limegreen

xterm*pointerColor: limegreen

or

xterm*Foreground: limegreen
```

Capitalizing the first initial differentiates class and instance names. Class will always begin with an uppercase letter and instances in a lowercase one. However, if the instance name is a compound word such as `pointer-Color`, the latter is capitalized.

The effect of class and instance naming cannot be felt in applications such as `xterm` because they have a simple widget hierarchy. In other complex applications made with the X Toolkit, this naming allows you to do more customization. Just remember that the instance name specification always overrides the class name for that instance. Class names, therefore, allow for default values to be set for all instances of a particular element. It can also be used with loose binding to specify a resource for all clients. Instance names specify the exception to the class names specifications.

# Precedence Rules for Resource Specification

Resource specifications can conflict even on a singular resource file such as `.Xresources`. For instance, do you recall this example from earlier?

```
xclient*Buttons.foreground: yellow
```

```
xclient*help.foreground: green
```

The first specification makes the foreground color for all buttons in the Buttons class yellow. The second one overrides the first specification in a single instance where it makes the foreground color of the Help button green. In such a case where specifications clash, several rules assist the resource manager in deciding which specification takes effect. These include:

- Instance names take precedence over class names

- Tight binding takes precedence over loose bindings

From the two rules, it is clear that the more specific a resource definition is, the higher it ranks and thus takes precedence. However, if you want to set things up very carefully in your system, you should know how programs interpret resource specifications. For every resource variable, a program has both a complete, fully-specified, tightly bound instance and class name. In analyzing ambiguous specifications, the program compares them against the full instance and class name. If there is a match, it is accepted. However, if more than one part in either name matches, the following rules in addition to those mentioned earlier apply.

- The hierarchy levels specified by the user must match the program's expectations or be ignored. If, for instance the program expects:

```
xterm.vt100.scrollBar: value instance name

XTerm.VT100.ScrollBar: value class name
```

The specification *xterm.scrollBar: True* won't work because the tight binding is incorrect. The elements in the `xterm` and `scrollBar` hierarchies are not adjacent. It would work if it was a loose binding.

- A class or instance name that is explicitly mentioned takes priority over one that is omitted. For instance, *xterm*scrollBar* is more specific than **scrollBar*

- Elements on the left carry more weight over those on the right, just as in the above example.

# Chapter Summary

In this chapter, we looked at what a desktop environment is, the different types of DE, and their implementation. We also took a more in-depth look at the X windows system, its makeup, and configuration. It is important to note that desktop environments are preferred because they make configuring your system a lot easier compared to using the command line.

We also learned that X is a client-server, multi-user system, not just a graphical user interface. It is not integrated into the OS but instead operates on top of it like other servers. It is also an open standard that runs on many platforms. What you see on the screen is a combination of many components working together: OS, X, Window manager, and a DE if you have installed one. They are plug and play elements that let you interchange what you want without interfering with the rest. Since they all have their configurations, this makes the system very robust and flexible, although it makes it quite complex.

# Exercises

1.  Explore the menus in your desktop environment. What happened?

2.  Customize your terminal window. Were you successful?

3.  Configure your window manager and try out different workspaces (virtual screens).

4.  Apply a different theme. Were you successful?

5.  Switch to a different window manager. What happened?

6.  Log out and pick a different session type, like Cinnamon, if you were using Gnome earlier. Repeat the previous steps.

# CHAPTER 3

## The Shell and Its Utilities

By now, as a Linux user, you are already aware of the basic makeup of a Linux system. It is comprised of a kernel, Shell, commands and utility programs, files, and directories. The kernel is the core of the operating system. It interfaces with the computer hardware and other core functions such as memory management, file management, and task scheduling. Shell is a utility program that handles your requests. When a user enters a command into the terminal, Shell deciphers the commands and initiates the program you want to helps generate the result you wanted. It uses a standard order for all its commands. There are several shells available for Linux distros such as C shell, Bash, Korn Shell, and many more.

The commands and service programs comprise the commands mentioned above and other utility programs that the user uses. These include mkdir, sudo, cp, cal, and so on. There are over two hundred and fifty standardized commands plus numerous troves of those supplied through 3rd party software. All of the data in a Linux system is arranged in files. These files are then arranged into directories. This organization structure further arranges the directories into a tree-inspired structure known as the file system.

In this and subsequent chapters, we will take a more in-depth look into these various components and see how they work on a Linux system, as well as how you can utilize them. The first one you will tackle is Shell and its utilities.

# Shell

As a refresher, the Shell is, in essence, an interface between the OS and the user. It is a command-line interpreter through which you can issue various instructions to the system. The Shell interprets these instructions, and it tells the system what actions to take. Therefore, the command prompt is where you input these instructions or commands. Before GUIs were developed, the only way to input commands was via the Shell prompt. All these shells have similar input attributes. You have to issue commands to get the device to carry out any task.

Some commands do not require any input to work, such as the date command; however, others require an argument or option to work. Anything included in the command line after the command is an argument. An option affects this behavior, whereas an argument is acted upon as is by the command. It is important to note that some arguments are optional, and other options are needed. For instance, you don't always require an argument for the date command, whereas the tar command requires an option.

The basic Shell of all Unix systems is the Bourne shell, simply denoted as (sh). Other shells such as bash, csh, ksh, and more have evolved from this. Every Shell has a certain order in which the internal functions such as the variables, redirection of input and output devices, etc. are executed. There are many advantages to learning how to use the Shell and its functions. Let's take a look at some of its components below.

# Environment Variables

The shell environment consists of everything it will need as it runs. These components are referred to as environment variables and include the search path, the user's logname, and the type of terminal you are using. When a user logs in, many of these variables are already set by a shell mechanism.

An environmental variable is a variable with a name and value. This value can be anything from the default editor, system locale settings, to even directories. PATH is an example of such a variable. New Linux users find these settings' management somewhat hard to handle. Environmental variables, however, offer a simpler way to share configuration settings among many programs and processes. The following are some important variables you should know and how they are set and accessed.

1. DISPLAY – has the identifier for the default display that X11 applications use

2. HOME – shows the home directory of the current user, and it is the default argument for the built-in cd command

3. IFS – shows the Internal Field Separator used by the parser for word splitting after expansion

4. LD_LIBRARY_PATH – a Linux system containing a dynamic linker has a colon-separated directory list that the dynamic linker should look in for shared objects when constructing a process image after exec, before looking in other directories

5. PATH – shows the search path for commands

6. PWD – shows the current working directory as set by the cd command

7. RANDOM – produces an arbitrary integer within 0 and 32,767 every time it is referenced

8. SHLVL – increases by one every time a bash instance is initialized; it is ideal for monitoring if the built-in exit command ends the current session

9. TERM – indicates the display type

10. TZ – indicates the Time zone such as CAT, GMT, etc

11. UID – expands to the numeric user ID of the current user, initialized at the shell startup

With that in mind, let us dive into the PATH environmental variable.

# Paths

PATH is an environmental variable used in Linux that instructs the Shell in which directories to look for ready-to-run files as a response to user issued commands. It enhances the ease and safety of Unix-like operating systems and is thus considered quite valuable.

If, for instance, you know that there is a particular application in your system, but when you try to initialize it, the system responds with a "file not found" message. You might attribute this to you not remembering the right name or spelling. But in fact, the reason behind it is because the application was not in the search path. A user's search path is a predetermined directory set where the system searches for the application when you typed in the command line or which was initiated by another command. The search path saves the system a lot of time because it does not have to look through all the directories for what you want. By searching in specific areas, you can get faster results. The downside, however, comes when the program is not in any of the specified directories. To instruct the Shell where to look for your file, you must issue explicit commands that require you to specify either the path to the file relative to where you are or the full command path.

PATH, which is denoted in upper case letters, should not be confused with path, which is a file's or directory location in a file system. A *relative path* is a location relative to the directory which the user is currently working in. An *absolute path*, also known as a *full path*, is a location relative to the root directory. The root directory is the directory at the topmost level of the file system, and it contains all other directories and files.

A user's PATH is therefore comprised of a series of colon-separated absolute paths that are kept in plain text files. Every time a user types in commands at the command line (CL) that isn't built into the Shell or doesn't include its absolute path and hits *Enter*, the Shell looks through the directories that make up the user's search path until it finds an executable file with that name. By concentrating most executable files in a few directories and using PATH to find them, it removes the need for users to recall which directories they are in and type their absolute paths. This means that any application can be run by just typing its name, such as `ls` instead of `/bin/ls`. This execution happens regardless of whether the user is currently working on the file system. It also reduces the chance of causing damage to the data or the system by accidentally running a script named similarly to a standard command.

By running the `env` command, a user can see a list of all the current environmental variables, their values for the current user, and all the directories in the PATH variable. This command can be run without any options or arguments. Since this can be quite a bit of information, you can change the command so that it only shows the PATH variable and its value. You can do this by using a pipe that is represented by a vertical character to switch the `env` output to the `grep` filter while using PATH as an argument to `grep`, i.e., `evn|grep PATH`.

You can also use the echo command to view PATH, i.e., `echo $PATH`

Echo duplicates whatever follows it on the command line. The $ sign before PATH instructs echo to repeat the value of the PATH variable instead of the name.

Every user can have a different PATH variable. When an OS is installed, the default PATH variable, known as the root account, is created. Another default is also established that will be used as a template for other normal user accounts as they are added. The root PATH variable has more directories than the user PATH variable. This is because it contains directories such as `/sbin` and `/usr/sbin,` which contain applications used by a particular user.

PATH variables can be altered easily. You can modify them for a particular login session or alter them permanently. You can include a directory into a user's PATH variable and thus into the search path by using `PATH="directory:$PATH"` command. For example, you can add `/usr/sbin` to the PATH variable. The command will look like this:

`PATH="/usr/sbin:$PATH"`

You can also use the export command to add a directory, i.e., export `PATH=$PATH:/usr/sbin`

A user's PATH variable can be made permanent by including it in the user's `.bash_profile` file. The `.bash_profile` file is a hidden file in each user's home directory that explains any particular environmental variable and startup applications for that specific user. It is important to note that a colon with no spaces should precede each absolute path. For example, `PATH=$PATH:$HOME/bin:/usr/test`

You might want to run an application or script that has been installed in another user's home directory or a different location other than the default search path. You can run this application or script by typing in its absolute path or preceding its command name with a dot slash, which is a period followed by a forward slash and no spaces. The dot is used to show the current directory, and the slash is a directory separator and to distinguish file and directory names.

## Permissions and Access Modes

In Linux, you have to have the right permission to gain access to a file. This is important because it allows you to locate, edit, and execute commands. For instance, if you want to read a file, you must have read permission to write or edit a file, write permission, execute or run a file, or execute permission. These authorizations or access modes are set using the chmod command or during file creation. You can view a file's permissions via the l or ls -l commands

In Linux, file permissions are essential because they provide a secure method for file storage. Every Unix file has the following attributes: owner, group, and other or world permissions. Owner permissions define what the owner of the file can do. The group permissions show what actions can be taken by a user who is a member of the group that owns the file. Lastly, the other permissions show what actions other users can perform on a file.

As stated before, a file's permissions can be viewed through the ls -l command. To better comprehend what these permissions entail, let's take a look at the following example.

```
$ls -l /home/fiona

-rwxrw-r--  1 fiona  users 1024 Jan 2 00:20 myfile

drwxr-xr--  1 fiona  users 1024 Jan 2 00:20 mydir

$
```

There are ten characters at the beginning of each line, and they can either be dashes or letters. Let's break down each position accordingly.

The first place shows the file type. It can be a d for directory, r for a regular file, c for a character device, etc. The other nine places are divided into groups of three, and each group has three places to indicate the permissions granted to that group. The order for these permissions is r for read, w for write, and x for execute. The first group of three positions shows the owner's permissions, the second one shows the group permissions, and the last one shows the permissions for everyone else. If certain permissions are not granted, there will be a dash (-) in its place.

As per our above example:

d – this indicates the file type, which in this case is a directory file

rwx – this shows that the owner has all three permissions to read, write, and execute

r-x – this shows that the group can only read and execute the file

r-- – this indicates that all the other users can only read this file

For directories, if you don't have read permissions, you cannot view a directory's contents. If you lack write permissions, you cannot write to this directory. This means that you can't create a new file in that directory, either. Execute permissions mean you can search the directory and list its contents; for example, if you don't set the execution permissions, you can view directory files. Still, you cannot execute them or change into that directory. Also, if you have execute permissions but no read permissions, a user can execute files and change directories but not view the files.

Write permissions affect directories differently too because a user must have these authorizations to create a new file or remove an existing one. Even without the write permissions for the specific file, if you have directory write permissions, you can erase the files.

## Modifying Owners and Groups

As you make an account in Linux, the system assigns you both an owner and group ID. These IDs influence the kind of permissions you are granted as a user. Two commands can alter the owner and group of a file. These are chown and chgrp. The first command, chown, means change owner, and it is utilized to change a file's ownership. The `chgrp` one stands for change group, and it changes the group of a file.

This is the basic syntax of using `chown`: `$ chown user filelist`

The value of the user can be the username or user id. Thus the above command will look something like this:

```
$ chown fiona test

$
```

This changes the file ownership to the user named Fiona. It is important to note that superusers or root users have the unrestricted ability to change file ownership, while normal users can only do so for files they own.

The syntax for chgrp is `$ chgrp group filelist`

Just like the previous command, the value can either be the group name or group id. The `chgrp` command for the above example would then be:

```
$ chgrp minor test

$
```

This changes the group of that file to minor group.

# Set User ID and Set Group ID

As a command executes, it can do so with special privileges to fulfill its task. For instance, when you use the `passwd` command to alter your password, the new password is stored in the `/etc/shadow` file. As a regular user, you lack read and write permissions to these files because of security reasons. However, to change your password, you need these permissions. This means that the `passwd` command has to grant you this authorization to write in the `/etc/shadow` file.

This additional permission is given to such programs through mechanisms known as Set User ID (SUID) and Set Group ID (SGID).

When a program is SUID or SGID enabled, you get the permissions of the owner and group, respectively. If they are not set, the programs use the permissions granted to the user who started them. These programs are indicated by the letter "s" if the permission is available. The "s" will appear in the slot where the owners' execute command is. Let us look at the following example:

```
$ ls -l /usr/bin/passwd

-rwsr-xr-x  1   root   bin   69531 May 7 15:49  /usr/bin/passwd*

$
```

As you can see, the SUID bit is set, and the command is a root command. An upper case "S" in place of the lowercase one would show that it is not set.

## Pipes and Redirection

The | character — or as it is more commonly referred to, the pipe symbol — is quite prevalent in commands. Pipe lets you pass the output of one command through the input of another. For instance, let's say you want to make a long listing, such as the /bin directory. By inputting ls -l and hitting enter, the list appears, but the names pass by too fast to read. The entries you get to see are the last ones. If you instead input ls -l | more, the search results of the list command will be piped through more. This enables you to go through the results one batch at a time. Here the standard output of the ls command points to the pipe and becomes the standard input of the more command since it is also altered to point to the pipe.

The pipe symbol simply tells the Shell to use the files indicated instead of the standard input and output files. Every Linux system has the concepts of standard input, output, and error. Standard input is taken when a user logs in and uses the command line. Both standard output and error are sent to your screen. That is, your system expects to receive input from a keyboard or mouse and display the results or error messages on the screen.

As your system initiates, it opens these three files first. If a user, for instance, runs a command such as `find`, it gets its input from a file and shows the result on the screen. Even though it looks like the standard input is coming from the file, it's not. It is instead still coming from the keyboard. That is why, even for large files, you still use the keys to go through the results.

## Filters

When an application gets input from another program or file, acts on the input, and displays the results on standard output, it is referred to as a filter. Let's look at a few of these filter commands.

## The `grep` Command

This command searches a file or files for lines that exhibit a specified pattern. Here is the syntax: `$grep pattern file(s)`. The term *grep* is derived from *g/re/p*, which stands for "globally search for a regular expression and print all lines containing it." A regular expression consists of plain text and/or specialized characters used to match the patterns. The most basic use of `grep` is in searching for patterns containing single words. It can be added in a pipe so that only the input files with a certain string are output. If it doesn't have a file name to read, `grep` reads its standard input. This is also how all filter programs work.

You can also use several options with `grep`:

- -v – shows all lines that don't match the pattern

- -n – shows the matched line and its number

- -l – (letter "l") only shows file manes with matching lines

- -c – shows the matching lines count

- -i – matches either upper or lowercase

# The `sort` Command

This command organizes text lines alphabetically or numerically. For instance:

- `$sort cars`

- `Alpha Romeo`

- `Chevy`

- `Ford`

- `Isuzu`

- `Mercedes`

- `$`

However, there are several options for controlling this sorting. They include:

- `-n` – sorts the lines numerically and ignores blanks and tabs

- `-r` – reverses the sort order

- `-f` – sorts both upper and lowercase lines together

- `+x` – ignores the first x fields when sorting

You can link several commands into a pipe such as `ls -l | grep pattern file | sort +4n`

# Chapter Summary

In this chapter, we looked at several things.

- The Linux Shell and what we already knew, such as its various components, and we got deeper into these elements.

- Environmental variables contain everything a shell needs to operate. An example of an environmental variable is PATH.

- We also looked at search path, absolute, and relative path too.

- The three access modes in a Linux system: read, write, and execute. These modes are also permissions as to what a user is allowed to do to a file or directory.

- There are also various commands attributed to all the actions discussed in this chapter and some examples of them in use.

# Exercises

**Exercise 1**

a) Run `echo $SHELL` to find out what Shell you are using.

b) What `init` files does your shell use, and when are they used?

c) Try out these commands and take note of the differences

- `ls`

- `ls -l`

- `ls *`

- `ls -ld*`

d) List the contents of directories containing a *4* in their name.

**Exercise 2:**

a) Use the `echo` command to display what is in your current PATH (remember it needs to be named `$PATH` when using it). Which of the directories are being searched as the command executes?

b) Enter the following commands and observe what happens.

- `cd blah`

- `cd ..` remember to mind the space between "cd" and ".."!

- `pwd`

c) Detail the directory contents with the `ls` command. What do you see, and what do you think these could be? Use the `pwd` command to check.

d) Type in the `cd` command and repeat the step twice as you observe what's happening.

e) Try `cd root` and observe what happens. Check to see which directories you have access to?

f) Repeat the `cd` command input step, is there another way you can get to your directory?

g) Read `man intro, man ls, and info passwd`

h) Enter the pertinent `pwd` command.

i) Try `man` or `info` on `cd`. Which one showed more information about `cd`?

# CHAPTER 4

## System Administration

System administration encompasses a lot of areas, and thus it becomes quite hard to clearly define what it is precisely because all aspects of a computer fall under system administration. This includes software, hardware, networking, and even programming, to mention a few.

System administration allows a user to get a better understanding of the system and thus utilize it better, from starting the system, creating and managing accounts, installing software, configuring hardware, device management, automating the system, backing it up, etc. You can see that a system administrator wears a lot of hats. You are your system's administrator, and these responsibilities fall on you.

In this chapter, we'll examine some of those system administration tasks. We will not dive deep into the nitty-gritty, but we will cover the basics — i.e., the functional areas of system administration — so that you can use the programs and utilities at your disposal.

### System Start-Up and Shut Down

Starting up a Linux system is quite simple, and it involves pressing the power button and watching your system boot. Almost all users and many system administrators have no idea of what is happening as the system boots. From switching the power on to getting to the login prompt, a lot of things must take place. Knowing what is happening in the boot process can be quite useful because you can easily tell what went wrong if a system does not start how it should. Starting up your system can be as easy as turning it on and letting it boot. However, you can alter this behavior by changing the boot process. We will not get too deep into the boot process, but here are some important things to keep in mind when shutting your system down.

Linux is unlike the other operating systems, and even with the many efforts to make it look superficially like these other operating systems, they still differ, especially when shutting the system down. In other systems, you are always aware of what's going on, and you have complete control over everything. You can decide to turn the computer off once you feel you are done. However, since Linux is a multi-user system, there are other users working or using its resources, so simply switching off the machine is not advised. Other than annoying other users, you could damage your system depending on what was running when you switched off.

On a multi-user system, there are many things that are going on without the user's awareness. For instance, the system could still have data in the buffer waiting for a chance to write it on the hard drive. If you switch off the power, this data will be lost, and the data left on the drive will be inconsistent. To prevent this, you need to shut your system down properly. What a proper shut down consists of will depend on the conditions. Linux nonetheless does have tools to help with the shutdown; switching off the power is not considered a proper shutdown.

## User Account Management

When many people use a device such as a workstation, it's vital to differentiate between the users. This, for instance, helps keep their personal files private, whether it is used by many users simultaneously or only by one user at a time, such as in microcomputers. Every user is assigned a unique identifier known as a username that they use to log in.

In Unix-like systems such as Linux, there are three types of user accounts: the root, system, and user accounts. The root account, also called the super user, is automatically created when you install your Linux OS and has complete, unrestricted control over the system. In other words, it has administrative privileges for all the operating system services. A root account can run any commands, and this account is often referred to as the system administrator account. System accounts are required for the running of system-specific elements such as mail or the sshd accounts. These accounts are required for particular functions, and any modifications could affect the system badly. For instance, services such as games, mail, and printing have individual system accounts that allow them to interact with your computer. Finally, user accounts give users or groups of them interactive access to the system. These accounts have the necessary privileges to undertake standard tasks in a Linux system, such as run programs, store data in files and databases, etc. These accounts, however, do not have admin privileges, so they cannot, for example, mistakenly delete core operating system configuration files. General users are usually assigned these accounts.

Unix also supports the group account concept, where several accounts are logically grouped, making them part of the group account. This group account plays an important role in file permissions and process management. Users can be members of multiple groups. For instance, in the Red Hat Enterprise distro, when a user is added, a private user group is created. This means that a user group named after the user has been created and the new user is the only member.

## Creating an Account

The Linux system views users as numerals, and each one is assigned a unique identifying integer known as the user ID or UID. This is because, for a computer, numbers are easier and faster to process compared to textual names. There is a database outside the kernel that gives the textual name, the username, to every user ID. Every UID is assigned at least one group, with one designated as their login group.

All groups have a group ID or GID, which helps identify the user's login group. These two sets of identification help keep track of the user and define what files they can access. Applications and commands that engage with users report user data by logname or group name. However, the OS uses the UID and GID for most identification requirements. These are the primary administrative files:

1. `etc/passwd` – stores the user account and password data; this file contains the most information about accounts on the system

2. `/etc/shadow` – contains the encrypted password of the corresponding account; note that not all the systems support this file

3. `/etc/group` – **this file has the group's data for every account**

4. `/etc/gshadow` – **this file has secure group account data**

As stated above, the `/etc/passwd` and `/etc/group` files define both the user and group accounts, respectively, and everyone has access to them. To create a user, information about the user needs to be added to the user database and make a home directory for them, `/home/<username>`, which is also their default directory once they log into the system. It is important to note that the parent directory might differ. You might need to teach the user about a few things and set up the environment for them. There are several applications for creating user accounts available with most distributions. However, you can also use the command line to create them with the `adduser` and `useradd` commands. Let's see how to go about it.

The basic syntax for creating a new account is `useradd [options] username`. When expanded it looks something like this: `useradd -d homedir -g groupname -m -s shell -u userid account name`

- `-d homedir` – defines the home directory for the account

- `-g groupname` – defines the group account for the account

- `-m` – creates the home directory if it is non-existent

- `-s shell` – defines the default shell to use for this account

- `-u userid` – this is where you define a user id for the account

- `account name` - this is where you input your preferred account name to be created

To use this command, you must have sudo access or be logged into a root account. The `useradd` command makes a new user account using the options detailed on the command line plus the defaults in the `/etc/default/useradd` file. These values are different in each distro; thus, running the useradd command might display varying results on each distro. The command also reads the `/etc/ login.defs` file because it contains the shadow password suite configuration. These include user ID ranges used in creating accounts, password expiration policies, etc.

Type in `$ sudo useradd username` and hit enter. The command will read the default file and create an entry in the `/etc/passwd, /etc/shadow, /etc/group` and `/etc/gshadow` files. So for example, to create a new (ordinary) user account for Fiona, type in `$ sudo useradd fiona,` or `$ useradd -d /home/fiona -g minor -s /bin/ksh fiona`

Don't forget to create the minor group before issuing this command.

# Changing Passwords

To log in using your new account, a password must be set using the passwd command. Here is the syntax: `$ sudo passwd username`

After running this command, you will be requested to input the password and confirm it. Ensure that you set a strong password to safeguard your account. Here is the basic syntax and an example.

```
Changing password for user username

New password:

Retype new password:

passwd: all authentication tokens updated successfully
```

Here's the example

```
$ passwd Fiona

Changing password for user fiona

New password:
```

```
Retype new password:

passwd: all authentication tokens updated successfully
```

## Modifying Accounts

You can make changes to an existing account from the command prompt via the usermod command. It employs the same argument as the useradd and the -1 commands which allow you to alter your account name. To change the account name fiona to fiona23, and alter the home directory too, you will type in: $ usermod -d /home/fiona23 -m -l fiona fiona23

## Removing Accounts

You can also delete a dormant, unused, or existing account using the userdel command. Please note that this is a dangerous command and should be used cautiously. It uses only one argument or option, .r, to remove the account's mail file and home directory.

For example: $ usermod -r fiona23

If you want to retain the home directories for backup, you can omit the -r option.

## Group Accounts

All the existing groups in your system are located in the /etc/groups file. However, as defaults, they are system account specific, and they are not recommended for use with ordinary accounts. To create a new group, you will use the groupadd command in the following syntax: groupadd [-g gid [-o]] [-r] [-f] group name

- -g GID – represents the numerical value of the group's ID

- -o – the option permits the user to add a group with a non-unique GID

- -r – the flag instructs the groupadd command to add a system account

- `-f` – this option causes an exit with success prompt if the defined group already exists. With `-g`, if the defined GID already exists, other (unique) GID is selected.

- `groupname` – this is the actual group name to be created

To modify a group, utilize the groupmod command in the following syntax: `$ groupmod -n new_modified_group_name old_group_name`

For example: `$ groupmod -n minor minor¬_2`

To delete a group, you require the groupdel command and the group's name, i.e., `$ groupdel group_name`. This will only remove the group and not the files.

# Process Management

A process is an executable application that's operating in its own location. It is distinct from a job or command as they can comprise of several processes working together to achieve a singular task. A singular process executes simple commands such as `ls`. A command containing pipe symbols, for instance, is a compound command and requires the execution of several processes. By controlling the processes, you can manage the CPU resources on Unix based systems.

Don't forget that Linux is a multi-user system, so you can have several users running multiple commands simultaneously on the same system. This can present quite a challenge, and measures have to be taken for the CPU to manage all these processes while retaining functionality so users can switch between and also retrieve interrupted processes. There are cases where processes continue running even after the user who initiated them logs out.

To better understand how this works, let's examine the process structure.

## Process Types

Several kinds of processes exist; here, we will look at interactive, daemons, and automatic batch processes.

## Interactive Processes

These are started and controlled through a terminal session. This means a user has to be connected to the system to initiate them since they are not automatically started as part of the system functions. They can either run in the foreground or background. Processes running in the foreground remain attached to the terminal because it communicates directly with the terminal. For instance, a command that has been run and is awaiting output means it is a foreground process. While a foreground process operates, only it can get input from the terminal.

This means that if you run a command on a large file, you will not be able to run another one until the command ends, or you kill it with CTRL-C. Alternatively, you can run it as a background process. This way, the user can still use the terminal as the other program runs. This way, the system does not remain idle or generate error messages.

The shell has a feature known as job control that eases the handling of several processes. This feature switches processes from the fore to the background and vice versa. You can also start applications in the background. Running a process in the background is only useful if it does not need user input and its execution might take a while. A background process can be resumed and executed unlinked to the terminal that began it. Here are some of the ways the job control feature works in most shells.

- `regular_command` – runs a command in the foreground

- `&` - adding this to a regular command tells the shell to run the command in the background. (e.g. `$ long_cmd &`)

- `jobs` - shows a list of background processes

- Ctrl+Z – suspends, meaning it temporarily stops — but does not quit — a process running in the foreground

- Ctrl+C – interrupts, meaning it terminates and quits a foreground process

- `%n` – assigns each process running in the background a number; by using the `%` expression a job can be referred to using its number, for instance, `$ kill %4`

- `bg` – reactivates a suspended background process

- `fg` – restores a process to the foreground

- `%? str` – used to reference the background job command containing the specified characters

- `kill` – ends a process

## Batch or Automatic Processes

These processes are independent of the terminal, but they can be queued in a spooler area as they await execution on a first-in, first-out (FIFO) basis. These processes can be run by applying either of these two criteria: these tasks are executed at a specific time and date, or this is done using the at command.

The tasks can also be executed when the system load is low enough to allow extra jobs. This is done using the batch command. By default, these processes are queued and await execution when the system load is below 0.8. In larger systems, batch processing can be used when there is a lot of data that requires processing, or the task load is too demanding on the current system. It can also be used

## Daemons

These are continuously running server processes. They are initialized at start-up and wait in the background until they are needed. An example would be the networking daemons which lay dormant until needed by a client application. There are several Unix daemons such as `syslogd`, `sendmail`, `lpd`, `rlpdaemon`, `crond`, `syncd`, `pagedaemon`, and many more.

## Process attributes

Linux processes have several characteristics that can be seen using the ps command. These include:

- The process ID or PID – a unique identification number used to reference a process

- The parent ID or PPID – the PID of the process that initiated the current process

- Nice number – indicates the friendliness of the current process to other processes. It should not be confused with process priority, which is calculated based on the nice number and the process's CPU usage.

- Terminal or TTY – indicates the terminal to which the process is linked to

- Real and effective user ID (RUID, EUID) – a process's RUID is the user ID of the owner or the user who started it. Its EUID is the user ID used to define the access the process has to system resources. They are usually the same and grant the process the same access rights as the owner, except when setuid access mode is set.

- Real and effective group owner (RGID, EGID) – the real group owner is the main group of the process owner. The effective group owner, which determines access, is usually the same, except when setgid (SGID) access mode has been applied.

# The Life Cycle of a Process

A new process is created when an existing one, its parent process, makes an exact copy of itself in a procedure known as forking. This new process is referred to as the child process and shares the same environment as the parent process but with a different PID. After forking, the child process's location is overwritten with the new process data through the exec system call, hence the popular phrase fork-and-exec. A new program completely replaces the parent duplicate, even though the parent process remains with its environmental variables, standard input, output, and error assignments, along with its execution priority.

Let's use an example to help you better understand this concept. When a user runs a command such as `grep`, the user's shell process forks, creating a new process to execute the command. This new shell process execs grep begins executing the command since it overlays the shell's executable image in the memory with `grep`'s. Once the `grep` command completes, the process dies.

This is basically how all Unix processes are created. The overall process ancestor, PID 1, init, is created during the boot process. It creates other processes through fork-and-exec, and among them are processes executing the getty command. They are assigned to different serial lines and display the login prompt, waiting for someone to respond to it. When a user logs in, the getty process execs the login program, which then validates the login credentials, among other activities. Once verification is done, login execs the user's shell.

You don't always need to fork to run a new program such as is the case with the login program above. After logging into the system, the user's shell is the same process as the getty that was monitoring the unused serial line. That process switched programs two times by execing a new executable, and it will proceed to create new processes to run the commands inputted by the user. When a process exits, it sends a signal that informs the parent process that it has been completed. When a user logs out, the login shell will signal its parent, init, as it closes, informing init that it should create a new getty process for the terminal. Then init forks again and initializes getty, and the whole cycle repeats.

## Controlling Processes with Different Signals

As mentioned before, processes use signals to terminate. There are, however, a lot of signals that can be used to control the behavior of a process. For instance, you can use the `kill` command to send a process a signal. Most signals are used by the system internally or by programmers when they code. Here are some examples.

- SIGTERM – signal number 15 – signals a process to terminate in an orderly way

- SIGINT – signal number 2 – interrupts a process; a process can choose to ignore this signal

- SIGKILL – signal number 9 – interrupts the process; this signal cannot be ignored

- SIGHUP – signal number 1 – this is for daemons; it instructs them to reread the configuration file

You can get the full list of signals by typing in the `kill -l` command. The list varies according to your distribution.

## SUID and SGID

The setuid and setgid access modes enable regular users to carry out tasks that require privileges and access rights, which they don't have. Take, for example, in many systems, the write command belongs to the tty group. This group also owns all the terminal and pseudo-terminal files. The write command, therefore, has setgid access, which allows users to write messages to another user's terminal or window, which they normally have no access to. As the user writes, their EUID is set to that of the group that owns the executable file (`/usr/bin/write`) for the command duration.

SUID and SGID are also utilized by the printing subsystem, mailers, and other system facilities, but they are prone to causing security risks. Setuid almost always sets the user ID to root; you can see the danger this poses to the system. Programs and users can find ways to perform extra unauthorized actions, while setuid is active to retain this access after the process ends. Setuid should be avoided since it poses a greater security risk than setgid. You can perform any task with setgid in conjunction with carefully designed groups. This, however, doesn't make them completely risk-free.

# System Performance Monitoring

Another important duty of a system administrator is to monitor and manage the system's performance. Linux provides tools to help with this, and these tools also give guidelines on how to diagnose and fix system performance errors. There are major resources that require monitoring and management. These include the CPU, memory, hard drive, lines of communications lines, I/O time, network time, and application programs.

Performance components are used to gauge how the system is working. Below are five major components that make up system time.

1. User State CPU

   This indicates the actual time the CPU spends running the users' applications in the user state. It includes the time spent executing user-initiated processes such as library calls but doesn't include the time spent in the kernel on behalf of the process. Every CPU time used by anything else other than the kernel is marked as a user time, even if the user did not launch it. If, for instance, a user-process needs to access some hardware, it has to put a request in through the kernel, meaning this would count as system state time instead.

2. System State CPU

This shows the amount of CPU time is taken up by the kernel. The kernel handles all low-level tasks such as memory allocation, communication between operating system processes, running device drives, managing the file system, and interacting with hardware. This means that all I/O routines require kernel services. A programmer can alter this value by blocking any I/O transfers during a session.

3. I/O Time and Network Time

This indicates the time spent transferring data and attending to I/O requests from various processes. An iowait is a subcategory of I/O time that shows the time spent waiting for I/O operations, such as a read or write to disk. As a processor awaits a file to be opened, the time spent is marked as iowait. High iowait times can indicate issues in the system that are outside the processor's control.

4. Virtual Memory Performance

This includes time spent context switching and swapping.

5. Application Program

This is the time spent running other application programs. That is when the system is not attending to this application because another application currently has use of the CPU.

# Performance Tools

Remember the tools mentioned before that help users measure, monitor, fine-tune, and manage system performance? They include:

- `nice/renice` – runs a process with modified scheduling priority

- `netstat` – prints network connections, routing tables, interface statistics, mask connections, and multicast memberships

- `time` – helps a user time a simple command or gauge resource usage

- `uptime` – shows the system load average

- `ps` – reports a snapshot of the current processes

- `vmstat` – reports statistics on virtual memory

- `gprof` – displays the user's call graph profile data

- `prof` – facilitates user process profiling

- `top` – shows all the system tasks

You can use the Manpage Help to get the syntax of these and more Linux commands.

# System Logging

Linux has an extremely flexible and powerful logging system that enables a user to log or record just about anything and manipulate these records to get the information they need. This is through the syslog facility. Programs that require their data to be logged send this information to the syslog facility. syslog is a host configurable, uniform system logging facility that uses a centralized system logging process that runs the `/etc/syslogd` or `/etc/syslog` program files.

The way it works is that programs send their log entries to syslogd, which then creates the `/etc/syslogd.conf` or `/etc/syslog` configuration file. When a match is found, it writes the log data into the wanted document. The following are some basic syslog terms you should know.

The first one is the facility. It is an identifier used to define a program or process that presented the log message. It can be the kernel, mail, FTP, etc. Next is the priority, an indicator of the log message's importance. Priority levels within syslog are defined as guides for events such as debugging or error reporting. The term "selector" refers to a combination of one or more facilities and levels. The last term is the action. This refers to what takes place when an incoming message matches a selector. They can be a write to log file, echo log message to console, send the log message to another syslog server, and so on.

Syslog facilities are programs for the selector, such as auth, which shows any activity related to requesting username and password, like getty, login, etc. Console captures messages directed to the system console. Cron shows messages from the cron system scheduler. FTP shows messages for the FTP daemon. There are quite a few facilities, and not all of them are present on all Linux distributions.

Syslog priorities show the importance of the log messages that come in. They include:

- `emerg` – for emergency conditions such as a system crash that all users are informed about

- `alert` – indicates that the message condition needs to be addressed immediately

- `crit` – shows that the message condition is critical such as a hardware error

- `err` – shows a normal error message

- `warning` – shows a warning message

- `notice` – shows that even though the condition is not an error ir should be handled specially

- `info` – for information messages

- `debug` – for debugging messages

- `none` – for pseudo-level messages that don't need logging.

These facilities and their priorities help the user discern the system logs and knows where to find the information they need. The system logger decides what to keep or discard depending on the selector priority level.

## Chapter Summary

- You learned what system management is and a bit of what it entails.

- A system administrator does a lot of things and thus should also be well informed. A system admin needs to know how things work, especially today, with systems being touted as easier to use and requiring little or no system administration. Simple-to-use tools are being created every day attempting to make system administration simple even for a novice.

- However, if someone has to understand the nuances and details of how things really work, it should be you.

- Before taking any actions, make sure to plan ahead.

- Remember to make the process reversible and have backups. Various tools can assist you with this.

- Implement any changes gradually and test out whatever tool you want to add thoroughly before releasing or implementing it.

# Exercises

## Exercise 1:

Check all the following files using the `cat` command.

- etc/passwd

- /etc/shadow

- /etc/group

- /etc/gshadow

## Exercise 2:

- Connecting and disconnecting from the system

- Figure out if your system is in text or in graphical mode.

- Find the login prompt and log in with the username and password you created during installation.

- Log out and try logging in again, using a made-up username and observe your terminal.

## Exercise 3

- Log in again with your username and password and change your password to K5js3.tt!, hit enter and observe what happens.

- Try it again but this time, set your password to something easy like 0000 and see what happens.

- Change your password a third time but don't input anything and see what happens.

- Try using the passwd command instead of passwd and observe what happens.

- Remember to change your password back from K5js3.tt!, after this exercise. Some systems might not allow you to recycle passwords, i.e., restore your original password within a certain time frame or a certain amount of password changes, or even both.

# CHAPTER 5

## Security

E ven though Linux has some inherent advantages over other operating systems when it comes to security, it is still vulnerable to security issues that need to be addressed just like in any other system. Regardless of the measures you may have in place, the concepts are the same. Think of it this way: the basic principles you would use to secure for your home or office will apply when it comes to computer security. You only want to let in authorized people and give them access to the areas they are allowed in. Most people think security is being risk- or danger-free. They also think that it includes the methods used to keep this danger or risk away, such as getting an alarm to keep burglars out. When it comes to computers, both these definitions apply, albeit depending on what you are referring to.

If we consider computer or system security from the point of view of being risk-free, then we are referring to such things as having reliable software, hardware, and backups. While these issues are important, this is not everything that is meant by security. Computer security also deals with preventing someone from breaking into your computer. That is, another user gaining unauthorized access to your system.

# Why Is Security Important?

In today's world, almost all devices are connected to a network. Whether it is on an isolated or public network, you have to protect the system from other users and the users from each other. You don't want them altering or deleting system files accidentally or intentionally, or damaging their systems too. The odds are quite high that your Linux system will be connected to the Internet. You want to protect it from the danger that is present on the web. These intruders can impersonate a user and access a system to steal, destroy, or deny you access. This is referred to as a denial of service (DoS) attack.

An internet connection makes your system open to other systems on the Internet. While this can be great for a multitude of services, it also puts you at risk. You cannot have a truly secure system as long as it is connected to a network, but you can work to make your system more secure and robust to deter attacks.

There are many reasons why you should secure your system, and before undertaking any measure, it is important to know why you are doing so. As you look to secure your system, ask yourself what it means to be secure, what are the risks involved, the effects it will have on the users, and if there is any data on it. By considering these factors, you will know if you have met your goal of securing your system.

We keep talking about security and securing a system, but what aspects of security should be implemented to get this security? These aspects include:

- authorization for users, programs, etc. with the necessary permissions or access

- authenticity to verify users, programs, etc. as who they claim to be

- privacy to ensure personal data is not tampered with or compromised

- integrity in upholding the privacy of the data and ensuring no corruption has taken place

- non-repudiation that the data is reputable

- availability of the system to perform its duties and functions

Now that you know the aspects a secure system should have, let's look at system hardening. This chapter goes through how to harden your system to make it more secure. Before we begin, let us define some terms. They embody the key concepts of securing a system.

## System Auditing

An audit is an inspection or assessment of a system. Therefore, a security audit can be defined as the inspection and assessment of a system's security capability. No system can be deemed as secure without testing. This is where a security audit comes in. You can assess the potential risks your system is under.

## System Compliance

Compliance can be defined as the ability to meet specified standards. When applied to computer security, system compliance then refers to the measures taken to ensure the system meets the requirements. For instance, your baseline requires that each system should have a firewall. A compliance check would involve testing for the presence of a firewall.

## System Hardening

As the name would suggest, system hardening involves strengthening your system's defenses to safeguard it better. It is similar to fortification, where you add new defenses and improve on existing ones. This fortification can also involve the removal of some components to keep the system safe. For example, if you have a security system that protects your home from thieves, you can harden it by adding other security features. These can include motion sensors, infra-red cameras, etc. to boost your defenses.

The first step is setting up a set of guidelines that explain what users on your system, even internet visitors, are allowed to do. The security level you set depends on how you use your system and the risk it is under if someone were to gain unauthorized access. A company system administrator, for instance, may want to involve the management in setting up these security policies. The system security requirements you set determine what you are securing. They identify the computer resources and data you have to protect, including the applicable laws such as privacy.

These requirements can include enabling authorized users to access data, implementing rules that define who has access to what data, and limiting access to public users. Use a robust user-authentication system tool. Refuse the execution of malicious or destructive actions on the information. Secure data from end to end as it moves across networks. Finally, impose all security and privacy needs that applicable laws require.

## Risk Analysis

Risk analysis helps assess the potential dangers that could harm your system. A risk analysis defines the risk, then it identifies and establishes the priority for handling these risks. Risk analysis looks at any possible threats, what you are protecting your system against, the vulnerabilities and weaknesses in your system that could be exploited by those threats, the probability or likelihood that a threat will exploit the weakness, and the impact such a risk poses and any mitigation measures that could be taken to reduce or remove these vulnerabilities.

## Threats

This is a list of typical attacks a Linux system can come under.

1. A DoS attack

   This attack ties up the computer and network so that legitimate users cannot use or access the system. Let's take a company; for instance, a DoS attack can cripple service and cause revenue losses. Since bringing an organization down with one computer attack can be hard, a common tactic is to redirect several computers to a single site and let them crash the system. This is referred to as a distributed attack, or DDoS.

2. Unauthorized hacking

   This is when an unauthorized user gains access to the system. They can steal, corrupt, or delete data. This can have adverse effects on the system, such as causing it to crash.

3. Disclosure of information

   To disclose is to release, show, or tell something that is private. A good example would be the disclosure of a password file that shows potential hackers your login credentials. This also applies to the leakage of sensitive data such as financial or medical reports.

## Vulnerabilities

Here are some of the areas in which systems and networks are vulnerable to attacks: by divulging and sharing user passwords and security credentials; through unsecured access points such as routers and network switches; the interconnections between the system and the Internet, such as gateways; loose or bad security from 3rd party network providers (ISPs); holes in the operating system's security such as internet holes associated with the `sendmail`, `named`, and `bind` commands; lastly, weaknesses in specific applications. All these vulnerabilities are potential entry points for security threats.

## Securing Linux

After determining a security policy, you can move on to securing the system as per your policy. As stated earlier, the exact steps of how you secure your system will depend on what you want to do with the system, whether it's a workstation or server, and how many users are expected to use the system. Linux security is covered in two broad categories, namely host security and network security issues, and to secure your system you have to handle both.

Important tip: if your host is connected to a large network, the directory services can present some security issues, so look into them.

## Host-Security

This involves dealing with issues related to securing the OS, files, and directories. Here are some guidelines on how to address host-security problems.

1. Don't install software you don't need. For instance, if your system is a workstation, you don't need web or news servers.

2. Create all the user accounts you will need in the beginning and ensure they have strong passwords. Linux has tools you can use to enforce strong passwords.

3. Set file ownership and access to safeguard important files and directories.

4. If your system has the capability of mandatory access control, enable it. This feature has been supported by kernels through the incorporation of Security-Enhanced Linux (SELinux)

since the release of kernel 2.6. Think of it as a layer wrapped around your system, thus adding more security.

5.  Use the GNU Privacy Guard (GnuPG) to encrypt or decrypt files with sensitive data and to authenticate downloaded files. GnuPG comes with most Linux distros, and you can use the `grp` command to encrypt, decrypt and even make a digital signature.

6.  Utilize file integrity tools to monitor any changes to crucial system files and directories.

7.  Check various log files periodically for any signs of tampering, break-ins, or attempted break-ins. These files can be found in the `/var/log` directory of your system. You can install stable security updates as soon as they are made available. They target the vulnerabilities of the system and fix them. Make sure you test this update out before updating your system and machines.

8.  You could spend a lot of time hardening your system and forget the physical aspect of security. What's the point of finally having a secure system if someone breaks in and steals it? You can set up your system in secure rooms where you can control access.

## Using GnuPG to Encrypt and Sign Files

Linux comes equipped with the GNU Privacy Guard (GnuPG or GPG) encryption and authentication utility. It lets you create a private and public encryption key, then uses the key to encrypt your files and sends a digital authentication to show that the message came from you. Someone with your public key can verify this. The idea of using public encryption keys is basically to have two keys that are related but cannot be used to figure out one from the other. Anything encrypted with any of the keys can only be decrypted with the corresponding key. You distribute the public key to other people, but keep the private one to yourself.

Let's use an example to help illustrate the use of encryption keys. Jane wants to send a secure message to Joe. Every user generates a public and private key, and they swap their public keys. If Jane wants to send Joe a message, she encrypts the data with his public key and sends the message to him. Since the message is encrypted, it is secure from eavesdropping because only Joe's key can decrypt it, and only Joe has that key. Once Joe receives the message, he used his key to decrypt the message and reads it. At this point, you might have noticed some vulnerabilities. These include, how could Joe be sure the message came from Jane? What if someone else has Joe's key and sent the message posing as Jane? This is where digital signatures come in.

## Digital Signatures

The purpose of an electronic signature is to help identify you. Unlike pen-and-paper ones, digital signatures depend on the message you are sending. You first start by applying a mathematical function to the message and then reducing it to a fixed-size message digest known as a hash or fingerprint. Despite the size of your message, the digest is either 128 or 160 bits, depending on your hashing function. Next, you apply your public key by encrypting the message digest with your private key and get your digital signature. It is normally added to the end of the electronically signed message.

Digital signatures let anyone who wants to verify that you signed the message to use the public key and decrypt it to see the message digest or encrypted hash. They can run the same hash function on the message and match the computed value with the decrypted one. Since your public key was used to verify and decrypt the message, it must have been meant for you.

## Using GPG

The GNU Privacy Guard (GnuPG) contains the tools you require to use public-key encryption and digital signatures. The first step is decryption, and you can get the hang of using GPG as you progress gradually. With GPG, you can generate encryption keys, exchange keys, sign files, encrypt, and decrypt documents. Let us take a look at each of these functions.

## Generating Key Pairs

Type in the `gpg --gen-key` command. If this is your first time using GPG, it will create a .gnupg directory in your home directory, and a file named .gpg.conf will be created in that directory. It will then ask what kind of key you want. Either DSA and ElGamal (which is the default), DSA (sign only), or RSA (sign only).

After selecting a key type, hit enter. You can also hit enter to select the default choice. You will be prompted to enter a key size in bits, i.e., 128, 160, 256, etc. Press enter to accept your choice or leave it blank then hit enter to use the default value of 2048. If you want to use default settings, keep hitting enter.

When asked whether you really never want the keys to expire, press Y to confirm, you will then be asked to type in your name, email address, and a comment to link the key to you. Hit enter. When asked to change or confirm this data, go over it then hit enter. You will be asked for a passphrase that is used to protect your private key. The passphrase should contain both uppercase and lowercase letters, numbers, and even punctuations marks. The longer, the better, then hit enter. Be careful as you set the passphrase because you need to be able to remember it easily.

## Exchanging Keys

To communicate securely, you have to give other people your public key and get their public keys. GPG stores your keys on your key ring, a file containing these keys. To list the keys on your key ring, input `gpg --list-keys`. To send your public key, you have to export it to a file first. The best way to document it is in the ASCII-armored format like this:

```
gpg --armor --export spadelanny@boomee.com > spadelanny.asc
```

This command will save the public key in ASCII-armored format in the spadelanny.asc file. The key is now ready to be sent. You can also receive key files which you will import using the `gpg --import file_name` command. The `gpg -list-keys` command verify the keys present in your key ring. Next, you will want to check the key's fingerprint by using the following command: `gpg --fingerprint file_name`. This will display the messages' fingerprints. You can then verify the fingerprint and validate it. This tells the system that the key is good, and you trust the key, but be very careful with key verification as they can make your system vulnerable. You can use the `gpg -sign-key file_name` command to sign the key.

# Signing Files

Signing files can be used as a way of assuring the file recipient that you have verified the information, no one has tampered with it, and you did indeed send the file. For instance, you can compress and sign a file named "urgent" using the following command: `gpg -o urgent.sig -s urgent`. Use `gpg --verify urgent.sig` to verify the signature. Sometimes you still want to sign a message to show that it came from you even though it is not secret. You can generate and include a clear-text signature with the following command: `gpg -o urgent.asc --clearsign urgent`

# Encrypting and Decrypting Files

To encrypt a message, use –encrypt or –e in the GPG command, that is, gpg -o urgent.gpg -e -r spadelanny@boomee.com message

This message named urgent is now encrypted using spadelanny's public key. It doesn't have a signature, though. You can add it using –s command. To decrypt the same file, for instance, the recipient must have the private key so that they can issue this command: gpg -o message --decrypt urgent.gpg

# Network Security

This involves dealing with issues related to threats or attacks over a network connection. Network security becomes relevant when you connect your system to a network, such as connecting to your company's internal network, even if you are dealing with a single computer connected to the Internet. Albeit the latter situation does not warrant you to worry too much, having the internal network system exposed to the world can cause you quite a headache.

You could be thinking that you can avoid putting your internal network at risk by connecting only the external servers such as the web or FTP servers to the Internet. This simplistic approach is not recommended. Liken it to an example of a person who will not drive because there is a chance they might get involved in an accident.

Not connecting your system to the Internet can have the following disadvantages. First, you cannot use file transfer protocols, or FTP, to company files from your system to the web browser. Users cannot access other remote servers that are connected to the network. The internal network users don't have access to web servers over the Internet. This makes resources such as the web inaccessible to you and your users.

A practical solution would be to use a firewall and place the webserver on a very secure host outside the firewall. You can also enable the internet services you require on your system and keep away from unconfigured services. Utilize Secure Shell for remote access and don't use the `r` commands such as `rlogin` or `rsh`. Secure and harden the internet services that you want to run on your system.

You can apply the TCP wrapper access-control files, `/etc/hosts.allow` and `/etc/hosts.deny`, to secure some of these internet services. Quickly fix any known vulnerabilities of the internet services you choose to run. You can download and install the current security updates for your distro from their online update websites.

## Monitoring System Security

Even a secure system requires constant monitoring of the log files periodically for signs of intrusion. You can use an excellent detection tool such as Tripwire to detect any changes made in the system files and monitor the integrity of critical system files and directories. Your Linux system may not come equipped with detection tools; you may have to download or purchase them. Once installed, you can configure the tool to monitor any log changes.

It is essential to occasionally examine the log files in the `/var/log` directory and its subdirectories. Many Linux programs, such as some servers, write log data by using the logging capabilities of syslogd or rsyslogd. The log documents written by syslogd and rsyslogd are found in the `/var/log` directory in most Unix systems, so ensure that only the root user can read and write these files.

# Securing Internet Services

For a Linux system connected to the Internet, or even one on a TCP/IP local area network (LAN) that is not connected to the Internet, a significant threat is that a user could use one of many Internet services to gain access to your system. These services, such as mail, web, and FTP, need to run a server program that responds to client requests arriving over the TCP/IP network. Some have vulnerabilities that an intruder could take advantage of to log in to your system, maybe even with root privileges. Luckily, Linux has facilities that you can help you secure your Internet services.

# Switching off Stand-Alone Services

To provide internet services, such as web, email, and FTP, your Linux system has to run server programs that monitor incoming TCP/IP network requests. Some servers initiate when your system boots, and they run in the background all the time. These servers are known as stand-alone servers, and examples include web and mail servers.

Another server, xinetd, begins other servers that are meant to work under xinetd. Some systems utilize the inetd server instead of xinetd to initiate other servers. Some servers can be designed to run on a stand-alone basis or under a super server such as xinetd. The vsftpd FTP server, for instance, can be set up to run as a stand-alone server or to operate under the xinetd control.

In certain distros such as Debian and Ubuntu, you can use the `update-rc.d command` to switch off stand-alone servers, and use the `invoke-rc.d` command to commence or terminate servers interactively. To understand more about the available services, type in this command: `ls /etc/init.d`, and view all the script files meant to turn services on or off. You have to apply these filenames whenever you want to switch services on or off. To turn off the Samba service, for instance, type in `update-rc.d -f samba remove`. If the process was already operating, type `invoke-rc.d samba stop` to terminate the service. You can utilize the `invoke-rc.d command` to terminate processes or services similarly.

In Fedora and SUSE, stand-alone servers can be switched on and off by using the `systemctl` command. Input the `ls /etc/init.d` command to acquire the service scripts, then switch off a service (such as xinetd or Samba) by typing `sudo systemctl stop smb` or the proper syntax for the `xinetd` command. If the service was already operating, use `/etc/init.d/smb stop` to halt the Samba service. You can operate scripts from the `/etc/init.d` directory with the halt argument to stop any service in a related manner.

## Internet Super Server Configuration

Along with stand-alone servers such as web and mail servers, the inetd and xinetd servers have to be configured individually. These servers are Internet super servers because they can launch other servers on demand. You can input `ps ax | grep inetd` to view which Internet super server, inetd or xinetd, your system operates. Debian and Ubuntu use inetd, and Fedora and SUSE use xinetd.

The inetd server is set up through the `/etc/inetd.conf` file. To disable a service, locate the appropriate line and comment it out by putting a pound sign (#) at the beginning of that line. After saving the set up file, type in `/etc/init.d/inetd restart` to restart the inetd server.

Setting up the xinetd server is a bit harder. This server reads a configuration file titled `/etc/xinetd.conf` at system initialization. This file, in turn, references configuration files saved in the `/etc/xinetd.d` directory. The files in `/etc/xinetd.d` show the xinetd command which ports to listen to and the server to launch for each port. Type in `ls /etc/xinetd.d` to view a list of the documents in the `/etc/xinetd.d` directory on your Linux system. Every file denotes a service that xinetd can launch. To switch off any of them, edit the file in a text editor, and add a `disable = yes` line in the file.

After making changes in the xinetd set up files, a restart of the xinetd server is required for the changes to take effect. To restart the server, input `/etc/init.d/xinetd restart` into the command line. This will terminate the xinetd server and then restart it. When xinetd restarts, it reads the configuration data and effects the changes.

## Configuring TCP Wrapper Security

An essential security feature of inetd and xinetd is their usage of the TCP wrapper to launch various services. The TCP wrapper is a code block that provides an access-control facility for internet services by acting like a shielding package for your message. The wrapper can initiate other services, such as FTP and Telnet. However, before launching a service, it confers with the `/etc/hosts.allow` file to discern whether the host requesting the service is authorized to use that service. If nothing about that host emerges in `/etc/hosts.allow` file, the wrapper checks the `/etc/hosts.deny` file to discern whether it should deny the service. If both files are empty, the TCP wrapper can provide access to the requested service.

Here are the steps on how to tighten access to the services that inetd or xinetd is set up to start:

1. Use a text editor such as vi to edit the `/etc/hosts.deny` file, to include the following line: `ALL:ALL` — this setting denies all hosts access to any Internet services on your system.

2. Edit the `/etc/hosts.allow` file and include to it the hostnames that can access services on your system.

3. To permit only hosts from the 192.168.1.0 network and the localhost (IP address 127.0.0.1) to obtain the services on your system, put the following line in the `/etc/hosts.allow` file: `ALL: 192.168.1.0/255.255.255.0 127.0.0.1`

4. If you want to authorize a specific remote host access to a specific internet service, use the following order for a line in `/etc/hosts.allow`: `server_program_name: hosts` — here, `server_program_name` is the title of the server program, and `hosts` is a comma-separated listing of the hosts that have access to the service. You can also enter `hosts` as a network address or an entire domain name, such as .myplace.com.

## Computer Security Tools

These are some common tools you can use as you secure your system,

1. `chage` – modifies the time between required password changes. You can set the minimum and the maximum number of days and the number of warning days to be given so that a change is made, and the expiration date

2. `find` – one of the most powerful all-rounded tools in this system. The command lets you find almost anything on a machine if you have the right syntax. Among the many choices, you can find files created by a user, by a group, or on a certain date, with certain permissions.

3. `lsof` – an acronym for the list open files utility. Depending on the parameters applied, you can choose to view files opened by a process or by a user.

4. `netstat` – lets you view the status of the network, network connections, routing tables, and statistics per interface, etc. There is a similar command, `ss`, that is intended to replace much of the functionality here.

5. `nmap` – scans the network and creates a map of what's available on it. This ability makes it ideal for port scanning and security auditing.

6. `passwd` – allows the user to change their passwords in the command line. It shouldn't be confused with the file by the same name that has user account information. Many users don't know of its existence and opt to change passwords via the graphical interface tools.

7. `su` – grants temporarily root access to another user, and can be used in the current user's session. Another shell is made; when a user exits this second shell, the user reverts to the original session. This utility can be used to become the root user or any other user as long as you have the password.

8. `sudo` – instead of starting a new session (as needed in `su`) to carry out a job with special privileges, `sudo` lets the user just run that task with elevated privileges

9. `ulimit` – sets the resource limits on shells to keep a single user from excessively hogging all the system resources

10. `usermod` – can be viewed as an enhanced version of `chage`. It can set or change password expiration parameters and used to specify a default shell, to lock or unlock a user account, etc.

# Chapter Summary

Let's recap:

- We established what underlying security is and why it is crucial to secure your system.

- We took a look at risk analysis and some of the threats your system might face.

- We looked at how to protect your files and system in general by assigning users the appropriate ownership and permissions.

- We discussed some host-security issues such as access control, and how you could use GPG to encrypt your files.

- We discussed how to handle network-related security issues and some security tools you can use.

## Exercises

1.  Carry out a system security audit. Have you discovered any possible threats or vulnerabilities in your system?

2.  Check and see if your system is security compliant. Are there any ways you can reinforce your security?

3.  Download the GNU Privacy Guard (GPG) tool and install it. Try generating encryption key pairs. Were you successful?

4.  Now try to encrypt and decrypt a file. Were you successful?

# CHAPTER 6

## Networking with Linux

Linux and networking go hand in hand. Not only is Linux the operating system of choice, but it has a wide array of tools, features and applications that allow integration into all types of network structures. Linux is preferred because of its robust nature even under heavy loads which are a result of the many years of debugging and testing.

Networking is a broad subject, and we couldn't possibly cover everything in one chapter. However, in this chapter, we will take a look at what networking in Linux entails. We will explore some of the tools and fundamental mechanisms of networking. We will also take a look at how to configure your network.

## Network Protocols

The need to exchange data between machines gave rise to networking, and to be able to transfer data, computers must be able to talk to each other. However, with so many different pieces of hardware and software each speaking a different language, getting them to communicate seems complicated. How they interact is carried out in a predetermined manner referred to as a protocol. Basically, a protocol is a set of communication rules. These protocols define how each device behaves and how to react. The most common protocol in Unix-based systems is TCP/IP, which stands for Transmission Control Protocol/Internet Protocol.

# TCP/IP

TCP/IP is a protocol suite containing various protocols that were developed to allow communication between different brand devices. The TCP/IP protocol suite is based on a layered model, and it is focused on delivering interconnectivity rather than adhering to functional layers. This is the reason why TCP/IP has become the default standard opposed to Open Systems Interconnection reference model (OSI).

Take, for instance, your email program. It can communicate with the OS through certain protocols but not the hardware. It would require a special program to do this and still require more software to facilitate communication between the computer and the internet hookup method used. Don't forget that the network connection hardware also needs to talk to pass along your email to the destined computer. So if all these types of communications are classified into layers, only adjacent layers can communicate with each other.

This is how the OSI model works. Even though TCP/IP is structured similarly to this, as stated before, it allows for inter-layer communication. As per the example, the network connection hardware can communicate with the email-sending application. TCP/IP protocol suite is considered the industry standard because of its versatility.

Here are some examples of the protocols in the TCP/IP family:

- Transmission Control Protocol (TCP) – a connection-oriented secure protocol. The program first sends the information to be transmitted as a data stream then converted by the OS to the correct format. The data arrives at its destination in the original data stream format in which it was originally sent. TCP ascertains that there was no data loss or any kind of mix-up. This protocol is implemented wherever the data sequence matters.

- User Datagram Protocol (UDP) – a connectionless, insecure protocol. The data to be transmitted is sent in packet form already produced by the application. The order in which the information arrives at the recipient is not assured, and there is a possibility of data loss.

The UDP protocol is suitable for record-oriented applications and features a smaller latency period than TCP. For instance, Services, such as the Network File Service, or NFS, that use UDP must provide their own mechanisms to ensure packet delivery and their correct sequencing. Since it can broadcast or multicast, UDP also offers one-to-many services.

- Internet Control Message Protocol (ICMP)– this is not a protocol for the end-user, but a special control protocol that releases error reports and has control over how the machines participating in TCP/IP data transfer behave. Additionally, ICMP provides a special echo mode that can be viewed using the program ping.

- Internet Group Management Protocol (IGMP) – manages the computer's behavior when implementing IP multicast.

Most hardware protocols are packet-oriented. The data transferred to and from the hard drive is referred to in terms of data blocks known as packets. Depending on the application you are using the packet size can vary; however, they are small enough to transfer across networks quickly without any delays due to size. Also, since they are transferred so fast, you might not notice that your data is broken up.

## TCP/IP Layers

If we looked at the network communication process abstractly, every section supports and is supported by the other sections. These sections, also called layers, are stacked onto each other in the order below.

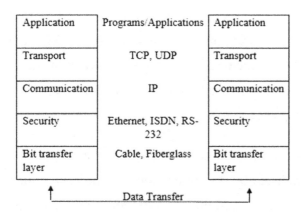

The bottom layer is responsible for the physical connection between the machines. It is known as the physical layer and deals with cable types, signal forms, codes etc. Next to it is the security layer or the data link layer. These layers handle accessing procedures such as which hosts can send data, error correction, and so on. The third layer, the network layer, handles remote data transfer and ensures that the data can be delivered and that it arrives at its destination. In more technical terms, this layer ensures that the packets either stay on the network or get transferred to the right network, all while ensuring they go to the correct network address.

The transport layer ensures that the data arrives in the right order and that no data loss occurs. It is important to note that the data link layer ensures that the data gets to the right destination while the transport layer ensures that no data loss occurs. The final layer is where the data is generated and processed by the application program. This is the layer the user sees, such as an email program.

Each layer is communicating with its counterpart on the other machine. This means that the communication between the matching layers is conceptual. The actual communication takes place between the different layers on each machine and not the matching layers on different machines. Additional data concerning each layer is added to the data packet to help each layer perform its job. This information is found in the packet header where every layer attaches a small data block, known as a protocol header, to every emerging packet.

When the application layer has information to send, it attaches the application header with the necessary information to get the data to the right destination on the receiving application. The app then calls up TCP to send the data. TCP wraps the information into a TCP packet with the TCP header added and passes it to IP. This is called encapsulation. Like the layers before, IP wraps the data packet up and adds the IP header, creating an IP datagram. The IP packet is then handed over to the hardware driver, such as Ethernet, which also adds a header and a trailer. This is called an Ethernet frame.

The network, through TCP, has a way of tracking what data belongs to what process. TCP ensures the packets are delivered in the right order and with all their content intact. It's also responsible for error detection. This is by comparing the checksum information of every data packet. If the checksum doesn't match the data packet contents or the packets fails to arrive, it is up to TCP to ensure the packet is resent. The TCP on the recipient machine must acknowledge receiving the packets; if not, the host TCP resends the packet. TCP is considered a reliable connection because of the checksum and resending data packets.

# TCP/IP Version 6

IPv6, as it is more commonly referred to, is an upgrade of the IPv4 protocol. This upgrade addresses several issues regarding its predecessor such as IP address shortages, network layer security issues, IPv4's lack of mechanisms to manage time-sensitive traffic, and so on.

# IP Addressing

The networking environment utilizes a diverse range of equipment to help unify them, TCP/IP determines an abstract interface through which the hardware is accessed. The interface provides a set of operations that is similar for all hardware types and basically handles the sending and receiving packets. Every peripheral networking device has a corresponding interface present in the kernel. For instance, Linux Ethernet interfaces in Linux are titled by such names as eth0 and eth1, ppp0 and ppp1 for PPP interfaces, and fddi0 and fddi1 for FDDI interfaces. These names are used for configuration purposes when you want to specify a particular physical device in a configuration command, and they have no meaning beyond this use.

Before use in TCP/IP networking, an interface must be assigned an IP address. It serves as its identification when communicating with other components. This address varies from the interface naming mentioned previously. Think of it this way: if you liken an interface to a door, the address is like the nameplate pinned on it.

The IP networking protocol recognizes addresses as 32-bit numbers, and every machine is assigned a number unique to the network environment, mainly IPv4. These addresses usually appear in the format below.

IP Address (binary): 11000000 10101000 00000000 00010100

IP Address (decimal):     192.     168.     0.     20

The IP address is written as 4 decimal numbers each 8-bits long separated by dots. For instance, a machine with an IP address of 0x954C0C04 would be written as 149.76.12.4. This format is also known as dotted decimal notation or dotted quad notation. It is increasingly going under IPv4 because IPv6 offers much more flexible addressing, as well as other modern features. The notation is split into a network number, which is found in the leading octets, and a host number found in the rest of the notation. When you apply to the NIC for an IP address, you are not assigned an address for every host you plan on using. Instead, you are assigned a network number and allowed to assign all valid IPs within this range to your hosts.

The host part depends on the network size and to accommodate the various needs several network classes showing different places to split IP addresses have been defined. Here are the class networks:

- Class A – `consists of networks 1.0.0.0 through 127.0.0.0. with the network number included in the first octet section. This class has a 24-bit host part, allowing roughly 1.6 million hosts per network.`

- Class B – contains networks 128.0.0.0 through 191.255.0.0 with the network number in the first two octet sections. This class provides for 16,320 nets with 65,024 hosts respectively.

- Class C – its networks range from 192.0.0.0 through 223.255.255.0, with the network number contained in the first three octet sections. This class permits for nearly 2 million networks with up to 254 hosts.

- Classes D, E, and F – IP addresses in this classes range from 224.0.0.0 through 254.0.0.0 and are either experimental or are reserved for special use and don't stipulate any network. IP Multicast, a service that allows data to be transmitted to many points on a network at one time, has been assigned addresses from within this range.

You may have discerned that not all possible values in the previous list were allowed for each octet in the host section. This is because octets 0 and 255 are reserved for special purposes. An address where all host part bits are 0 refers to the network and an address where all the bits are 1 is known as a broadcast address. This refers to all hosts on a certain network concurrently. So, for instance, 148.79.255.255 is not a valid host address but instead refers to all the hosts on the 148.79.0.0 network.

There other network addresses that are reserved for particular purposes such as 0.0.0.0 and 127.0.0.0. The first one is called the default route and the latter a loopback address. The loopback address is reserved for IP traffic local to your host. The address 127.0.0.1 will be given to a special interface on your host, referred to as the loopback interface, which acts as a closed circuit. Any packet from TCO or UDP will be returned as if it has arrived from another network.

# Network Configuration

Most Linux distros come with various graphical tools that allow users to easily set up a computer in a local network, connect it to an ISP (Internet Service Provider) or set it up for wireless access. These tools can be launched from the menu or the command line. For instance, RedHat Linux has `redhat-config-network`, which has both a graphical and a text-mode interface. Check your distribution's documentation for more information about the tools available and their use.

The tools referred to above edit particular network configuration files using several commands. The exact names and location of these files are dependent on your distro; however, there are some common network configuration files common in all systems.

```
/etc/hosts
```

The `/etc/hosts` file contains the localhost IP address used for interprocess communication. Do not remove this line! The file can sometimes contain addresses of additional hosts which can be contacted without using a naming service such as the Domain Name Server (DNS). You can read more about host files in the man pages, i.e., man hosts.

Here is an example of a host file:

```
# Do not remove the following line, or various programs

# that require network functionality will fail.

127.0.0.1      localhost.localdomain    localhost

223.168.53.10 pin.mylan.com            pin
```

```
223.168.53.11 winxp.mylan.com          winxp
```

**/etc/resolve.conf**

This file sets up access to a DNS server and contains your domain name and the names of servers to contact. You can get more information on the man resolve.conf page

**/etc/nsswitch.conf**

This file defines the order in which different name services will be contacted. The DNS needs to appear in the host's line if you plan to connect to the Internet. You can get more information on its man page.

# The `ip` Command

This command is used to assign IP addresses to interfaces, set up routes to networks including the Internet, display TCP/IP configurations, etc. It is important to note that for two network interfaces, even on a system with only one network interface card, "lo" is the local loop, used for internal network communication; "eth0" is a common name for a real interface. Don't ever change the local loop configuration as it will lead to malfunctioning.

Wireless interfaces are normally defined as "wlan0" and modem interfaces as "ppp0", but there might be other names as well. For IP addresses, marked with "inet", the local loop always has 127.0.0.1 and the physical interface can have any other sequence. The address of your hardware interface, which might be needed as part of the authentication method to connect to a network, is labeled with "ether". The local loop contains 6 pairs of all zeros, the physical loop has 6 pairs of hexadecimal characters, of which the first 3 pairs are distribution vendor-specific.

# Using `netstat`

This command, an alternative to `ip`, is used to check the host network configuration. It has a lot of options and is useful in any Unix system. You can display the routing information by using the – nr option of the `netstat` command.

Other commands you can use include:

- `/bin/hostname` – shows the name of current host.

- `/bin/ping` – sends `ICMP ECHO_REQUEST` packets to network hosts.

- `/etc/ftpaccess` – FTP access configuration file

- `/etc/ftphosts` – FTP individual host access file

- `/etc/ftpusers` – lists users who have been automatically denied FTP access

- `/etc/gated` – gateway routing daemon.

- `/etc/hosts` – lists the hosts on network.

- `/etc/hosts.equiv` – lists trusted hosts.

- `/etc/http/conf/*` – shows HTTP configuration files

- `/etc/inetd.conf` – shows the inetd configuration file.

- `/etc/named.boot` – shows the server configuration file of a named server

- `/usr/bin/rlogin` – launches the remote login program.

- `/usr/bin/route` – lets the user manually manipulate routing tables.

- `/usr/bin/rwho` – shows who is logged in on local network.

- `/usr/sbin/in.rlogind` – remote login rlogin daemon

- `/usr/sbin/in.rshd` – remote shell rsh daemon

- `/usr/sbin/in.telnetq` – the telnet Daemon

- `/usr/sbin/in.tftpd` – the trivial FTP TFTP Daemon

- `/usr/sbin/in.fingerd` – the finger daemon

- `/usr/sbin/traceroute` – traces packet routes to remote computers.

# Networking Applications

Linux is a great platform for networking services and here are some of the many applications.

# Server Types

You can provide a service to users in two ways: by letting the service run in standalone mode or make it dependent on other services for activation.

Standalone mode is mostly for those network services that are used frequently and continuously. They are independent programs that start up at system boot time, and they await requests on particular connection points or ports they are configured to listen to. When a request comes through, it is processed and the program continues listening for the next request. A good example is a web server. It should be available all the time, and if there are too many requests, it could create more listening instances to serve users simultaneously.

Program-service activation mode is for services that don't have server processes running in the background. The Internet Daemon (inetd) listens in their place and calls them up when needed, because starting all the processes you would need in a session would lead to a waste of resources and time. These services include FTP, Samba, Telenet, the secure copy or finger service, and more. The super server, Internet Daemon, is initialized at system boot and is implemented in two ways, inetd and xinetd. The latter is called the Extended Internet Daemon service, and one of the two is always running in the system.

The services the inetd daemon is responsible for are listed in its configuration file `/etc/inetd.conf` and `/etc/xinetd.conf`. When a connection request is received, the central server starts an instance of the required server. Thus when a user starts an FTP session, for instance, an FTP daemon will be running for the duration of the session. This also applies to any open connection on remote servers; either a daemon answers directly or a remote (x)inetd launches the service when required and kills it when you quit.

Other applications include email programs, web servers and browsers, FTP services, terminal emulation (Telenet), groupware applications for chatting and conferencing, news services, and so forth.

# Chapter Summary

We looked at:

- The TCP/IP network protocol and application.

- IP addressing and how to configure your network.

- Applications of networking in Linux.

## Exercises

- Display the network information of your workstation that is the IP address, routes, name servers.

- How do you display your system's hosts file?

- What does your `/etc/hosts` contain?

- How can you see who connected to your system?

# CHAPTER 7

# Linux and Cloud Computing

Clouds can be defined as information technology environments that are abstract, pooled, and that share scalable resources across a network. They are created to enable cloud computing. Cloud computing can then be defined as the on-demand availability of these computing resources such as storage, servers, databases, analytics, networking, processing power, and more, over the Internet. Cloud computing offers flexible resources and fosters faster innovation and economies of scale. The term is used to describe data centers that are available to many users over the Internet. Here, cloud computing is an application-based software infrastructure that keeps data on remote servers that are accessed through the Internet.

## Why Is Cloud Computing Critical?

The applications of cloud computing are so vast that you could be using it and not even realize it. If you use any online services to send mail, work on documents, stream media, play games, or store files, it is all thanks to cloud computing. Even though the technology is still relatively new, you can see how vast the applications are. Cloud computing is a significant shift from the traditional way everyone thought about IT resources. Here are some of the reasons why.

1. **Cost**

Cloud computing has eliminated the capital expense of purchasing computer infrastructure and setting up and operating on-premise data centers. These include the endless server racks, expensive software purchases, round-the-clock electricity to power and cool these giant machines, and the IT experts required to monitor and manage the infrastructure. The math adds up quickly. With the cloud, you only pay for applications when you need them, and many are free.

The usage of these services can be adjusted to fit your needs. This pay-per-use model eliminates extra costs, such as in-house maintenance. With certain models you don't need to install software to your desktop, eliminating the need to purchase pricey software.

2. **Scalability, agility, and flexibility**

Cloud computing offers more diversity, flexibility, and agility compared to other computing methods. It allows you to obtain your files from any location at any time. This can have a lot of advantages for organizations since employees can access their files from anywhere. You can also scale your usage depending on your needs. For instance, if you have a small company with only five employees, you pay for the services those five employees use. If you were to add more, you would then have to purchase more computing power depending on your needs. This would have taken quite some time in the past, but with the cloud, it is as easy as clicking a button.

3. **Speed**

Many cloud computing services are provided self-service and on-demand. This means that vast amounts of computing resources can be provisioned in minutes, typically with just a few mouse clicks. This gives companies and organizations a lot of flexibility and takes pressure off capacity planning.

4. **Productivity**

On-site data centers need a lot of work, from setting up the hardware, to patching the software, to configuring the servers, among other IT management chores. Cloud computing eliminates the need for these tasks. For companies, this is great because it frees IT teams to spend more time on worthwhile projects.

5. Performance

The most important cloud computing services run on a worldwide network of secure data centers, which are regularly upgraded to the latest version of fast and efficient computing hardware. This provides several benefits over a private corporate data center, including reduced network latency for applications and more significant economies of scale.

6. Security

Many cloud providers offer a broad set of policies, technologies, and controls that strengthen your security posture overall, helping protect your data, apps, and infrastructure from potential threats. The cloud also offers backups of all your data. It provides you with a way to safeguard your data.

7. Reliability

Cloud computing makes data backup, disaster recovery, and business continuity more manageable and less expensive because data can be mirrored at multiple redundant sites on the cloud provider's network.

8. Good for the environment

Cloud computing's ability to virtualize and share resources among different programs results in better server utilization. Take, for example, three distinct platforms that existed for various applications and each run on its own server. If they were to be shifted to the cloud, server resources would be shared, virtualized for the operating systems and programs to utilize the servers better. This would result in fewer servers, which would require less space, which reduces the data center size and lowers the amount of power needed to cool the servers. This, in turn, reduces the carbon and greenhouse gas emissions, thus reducing the carbon footprint. This system is not devoid of flaws, but we will take a look at those later on.

# Cloud Computing Models

Cloud computing can be viewed in two ways: either as a service the cloud is offering or based on the deployment model used. Based on the deployment method used, clouds would thus be classified as public, private, hybrid, and community. Based on services offered, the classification would be as follows: Software as a Service (SaaS), Platform as a Service (PaaS), and Infrastructure as a Service (IaaS).

# Public Cloud

This means that the computing infrastructure is located, owned, governed, and run by governments, academic institutions, or business organizations, and the customer has no physical control over the computing infrastructure. This cloud environment is created from resources not owned by the end-user, and they can be redistributed to other users. This type of cloud is used for business-to-consumer type interactions and excels in performance. Due to their public nature, they are prone to attacks.

Examples of public cloud service providers include Amazon Web Services, Google, Microsoft, and so on. Some of these companies also offer direct connect services that require customers to buy or lease a private connection to a peering point they offer.

# Private Cloud

This cloud infrastructure is run solely for a singular person or organization. It could be managed internally or by a third party with internal or external hosting. They have the same benefits as public clouds, but they utilize private hardware. The hardware is not shared publicly, but the servers are located remotely. There are options for on-site servers, but these tend to be more expensive even though they give the user control over the physical infrastructure. This type of cloud has the highest security, although the cost reductions are minimal if the company uses on-site cloud infrastructure. Private clouds are solely dedicated to the user, and this method is used for many intra-business interactions

# Hybrid Cloud

As the name implies, this cloud merges private and public cloud infrastructure according to their purpose. For instance, a public cloud can interact with consumers while storing their data safely in a private cloud server. The public cloud is associated with scalability and flexibility in its ability to handle demand shifts. However, specific data-intensive or high-availability workloads can cause performance issues. Hybrid clouds can be used for business-to-business (B2B) and business-to-client (B2C) interactions

# Community Cloud

This refers to computing resources provided for a community or organization with shared data and data management. For instance, a community cloud can belong to a government of a single company. The computing infrastructure can be located both on- and off-premises

# Software as a Service

As the name implies, SaaS is the ability to access software as a service over the Internet. Application Service Providers (ASP) were a precursor to SaaS. ASPs offer subscriptions to software that is hosted or delivered via the web. The software and fees charged are based on its use. This way, the user doesn't purchase the software, but leases it as needed. You can also think of SaaS as the use of software over the web that executes remotely. The software can be in the form of services used by local programs such as web servers or remote applications accessed through a web browser. These cloud services are ideal for end-users.

Examples of remote application services include Google Apps, which provide various enterprise applications such as word processors through a standard web browser. Remote execution of applications relies on an application server to provide the services needed. A software framework that uses Application Programming Interfaces (API) for software services such as database access or transaction management is called an application server. Examples include IBM's WebSphere application server, Apache Geronimo, and more.

# Platform as a Service

This service, PaaS, can be described as the virtualization of an entire platform where one or more servers have been virtualized over physical servers, operating systems, and specific programs such as Apache, MySQL, for web-based use. These platforms can be predefined and selected in some cases. However, in others, the user can provide a virtual machine image containing all the required user-specific programs. In other terms, it allows users to run applications on cloud infrastructure. The infrastructure is completely controlled by the service provider, and the user doesn't need to worry about its management or the infrastructure it is running on. The user may not know whether the underlying platform is operating on Linux, Windows, a mixture of systems, or something else entirely. All they are required to know is the interface and how to run jobs on the virtualized platform. These cloud services are ideal for software and application developers.

A good example is Google's App Engine. This service lets users deploy web applications on Google's very stable architecture. It provides users with a sandbox for their Python applications that can be referenced over the web. It provides Python APIs for data storage and maintenance using Google Query Language, in addition to supporting user authentication, image manipulation, and email sending. The sandbox restricts access to the underlying operating system. Even with limited functionality available to the user's application, the App Engine supports the building of useful Web services.

# Infrastructure as a Service

IaaS is cloud computing that delivers on-demand, scalable services over the web to organizations or users who deploy workloads that can expand or shrink depending on their needs. It is the distribution of computer infrastructure as a service. This lets users run operating systems or other infrastructure over computing services. The users don't managed or have control of the underlying hardware or platforms the infrastructure is running over. They only define what service level they require and run their infrastructure over it. These cloud services are ideal for system administrators.

IaaS differs from PaaS because the virtual hardware comes without a software stack. The user then provides a virtual machine image invoked on one or several virtualized servers. This makes it the rawest form of computing as a service other than physically accessing the infrastructure. A prime example would be Amazon's Elastic Compute Cloud (EC2). In this IaaS, the user can specify a certain VM and deploy their applications or provide their VM image to be executed on other servers. The user is then simply charged for computing time, storage, and network bandwidth used.

Another example is the Elastic Utility Computing Architecture for Linking Your Programs To Useful Systems, or "Eucalyptus project" for short. It is an open-source implementation of Amazon's EC2 that's interface-compatible with the commercial service. Just like EC2, it relies on Linux using Xen to virtualize the operating system, and it was developed for cloud computing research.

Other forms of cloud computing services include security-as-a-service, data-as-a-service, test environment-as-a-service, data-storage-as-a-service, desktop-as-a-service, and API-as-a-service.

# Anatomy of Cloud Computing

The cloud is a collection of services grouped in different layers, which include application, platform, infrastructure, virtualization, server, and storage. It is comprised of two major components, the front and the back end. The front end consists of the client or user part of the cloud computing system. It includes interfaces, applications, and everything needed to access the cloud computing platform. The back end, on the other hand, contains the cloud itself. It is comprised of the resources needed for cloud computing services such as virtual machines, servers, storage, and security mechanisms like traffic control and protocols. This end is under the control of the cloud computing services provider. It spreads the file system over multiple hard disks and machines. This means that the data is never stored in a singular place, and in the case a unit fails, another takes over automatically. In the distributed file system, the algorithm for resource distribution and user disk space are assigned. Since cloud computing is a distributed environment, it depends heavily upon a robust algorithm.

# Virtualization and Cloud Computing

Cloud's computing ace in the hole is virtualization; it is its main enabling technology. Virtualization can be defined as the partitioning of a single physical server into many logical servers. Once the partitioning is complete, each logical server behaves like a physical server and can perform the same duties as a real physical server. Some of these duties include running an operating system and other programs independently. A lot of companies provide virtualization services, where they let you use their servers instead of partitioning your PC for storage and computing. This is ideal because they are fast, consume less time, and are cost-effective.

For software developers and testers, virtualization allows them to write and run code in multiple environments. It also comes quite in handy when testing code too.

In cloud computing, virtualization is mainly used for three reasons; network, storage, and server virtualization.

- Network Virtualization is a way of putting together the available resources in a network by splitting up the available bandwidth into channels, each of which is independent of the others and can be assigned to a specific server or device in real-time.

- Storage Virtualization is the collection of physical storage from many network storage devices into what looks like a single storage device that is run from a central console. Storage virtualization is usually used in storage area networks (SAN).

- Server Virtualization masks server resources such as processors, RAM, operating system, etc., from server users. It intends to increase the resource sharing capacity and reduce the burden and complexity of computation from users.

Virtualization is the key to unlocking the cloud system, and it is vital because it separates the hardware from the software. For example, computers can use virtual memory to borrow extra memory from the hard disk. Normally the hard drive has a lot more space than memory. Virtual disks are slower than real memory, but if managed properly, the substitution works perfectly.

## Cloud Security

Even though cloud computing offers great opportunities, it is not devoid of challenges. There are plenty of areas at risk of being compromised and which require fortification. Below are some risk considerations that represent a potential area of attack or a source of failure. Let's examine some of the security threats and vulnerabilities the cloud comes under.

1. Organizational Security Risks

   Organizational risks are defined as the risks that can impact the structure of the organization. If a cloud service provider goes out of business or gets acquired by another company, it can have adverse effects on their cloud services.

2. Physical Security Risks

   The cloud data center's physical location must be secured by the service provider to prevent unauthorized on-site access to cloud service customer data. Firewalls and encryption cannot protect against the physical theft of data. It is upon the service provider to secure the data centers. They should take the appropriate measures such as controlling authorized personnel, the security of the physical location, and network firewalls. The service provider is not only responsible for storing and processing data but also sticking to privacy regulations.

3. Technological Security Risks

   These are the failures caused by the hardware, technologies, and services provided by the cloud service providers. These include resource sharing isolation issues and risks linked to changing service providers - i.e., portability. Regular maintenance and audit of infrastructure by the service providers is recommended.

4. Compliance and Audit Risks

   These are related to the law, and they include lack of information jurisdiction, jurisdiction changes, illegal contract clauses, and ongoing legal cases. For instance, in some areas, cloud service providers are required by law to hand over sensitive information if the court or government demands it.

5. Data Security Risks

   There are many data security risks involved in cloud computing, but data integrity, confidentiality, and availability are the main ones. This is the area most at risk of getting compromised, and a majority of the security efforts are focused here.

At the core of all computing is the processing of raw data into meaningful information. When the processing of this data is outsourced to computing infrastructure owned and maintained by third parties, it can lead to several issues concerning the security of the data. With data security, these four properties have to be kept in check.

- Privacy – ensures that the personal information and identity of the cloud user is not revealed to unauthorized persons, especially when dealing with sensitive data. This is the most prominent problem when it comes to cloud security.

- Confidentiality – closely related to privacy. It is the service provider's guarantee that the cloud user's data will remain anonymous and safe. This can be especially hard in systems where many users have access to the same system.

- Integrity – refers to the confidence that the cloud user has that their data will not be corrupted or altered in any way by unauthorized persons as it is being retrieved.

- Availability – ensures that the cloud customer has access to their data and is not denied service due to a malicious attack on the cloud. An example of this would be a denial of service (DoS) attack.

There are three stages at which the data in the cloud can be in at any given time. The first is data-in-transit, where it is in the process of being transferred. This could mean the user is uploading data to the cloud or downloading it to their computing device. This is where data is most at risk of interception. Encryption is usually used to prevent any data loss or corruption attempts. The next stage is data-at-rest. This refers to when the data is in cloud storage. The biggest risk here would be for the user to lose control over their data. This can mean anything from data corruption to the theft of files. It is up to the service provider to ensure that they keep the user's data safe and that all four properties are kept intact. The last stage is data-in-use. This refers to when the raw data is being processed into useful information. Some of the risks here would be with data corruption during processing. Some of the ways service providers can secure their cloud computing systems are as follows.

- Service providers can employ the use of data encryption and authentication methods such as two-step authentication before granting users access to the data.

- They can ensure that cloud data centers are secured from damage and intruders. Having strong deterrents such as armed guards, or restricting access and using keycards or biometric scans, can help keep the servers and in turn the data safe.

- To prevent having malicious insiders who want to use client data unlawfully, cloud service providers should conduct an extensive background check on their employees before hiring them and also have robust measures for dealing with breaches or data leaks.

- Cloud service providers need to understand the legal and regulatory responsibilities and regulations they have and ensure that their terms of service reflect this.

## Chapter Summary

We have looked at quite a lot of things in this chapter, including:

- Defining what cloud computing is, its structure, and various models

- How Linux has laid the infrastructure that made cloud computing possible

- How cloud computing is deployed as a public, private, community, or hybrid cloud

- How virtualization is the lifeblood of cloud computing and the three kinds of virtualization used in cloud computing, namely network, storage, and server virtualization

- The various security risks clouds are under, such as malicious individuals, bot attacks from malicious code that result in DoS attacks, data corruption, theft, and destruction

- Some of the ways to mitigate these risks and increase security

## Exercises

1. Build a cloud Linux instance

2. Create an Amazon AWS login for yourself.

3. Go through the process of creating and connecting to an EC2 Linux instance

4. Create a key pair and download the .pem file for it

5. Now create an EC2 instance and launch it

6. Use the key file to connect to your instance

7. Try out some of the previous exercises such as running some commands to see if they work in this environment

# FINAL WORDS

We have taken a long hard look at Linux in this book, and by now you know a little bit or a whole lot more about this wonderful and versatile operating system. It is the basis of significant software development in almost all industries ranging from technical areas to education. The vast applications of open-source software have given rise to countless new technologies. These include Android OS, which was developed by Google on the Linux kernel, not to mention all the distros like Ubuntu, RedHat, and Debian, to name a few. Every day more and more individuals like you are learning the benefits of using open-source software, the virus-free operating systems, and the ability to be flexible in every customization possible to suit every user's needs.

While we did not discuss the Internet of Things in this book, this is another area in which Linux is helping steer things into the future. The Internet of Things, or IoT, in summary, is the interconnection of computing devices found via the Internet that enables them to send and receive data from one another. An example is smart devices such as thermostats or air conditioning units. You can now control these and more devices using your phone. You might be wondering how all this ties into Linux. It's because the structures through which the thermostat can communicate with your phone is based on Linux and its various applications such as cloud computing.

There are several more emerging technologies that are mushrooming from open-source software such as Blockchain, which has been making big headlines with Bitcoin and other cryptocurrencies. You can see how open-source software, particularly Linux, is driving innovation. The benefits of learning Linux span further than just being able to keep up with emerging technologies. You will learn how hardware systems such as servers work since they mostly use Linux. You can even get a job or at least boost your employment chances by being Linux proficient. Its applications help companies reduce operating costs, become more reliable and resilient from attacks, and facilitate the integration of different equipment because Linux works across platforms.

The list is endless, and the vast collection of Linux distributions goes to show how limitless this system really is. There is a distro to fit any taste, and if you can't find one, build it and share it with the world. There is so much more documentation on everything you might want to know about Linux and the various distros. These include reading the man pages and the various HOWTOs available online.

This book is meant for anyone interested in Linux, whether you have no clue about it or you just want to polish up on some skills. The examples and exercises are meant to help you internalize the concepts taught in every chapter. And while it might take some time before you are called a Linux guru, reading this book is a step in the right direction.

# LINUX FOR HACKERS

*Unlocking Advanced Techniques*

*in Hacking with Kali Linux*

## Mark Reed & CyberEdge Press

# INTRODUCTION

## Why Linux for Hackers?

In today's rapidly evolving digital world, protecting systems and data from cyber threats is more critical than ever. As cybercrime is projected to cost the world $10.5 trillion annually by 2025 (Morgan, 2022), it's no longer an option to ignore cybersecurity—it's a necessity. One of the most effective ways to safeguard against these threats is through ethical hacking, which helps uncover and fix vulnerabilities before malicious actors can exploit them.

But, why should you, as a hacker, turn to Linux?

## Why Choose Linux for Hacking?

One of the core reasons ethical hackers and security professionals rely on Linux is that it is open-source. This means the code is available for anyone to view, modify, and share. For ethical hacking, this transparency is invaluable—it allows us to understand how systems work at their core and spot vulnerabilities with ease.

Here are a few other compelling reasons why Linux is the go-to platform for hacking:

- **Rich Availability of Security Tools**: Linux distributions, especially those designed for hacking (like Kali Linux), come preloaded with a wide array of security and penetration testing tools. This makes it easy for hackers to start right away, without the need for extensive setup.

- **Unparalleled Customizability**: Linux is known for its flexibility. Distributions can be customized to suit specific needs, allowing hackers to create lightweight, tailored environments that focus solely on their security tasks.

- **Stronger Security by Design**: Unlike other operating systems, Linux features more robust security frameworks, including advanced user permission structures and built-in security utilities that allow for better protection against threats.

- **Vibrant Community Support**: The Linux community is vast, active, and passionate. For ethical hackers, this community provides a wealth of resources, documentation, forums, and learning tools that can help you troubleshoot, learn new techniques, and stay up-to-date with the latest developments in cybersecurity.

## What Is Ethical Hacking?

Ethical hacking—sometimes referred to as "white-hat hacking"—is the practice of testing systems and networks for vulnerabilities in a lawful and legitimate manner. By understanding the methods that malicious hackers use, ethical hackers can defend against attacks and protect systems from being compromised.

Here's why ethical hacking is a crucial skill:

- **Thinking Like an Attacker**: To defend a system effectively, you need to think like an attacker. Ethical hacking lets you anticipate the strategies cybercriminals use and develop stronger defenses accordingly.

- **Quick Response to Security Breaches**: When you know how to identify and exploit vulnerabilities, you can respond to breaches faster. This knowledge helps secure critical systems, especially during emergencies when rapid action is needed to prevent further damage.

- **Protection Against Social Engineering**: Many cyberattacks aren't technical in nature—they exploit human weaknesses. By learning ethical hacking, you'll also become aware of social engineering tactics and how to defend against manipulation in high-pressure situations.

## What Makes This Book Different?

This book stands out because it is designed to be **self-contained**. Whether you're a seasoned Linux user or new to the system, each chapter is structured to stand on its own. While I encourage readers to explore my previous books for foundational knowledge, this book will guide you through more advanced topics, focusing heavily on Kali Linux and the world of ethical hacking.

Each chapter is designed to provide **in-depth** knowledge. The goal is not just to skim the surface, but to dig deep into the most critical ideas, concepts, and techniques. By the end of each chapter, you will have actionable insights that you can immediately apply in real-world scenarios.

## How to Make the Most of This Book

As you navigate through this book, the best way to learn is by **taking action**. As you encounter new ideas and techniques, break them down into actionable steps. Writing these down and creating a clear roadmap can help you turn theory into practice. The more you engage with the material through hands-on application, the quicker you'll internalize what you learn.

- **Persistence Is Key**: Not every hack or system analysis will go as planned, but that's part of the learning process. When you encounter challenges, don't be discouraged. Take the time to analyze what went wrong, adapt your approach, and keep pushing forward. Every failure is a stepping stone toward mastery.

- **Stay Practical**: While this book provides a wealth of theory and guidance, the real learning happens when you apply that knowledge. Don't fall into the trap of thinking that reading alone will make you a better hacker. Practicing what you learn, experimenting with real systems, and working through hands-on labs are crucial to truly understanding the material.

## The Journey Starts Now

If you're ready to elevate your hacking skills and dive deep into the world of Linux and cybersecurity, let's get started! This journey will not only teach you the technical skills you need but also cultivate a mindset of persistence, adaptability, and real-world application.

Turn the page and let's begin your exploration into the world of Linux for Hackers.

# CHAPTER 1

# Introduction to Kali Linux for Ethical Hacking

Before diving into the advanced concepts of ethical hacking, it's crucial to build a solid understanding of Kali Linux, the distribution at the heart of this course. Kali Linux isn't just another Linux distribution; it's a specialized platform designed to empower ethical hackers and security professionals. This chapter will cover the origins of Kali Linux, the role of the Linux kernel, process management, system architecture, and a glimpse into advanced bash scripting.

By the end of this chapter, you'll have a deeper appreciation of the core elements that make Kali Linux a powerful tool in the cybersecurity landscape. As cyber threats become increasingly sophisticated, the need for advanced defensive techniques grows stronger. Understanding these fundamentals will prepare you to meet those challenges head-on and take your skills to the next level.

## The Evolution of Kali Linux

Kali Linux is built specifically for ethical hacking and penetration testing, and its origins lie in a groundbreaking project known as **BackTrack**. Launched in 2006 by security experts Mati Aharoni and Max Moser, BackTrack combined an extensive suite of security tools into one convenient package. It quickly became the go-to platform for security professionals.

In 2013, BackTrack was reborn as Kali Linux, bringing with it even more robust features, regular updates, and improved hardware compatibility. The developers of Kali Linux designed it to cater to both beginners and advanced users in the cybersecurity field, ensuring the OS is always equipped with the latest tools and security features. Today, it is widely regarded as the most comprehensive Linux distribution for penetration testing and ethical hacking.

# Understanding the Linux Kernel

At the heart of every Linux distribution, including Kali, is the **Linux kernel**—the core that manages the interaction between hardware and software. Created by Linus Torvalds in 1991, the kernel started as a simple, monolithic system but has evolved dramatically over the decades. By 2020, with the release of **Linux 5.0**, the kernel brought in a host of performance improvements and enhanced support for modern hardware.

The kernel serves as the backbone of the operating system. It acts as a middleman between your system's hardware and the applications running on it, handling critical tasks like memory management, CPU scheduling, and input/output operations. Without the kernel, applications wouldn't be able to function—they rely on the kernel to access system resources safely and efficiently.

Here's a closer look at how the kernel works in practice:

- **Memory Management**: When you launch a program, the kernel allocates the necessary memory for it to run smoothly. It ensures that every application gets the memory it needs without overlapping with other running processes, maintaining system stability.

- **CPU Scheduling**: The kernel also manages which processes get access to the CPU and when. This is crucial for multitasking, allowing your computer to handle several applications simultaneously without lag or crashes. Think of it like an air traffic controller, guiding processes to the CPU and ensuring everything runs in an orderly fashion.

For example, if you're running a security tool like Wireshark alongside a web browser, the kernel ensures both applications receive enough processing power without one hogging all the resources. This multitasking capability is one of the reasons why Linux, and by extension Kali, is so well-suited for penetration testing.

### *Hands-On: Exploring the Kernel*

Now that you understand the role of the kernel, let's explore it directly in your Kali Linux environment.

1. Viewing Kernel Information:

Open a terminal and run the following command to view the current version of your Linux kernel:

```
uname -r
```

This command will display the kernel version running on your system. As an ethical hacker, it's important to know your kernel version since some vulnerabilities and exploits are tied to specific kernel versions.

2. Checking Kernel Modules:

You can list all the modules currently loaded by your kernel using:

```
lsmod
```

This command will show the kernel modules, which are pieces of code that can be loaded and unloaded into the kernel as needed. These are often used to support hardware or enhance system functionality.

## Process Management

Process management is a crucial component of the Linux kernel, responsible for the creation, management, and termination of processes. In simple terms, a process is a program in execution. Every time you open an application, whether it's your web browser or a text editor, the operating system (OS) creates a process for it. The OS ensures that each process runs correctly and efficiently.

When a process is created, it enters one of several possible states, such as **ready**, **running**, or **waiting**. A process begins in the **ready** state, meaning it's prepared to execute but is waiting for the CPU to become available. Once the CPU starts processing it, the process moves to the **running** state. If the process needs input from the user or another resource (like reading from a file), it transitions to the **waiting** state. Throughout its lifecycle, the kernel continuously monitors and manages the states of all processes to ensure they function properly.

The kernel uses **scheduling algorithms** to determine which process gets CPU time next. This is essential for multitasking, as it ensures that multiple processes can run concurrently without overwhelming the system. Two common scheduling algorithms are:

- **First-Come-First-Serve (FCFS)**: Processes are executed in the order they arrive.

- **Round Robin**: Each process gets a small time slice to run before moving on to the next, ensuring fair use of CPU time for all processes.

Efficient process management is vital to ensure that no single application consumes too many resources, which could slow down or crash the system.

### Key Concepts in Process Management

- **Process States**: A process can be in various states, including:

  - **Running**: Actively being executed on the CPU.

  - **Ready**: Waiting for CPU availability.

  - **Blocked**: Waiting for an event (such as user input or an I/O operation) to complete.

- **Process Scheduling**: The kernel uses scheduling algorithms to decide which process gets CPU time next. The **Completely Fair Scheduler (CFS)**, used in modern Linux systems, ensures that each process gets a fair share of CPU time.

- **Process Control Block (PCB)**: Every process has a data structure known as the PCB, which stores important information like the process state, priority, and resource usage.

- **Forking and Executing**: A new process is created by calling the `fork()` system call. This duplicates the current process, and the `exec()` function is used to replace the current process's memory space with a new program.

- **Inter-Process Communication (IPC)**: Processes need to communicate with each other for various reasons. Linux provides mechanisms like **pipes**, **message queues**, and **shared memory** for processes to exchange information.

- **Process Termination**: When a process finishes execution, it calls the `exit()` system call, and the kernel cleans up any resources the process was using.

### *Hands-On: Process Management in Action*

Let's get some hands-on experience with process management to solidify your understanding. Kali Linux provides several tools to interact with and manage processes in real time.

### 1. Viewing Processes:

Open your terminal and use the `top` command to view a live list of running processes:

```
top
```

This command shows a real-time, dynamic view of system processes, including CPU and memory usage, process IDs, and other important information.

### 2. Viewing Detailed Process Information:

Use the ps command to view detailed information about all the running processes:

```
ps -aux
```

This command lists every running process, along with detailed statistics like the user running the process, the percentage of CPU and memory it's using, and its process ID (PID).

### 3. Killing a Process:

Sometimes, processes need to be terminated (either because they've hung or because they're consuming too many resources). You can stop a process by using the `kill` command along with its PID:

```
kill <PID>

Use ps -aux or top to find the PID of the process you want to kill.
```

### 4. Changing Process Priority:

You can also adjust the priority of a running process using the `nice` command. A lower "nice" value means the process will get more CPU time, while a higher value makes the process run with lower priority:

```
nice -n 10 <command>
```

For running processes, use the `renice` command to change the priority:

```
renice <priority> <PID>
```

## System Calls

System calls are the critical interface between a program and the kernel of the operating system. They play a key role in enabling programs to perform tasks that require hardware access, such as reading from or writing to the hard drive, allocating memory, or creating processes. Since applications cannot directly interact with the hardware for security reasons, they rely on the kernel to handle such operations through system calls.

Let's break down how system calls work with an example.

### *Understanding System Calls*

Consider a simple case: you're using document editing software, such as Microsoft Word. When you edit a document and save it to your hard drive, Microsoft Word doesn't have the direct privileges to access the hardware. Instead, it makes a **system call** to the kernel, asking it to write the data to the hard drive. The kernel, which manages interactions with the hardware, handles this request, ensuring the data is written securely and efficiently.

This process allows developers to create applications without having to manage hardware details. The system call interface provides a layer of abstraction between the application and the hardware, ensuring that only the kernel has direct access to sensitive system components.

## Controlled Interface for Security

The main function of system calls is to provide a controlled and secure interaction between applications and the system's hardware. If applications had free access to the hardware, it could lead to instability or security vulnerabilities, such as malicious software modifying sensitive files or hardware behavior.

System calls serve as a gateway, where the kernel checks and controls every request. For example, when a program makes a system call, it must provide specific parameters, like the file's location and the data to be written. The kernel then validates the request, ensuring it meets security and system integrity standards before proceeding.

### *Benefits of System Calls*

System calls provide multiple advantages:

o **Abstraction**: Developers don't need to worry about hardware specifics. They can focus on application functionality, relying on the kernel to manage complex hardware interactions.

o **Security**: By mediating access to hardware, the kernel prevents unauthorized or malicious software from directly interacting with the system, thus maintaining overall system integrity.

## Types of System Calls

Different types of system calls serve various purposes. Here are some of the most common categories:

- **File Manipulation**: These system calls handle file operations such as creating, opening, reading, writing, and closing files. For example, `open()`, `read()`, and `write()`.

- **Memory Management**: These system calls are used to allocate and free memory. For instance, `malloc()` dynamically allocates memory for programs, while `free()` releases it when no longer needed.

- **Process Control**: These calls manage processes. Functions like `fork()` and `exec()` help create new processes and replace a process's memory space with a new program, respectively.

- **Inter-process Communication (IPC)**: These system calls enable communication between different processes, such as message passing and shared memory.

## How System Calls Work: The Execution Process

When an application makes a system call, the following sequence of events typically occurs:

1. **User Mode to Kernel Mode Switch**: The application switches from **user mode** to **kernel mode**, allowing it to execute privileged instructions.

2. **Validation by the Kernel**: The kernel validates the system call. For example, if an application is requesting to open a file, the kernel checks the file permissions to ensure that the application has the necessary rights to access it.

3. **Execution of the System Call**: If everything checks out, the kernel executes the requested operation, interacting with the hardware as needed. The data is read or written, memory is allocated, or a process is created.

4. **Return to User Mode**: After completing the system call, the process switches back to user mode, and the result of the operation is returned to the application.

# Key Features of Kali Linux Tailored for Penetration Testing

Kali Linux is uniquely designed for ethical hackers and penetration testers, offering an array of specialized tools and features specifically tailored for security assessments. Its robust framework allows security professionals to conduct various types of penetration testing, vulnerability assessments, and digital forensics. Let's explore what sets Kali Linux apart.

## 1. Comprehensive Tool Set

Kali Linux is preloaded with an extensive suite of tools for penetration testing and security auditing. From network analysis to web application testing, Kali's arsenal covers all aspects of cybersecurity assessments. These tools empower security professionals to perform deep assessments, exploit vulnerabilities, and reinforce system defenses.

Here are some key tools that make Kali Linux indispensable:

### SecOps Solution

An essential tool in Kali Linux, the SecOps Solution streamlines and automates security operations. It assists penetration testers and security analysts by automating workflows, improving incident response, and simplifying the orchestration of multiple security tools. This ensures quicker identification and mitigation of vulnerabilities.

### Wireshark

Wireshark is one of the most powerful network protocol analyzers available. It captures and inspects data packets as they traverse the network, making it an essential tool for detecting anomalies, troubleshooting network issues, and performing network intrusion detection. With its deep packet inspection capabilities, Wireshark enables testers to scrutinize network communications in detail.

### Metasploit

A leading exploitation framework, Metasploit is vital for ethical hacking. It allows penetration testers to simulate real-world attacks on network and application security. Metasploit includes a vast collection of exploit modules, payloads, and auxiliary scripts, providing flexibility in testing and reinforcing defenses against a variety of threats. This makes it an invaluable resource for identifying and exploiting vulnerabilities in controlled environments.

### Burp Suite

Burp Suite is a comprehensive web application security testing platform. It provides features such as intercepting traffic, scanning for vulnerabilities, and performing detailed security assessments of web applications. With both automated and manual testing capabilities, Burp Suite helps testers identify and exploit weaknesses in web applications, making it an essential tool for web security professionals.

### Forensic Tools

Kali Linux also includes a wide range of digital forensic tools that are critical for investigating and analyzing security incidents. These tools help security professionals conduct thorough investigations into breaches, data leaks, or suspicious activities. Forensics tools assist in gathering evidence, preserving data integrity, and understanding the scope of security incidents.

## 2. Customizability

One of Kali Linux's standout features is its high level of customizability. Users can tailor the operating system and its tools to fit their specific testing needs, improving both efficiency and effectiveness.

### Creating Custom Distributions

Kali Linux allows users to create personalized distributions by pre-installing frequently used tools and configurations. For example, if a security professional relies on specific tools or workflows, they can build a custom Kali version that includes those configurations out of the box. This streamlines the workflow and ensures that the system is optimized for the user's specific tasks.

### Integrating Additional Tools

Kali Linux facilitates seamless integration of additional tools, whether they are open-source or proprietary. This means users can install third-party penetration testing tools, scripts, or libraries based on their unique requirements. This flexibility ensures that Kali Linux remains adaptable and comprehensive, no matter how testing environments evolve.

### Modular Environment

Kali Linux is modular, which allows users to adjust core components like the kernel, services, and installed packages. This modularity is especially beneficial when testing specific aspects of a system, such as web application security or network penetration testing. Testers can fine-tune the OS to ensure peak performance and security, focusing only on what's relevant to the task at hand.

### Personalization and Configuration

Kali Linux also offers deep personalization options, from desktop environments to tool configurations. Security professionals can optimize their workspace by configuring tools, keyboard shortcuts, and terminal settings to suit their personal preferences, making the testing process more efficient and user-friendly.

## 3. Live Boot Capability

Kali Linux's live boot feature is particularly useful for penetration testers who need flexibility and portability. This feature allows Kali to run directly from a USB stick or CD/DVD without installing it on the host system, making it portable and disposable for security assessments.

### Portability

With Kali Linux, testers can carry a fully functional security assessment toolkit on a USB drive, allowing them to assess multiple systems without modifying the host OS. This portability is particularly useful in environments where installing software on the host machine is not permitted or practical.

### Disposability

Kali's live session ensures that once a test is complete, no trace of the session remains on the host machine. After rebooting the system, any changes made during the session—such as files created or tools installed—are discarded, protecting sensitive data and maintaining the integrity of the host OS.

### Ease of Use

The live boot feature simplifies the process of getting started with penetration testing. Users don't need to go through complex installation procedures; they can simply boot into Kali and start running their assessments. This low barrier to entry makes it ideal for both beginners and professionals who need a quick, fully-functional testing environment.

### *Testing Security Measures*

Using the live environment allows testers to bypass certain security measures on the host OS. This makes it especially useful when testing the resilience of target systems against unauthorized access or intrusions, all without affecting the underlying operating system.

### *Isolation*

Running Kali in a live session ensures isolation from the host system. This means that the tools and assessments you conduct will not interfere with or modify any of the running applications or configurations on the host. It ensures that testing is carried out in a controlled and contained environment.

## Support for Multiple Platforms

One of the key strengths of Kali Linux is its compatibility across various hardware architectures and platforms. Whether you're running it on high-performance servers, ARM-based devices, virtual machines, or even in the cloud, Kali Linux adapts to a wide range of environments. This flexibility allows penetration testers and security professionals to integrate Kali into their workflows, no matter the specific demands of their working environment.

Let's dive deeper into why this broad platform support makes Kali Linux such a powerful tool for security professionals:

### *Versatile Hardware Compatibility*

Kali Linux supports an impressive array of hardware architectures, allowing it to run on a wide range of devices, from resource-heavy servers to lightweight laptops. Whether you're conducting intensive security assessments on a high-performance machine or performing quick vulnerability checks on a portable device, Kali Linux can seamlessly adapt to your hardware.

This compatibility ensures that penetration testers can deploy Kali Linux on whatever system best fits their operational needs, maximizing the efficiency and scope of their security assessments. This versatility is particularly useful in situations where testers need to perform assessments on-site using whatever hardware is available.

### *ARM Device Support*

ARM architecture support in Kali Linux is particularly noteworthy due to the growing use of ARM-based devices in mobile computing, embedded systems, and the Internet of Things (IoT). ARM devices are valued for their energy efficiency, compact size, and cost-effectiveness.

Kali Linux's compatibility with ARM-based platforms makes it a preferred choice for conducting security assessments on mobile or embedded devices, which are increasingly becoming targets of cyberattacks. The ability to run Kali on ARM-based devices allows testers to broaden the scope of their penetration testing, ensuring they can secure everything from smartphones to smart devices in IoT environments.

### *Cloud Environment Integration*

Kali Linux is also highly adaptable to modern cloud computing environments, supporting platforms such as AWS, Microsoft Azure, and Google Cloud. Running Kali Linux in the cloud provides immense flexibility and scalability, enabling penetration testers to leverage powerful cloud resources for tasks that require significant computing power, such as large-scale security assessments or extensive vulnerability scanning.

Deploying Kali Linux in a cloud environment allows testers to simulate large-scale attacks on cloud-based infrastructure, test cloud application security, and assess vulnerabilities in virtual environments. Cloud integration enhances the agility and efficiency of penetration testing, allowing users to scale their resources as needed without being constrained by physical hardware limitations.

## Ethical Hacking Ecosystem

Kali Linux is a central tool in the ethical hacking ecosystem, providing a platform that supports both beginner and experienced hackers. Ethical hacking—finding and fixing weaknesses in systems and networks with the owner's permission—requires access to powerful tools and a flexible environment. Kali Linux delivers both.

### Tools for Beginners

Kali Linux offers a wide range of built-in tools that cater to beginners who are just getting started in the field of cybersecurity. Each tool is designed to address specific security challenges, giving novices a hands-on learning experience while providing practical exposure to real-world scenarios.

Some tools help beginners practice fundamental tasks like network scanning, vulnerability identification, and packet sniffing, while others introduce them to more advanced concepts in penetration testing. Beginners can use Kali's resources, including online tutorials, forums, and guided exercises, to sharpen their skills and advance their understanding of ethical hacking. Setting small, achievable goals, such as running a basic network scan or capturing network traffic, can help new users stay motivated and progress through their learning journey.

### Learning Path for Experienced Hackers

For seasoned security professionals, Kali Linux provides an environment rich with advanced tools that push the limits of their skills. Experts can leverage Kali Linux to tackle complex security challenges, perform deep penetration tests, and analyze vulnerabilities across various systems. Its comprehensive suite of tools—ranging from wireless network analysis to web application security testing—gives skilled hackers the resources they need to conduct sophisticated security assessments.

Advanced users often customize Kali Linux to suit their specific needs, adding additional tools, adjusting configurations, and automating repetitive tasks. This flexibility allows them to fine-tune Kali for their workflow, ensuring maximum efficiency during security assessments.

# CHAPTER 2

# Intermediate Networking Concepts for Penetration Testers

## The Importance of Network Security

To understand the importance of network security, let's revisit one of the most infamous data breaches of the last decade: the **Ashley Madison breach** in 2015.

Ashley Madison, a dating website catering to individuals seeking extramarital affairs, faced a devastating data breach when hackers, calling themselves "The Impact Team," infiltrated their network. The breach exposed millions of users' sensitive information, including names, email addresses, and payment details. What made this breach particularly catastrophic was not only the nature of the stolen data but also Ashley Madison's failure to implement even basic network security measures like proper encryption and secure coding practices.

The attackers exploited vulnerabilities in the company's web application and its network infrastructure. These vulnerabilities stemmed from poor **network defense strategies**, a lack of **secure coding practices**, and an overall **inadequate understanding of fundamental networking principles**. As a result, the attackers were able to navigate the network, collect sensitive data, and leverage that information to demand ransom, ultimately releasing the data to the public when their demands were not met.

This breach serves as a stark reminder of the potential consequences of **weak network security practices**. In this chapter, we'll explore **intermediate networking principles** that every penetration tester must understand to identify vulnerabilities in network infrastructures effectively. By mastering these principles, you'll be able to plan and execute penetration tests that target network weaknesses, enhancing your ability to defend against the kind of security failures that led to the Ashley Madison breach.

# Subnetting and Network Segmentation: Core Concepts for Penetration Testers

When performing penetration tests, understanding how a target network is structured and divided is crucial. Networks are often segmented and subnetted to limit the impact of potential security breaches and to improve performance. For penetration testers, these concepts are essential to uncovering **attack surfaces** and conducting efficient security assessments.

## Subnetting: Dividing Networks for Efficiency and Security

**Subnetting** is the process of breaking a larger network into smaller, more manageable subnetworks, or **subnets**. Each subnet operates independently within the broader network and is assigned its own range of IP addresses, controlled by a subnet mask. This approach helps improve network organization, performance, and security by controlling traffic within the network and limiting the exposure of systems.

### *Why Subnetting Matters in Penetration Testing*

For penetration testers, subnetting is more than just a way to manage IP addresses; it is a technique that plays a significant role in determining the network's **attack surface**. By understanding how a network is divided into subnets, you can focus on specific sections of the network during your assessment, allowing you to identify vulnerabilities in isolation rather than tackling the entire network at once.

For instance, in a flat network (without subnetting), a single compromise could allow attackers to move laterally across the network, gaining access to multiple systems. With proper subnetting, however, lateral movement can be restricted, limiting the damage caused by a potential breach.

Understanding how subnets are structured will help you identify critical points of entry and target specific vulnerabilities more effectively.

### *Hands-On Example: Analyzing Subnets*

To see subnetting in action, let's explore how subnets are structured in a real-world scenario.

1. **Check the Subnet Mask**: Use the `ifconfig` or `ip addr` command in a Linux environment to display the IP address and subnet mask of a given network interface.

```
ifconfig
```

2. **Calculate Subnets**: With a default Class C subnet mask (`255.255.255.0`), the network can accommodate up to 254 hosts. However, if you modify the subnet mask to `255.255.255.192`, the network is divided into smaller subnets that can each support fewer devices (62 hosts). Understanding this division helps penetration testers map out the network and identify which segments might hold more critical data or vulnerabilities.

3. **Practical Use in Testing**: During a penetration test, you can focus on one subnet at a time, scanning for open ports and vulnerabilities specific to that subnet. Tools like **nmap** can help you scan for live hosts and open ports within a subnet:

```
map -sn 192.168.1.0/24
```

This command scans all devices within the specified subnet, identifying live hosts and providing critical information about the network layout.

### *Benefits of Subnetting*

- **Improved Network Performance**: By reducing broadcast traffic within subnets, overall network congestion decreases, leading to faster and more efficient communication.

- **Enhanced Security**: Subnetting limits access to different parts of the network, making it more difficult for attackers to traverse the entire network if they breach one section.

- **Efficient IP Management**: Proper subnetting ensures that IP addresses are used effectively, minimizing the risk of address conflicts and making it easier to monitor network traffic.

## Network Segmentation: Isolating Network Segments for Security

While subnetting deals with dividing IP ranges, **network segmentation** is focused on dividing the network into isolated sections, typically using **firewalls**, **routers**, or **virtual LANs (VLANs)**. Segmentation enhances security by preventing direct communication between sections of the network, ensuring that if one segment is compromised, the rest of the network remains secure.

### *How Network Segmentation Works*

Imagine an organization with multiple departments—each department represents a network segment. By placing each department on a different segment, the IT team can isolate network traffic, control access between segments, and prevent attackers from moving laterally across the network if they compromise one segment.

- **Sales**: The sales team might have its own network segment, isolated from the rest of the organization.

- **Marketing**: The marketing team could operate on a separate segment, ensuring that their web-based services don't interfere with the company's internal services.

- **HR and Finance**: Sensitive data handled by HR and finance can be further isolated, ensuring that only authorized individuals can access this critical segment.

In the event of a breach, network segmentation acts as a containment strategy, limiting the damage to the compromised segment and preventing further intrusion.

### *Hands-On Example: Implementing Network Segmentation with Firewalls*

In a Kali Linux environment, you can practice setting up segmentation using **iptables**:

1. **View Current Rules**: List the current firewall rules on your machine with:

```
iptables -L
```

2. **Create a Segmentation Rule**: Use `iptables` to block traffic between specific IP ranges (segments). For example, to block all traffic from the `192.168.1.0/24` subnet to another subnet, you would use:

```
iptables -A INPUT -s 192.168.1.0/24 -j DROP
```

This command blocks incoming traffic from the specified subnet, creating an isolated environment where traffic cannot traverse between segments. By enforcing segmentation with firewall rules, you can prevent unauthorized access between different parts of the network.

### *Benefits of Network Segmentation*

- **Limiting Damage**: If an attacker breaches one segment, segmentation prevents them from accessing the entire network.

- **Improved Security**: Segmentation isolates vulnerable or outdated systems, protecting critical resources.

- **Enhanced Network Performance**: By reducing cross-segment traffic, segmentation improves the performance of critical applications and systems.

## Segmentation Techniques

Network segmentation is a fundamental concept in cybersecurity, and understanding its techniques is critical for penetration testers. There are two primary methods of segmentation: **physical segmentation** and **logical segmentation**. Each method has its own strengths and use cases, and both are important for maintaining a robust security posture.

Let's explore both techniques in greater detail.

### *1. Logical Segmentation*

Logical segmentation is a **software-based** approach, relying on technologies like **virtual local area networks (VLANs)** and **network addressing schemes** to create separate network segments. Unlike physical segmentation, this method does not require new hardware or major physical changes, making it more **scalable** and **flexible** for organizations as their network infrastructure grows.

- **VLANs**: Virtual local area networks allow network administrators to logically divide a network into isolated segments based on software-defined policies, rather than physical boundaries. VLANs can be based on factors like department, function, or even security level, making them an ideal solution for creating flexible and adaptable network segments.

- **Subnetting**: Another example of logical segmentation, subnetting uses **IP addressing schemes** to break a network into smaller subnets. Each subnet operates as an independent network within the larger infrastructure. This allows traffic to be managed and routed appropriately, based on logical criteria rather than physical hardware divisions.

**Why Logical Segmentation is Important**

Logical segmentation offers a **cost-effective** way to enhance network security. Since it doesn't rely on new hardware, it can be easily implemented within existing infrastructure. Logical segmentation allows administrators to adapt quickly to new security requirements without needing to physically rewire or rebuild the network.

For penetration testers, identifying **poorly configured VLANs** or **improper subnetting** can present an opportunity to bypass security controls. For instance, if traffic is allowed to flow freely between VLANs that should be isolated, attackers can move laterally between different parts of the network. Identifying these misconfigurations is a key task during a network penetration test.

### 2. Physical Segmentation

In contrast to logical segmentation, **physical segmentation** relies on hardware to divide a network into isolated segments. This can be achieved by using separate **routers, switches, firewalls**, or even physically distinct network infrastructure for each segment. Each segment has its own dedicated hardware, ensuring that the segments are completely isolated from each other.

- **Routers and Switches**: By placing different parts of the network on separate hardware, such as independent routers or switches, network administrators can enforce strict boundaries between segments.

- **Firewalls**: Physical firewalls are often placed between segments to control traffic and prevent unauthorized access. These firewalls can filter, monitor, and restrict traffic between segments, further strengthening the security of the network.

**Why Physical Segmentation is Important**

Physical segmentation is considered to be **more secure** because each segment has its own dedicated hardware, making it more difficult for attackers to move between segments. However, this method is more resource-intensive and **costly** compared to logical segmentation, as it requires additional hardware and infrastructure.

For penetration testers, physically segmented networks can present a tougher challenge. Breaking into a physically segmented network often involves finding **physical vulnerabilities** such as poorly secured hardware, misconfigured firewalls, or unsecured network cables. The isolation created by physical segmentation makes lateral movement more difficult, forcing attackers to rely on different strategies, such as gaining access to each segment individually.

## Impact on Security Posture

Both **subnetting** and **segmentation** significantly enhance an organization's overall security posture. By dividing the network into smaller, isolated segments, administrators can reduce the attack surface and contain potential threats more effectively.

When a network is properly segmented, even if an attacker manages to breach one part of the network, their ability to move laterally (i.e., from one segment to another) is greatly restricted. This prevents the attacker from accessing sensitive systems or data in other segments, as the traffic between those segments is tightly controlled by firewalls or other security measures.

Penetration testers often exploit poor segmentation or weak subnetting rules to **move laterally** within a network, allowing them to expand their foothold. On the other hand, well-implemented segmentation forces attackers to find new methods of bypassing controls, thus acting as a powerful defense mechanism.

## Practical Application for Penetration Testers

In real-world penetration testing engagements, effective use of subnetting and segmentation can either open doors for exploitation or present significant barriers. Here's how it plays out in practice:

- **Network Mapping**: During the reconnaissance phase of a penetration test, testers begin by mapping the network and identifying key subnets and segments. Tools like **nmap** can be used to scan for active hosts and understand how the network is structured. This helps testers pinpoint **critical assets** and **high-value targets** while also identifying potential attack vectors.

- **Exploiting Weak Segmentation**: Once the network layout is understood, penetration testers can exploit **misconfigurations** in segmentation to move laterally across the network. For example, a poorly configured VLAN might permit traffic between segments that should be isolated, allowing attackers to bypass security controls and access sensitive systems.

- **Testing Strong Segmentation**: On the flip side, strong segmentation practices can pose significant challenges for penetration testers. If segmentation is properly enforced, testers may encounter **strict isolation** between segments, forcing them to adjust their approach. They may need to find creative ways to **breach segment boundaries**, such as exploiting physical vulnerabilities, poorly configured firewall rules, or user-based weaknesses like shared credentials.

By thoroughly testing network segmentation, penetration testers provide valuable feedback that helps organizations **improve their security posture** and **harden their defenses**.

# Network Packet Analysis

Network segmentation and subnetting also play a crucial role in how data moves through the network. As part of their testing, penetration testers often analyze **network packets** to uncover vulnerabilities and anomalies within the network's traffic.

## *What is Network Packet Analysis?*

At its core, network packet analysis involves inspecting the small units of data—called **packets**—that traverse the network. Each packet contains critical information, including:

- **Source and destination IP addresses** (where the packet is coming from and where it's going).

- **Header information**, which helps identify the packet's type and ensures the data is delivered correctly.

- **Payload**, or the actual data being transmitted.

By examining these packets, penetration testers can understand how different systems on the network communicate with each other and detect potential security risks, such as unauthorized data transfers or attempts to exfiltrate sensitive information.

## *Why Use Tools for Packet Analysis?*

Manual monitoring of network traffic is nearly impossible due to the sheer volume of data transmitted in real-time. Advanced packet analysis tools automate the process, helping testers identify anomalies or malicious activity faster.

Here are more reasons to use tools:

- **Efficiency and speed**: Automated tools can analyze thousands of packets per second, promptly identifying potential issues like network slowdowns.

- **Comprehensive insight:** Tools can visualize data through graphs and reports, showcasing traffic patterns that would be difficult to discern manually.

- **Consistent accuracy:** Packet analysis tools use predefined criteria to flag anomalies accurately, reducing the risk of human error in manual inspections.

Some commonly used tools include:

- **Ettercap**: Known for its ability to support both active and passive dissection of live network traffic, Ettercap is particularly useful in conducting **man-in-the-middle (MITM) attacks** and analyzing **encrypted communications**.

- **Tcpdump**: A powerful command-line tool, Tcpdump allows users to capture and display TCP/IP packets being transmitted over the network. It is versatile and can be scripted to automate many aspects of packet analysis, making it ideal for penetration testers working in headless environments.

- **Tshark**: Essentially the command-line version of **Wireshark**, Tshark offers similar functionality but is designed for environments where graphical user interfaces are unavailable or impractical.

Using these tools allows penetration testers to conduct deep analysis of network traffic, uncover vulnerabilities, and respond to potential security breaches before they cause significant damage.

## Open Systems Interconnection (OSI) Model Deep Dive

The **Open Systems Interconnection (OSI) model** is a conceptual framework that standardizes how different network components communicate across different systems. It breaks down the complex process of data transmission into seven distinct layers, each with specific responsibilities, making it easier to understand, troubleshoot, and secure network communications.

Understanding the OSI model is crucial for penetration testers, as vulnerabilities may arise at different layers, and exploiting these weak points can provide access to sensitive information or unauthorized control over a network. Let's dive into each layer and explore its security implications.

## Layer 1: Physical Layer

The **physical layer** handles the raw transmission of data bits over a physical medium, such as copper wires, fiber optics, or radio waves. It is responsible for the physical connection between devices and ensures that the electrical signals representing data are transmitted properly.

From a security standpoint, the **physical layer** is often overlooked but remains highly important. For example, securing physical access to network hardware is essential to prevent tampering or hardware-based attacks. Attackers can easily bypass higher-level security measures if they have direct physical access to networking devices like routers or switches. Techniques such as shielding cables, securing access points, and implementing hardware-based encryption help protect the physical layer from threats.

## Layer 2: Data Link Layer

The **data link layer** ensures reliable data transfer across a physical network. It handles error detection, frame creation, and flow control. One of its key functions is managing **MAC addresses**, which are used to identify devices on a local network.

Security considerations at this layer include implementing **MAC address filtering** to restrict network access to authorized devices. This layer is also vulnerable to **man-in-the-middle (MITM) attacks** and **MAC address spoofing**, where attackers forge MAC addresses to gain unauthorized access. Penetration testers often assess how well a network is protected against such threats by testing ARP spoofing defenses and verifying that MAC address filtering is in place.

## Layer 3: Network Layer

The **network layer** is responsible for **logical addressing** and **routing** data packets between networks, which it does through IP addresses and routers. It determines the best path for data to travel and handles packet forwarding based on destination IP addresses.

Penetration testers need to be vigilant about security risks such as **IP spoofing**, where attackers disguise malicious packets with a legitimate IP address to bypass security mechanisms. Securing the network layer often involves configuring **firewalls**, **IPsec** (Internet Protocol Security), and routing protocols to prevent unauthorized access and ensure safe packet transmission.

## Layer 4: Transport Layer

The **transport layer** ensures the reliable delivery of data across a network by managing connections, breaking data into segments, and reassembling it at the destination. It also handles error correction and flow control.

Security at this layer focuses on **encryption and authentication**, which are essential for maintaining data integrity and confidentiality during transmission. Commonly used encryption protocols include **Secure Sockets Layer (SSL)** and **Transport Layer Security (TLS)**, which protect data in transit. For penetration testers, analyzing weaknesses in transport layer protocols—such as improper SSL/TLS configurations—can uncover vulnerabilities like **man-in-the-middle (MITM)** attacks and session hijacking.

## Layer 5: Session Layer

The **session layer** manages communication sessions between devices, including establishing, maintaining, and terminating connections. It ensures that sessions are synchronized and organized, which is essential for managing multiple communication streams.

Penetration testers must evaluate session management to prevent **session hijacking**, where attackers take over active sessions by stealing session tokens or cookies. Secure session protocols and implementing robust authentication methods can mitigate these risks. Tools like **Burp Suite** can be used to test session management vulnerabilities and ensure that sessions are properly secured.

## Layer 6: Presentation Layer

The **presentation layer** is responsible for translating data between the application layer and the lower layers. It handles tasks such as data encryption, compression, and formatting to ensure that the data sent by one application is correctly interpreted by another.

Security concerns at this level often involve weaknesses in **data encoding and formatting**. Attackers may exploit these vulnerabilities to inject malicious code or corrupt data, leading to severe consequences. Penetration testers focus on validating and sanitizing input data, ensuring that it is properly formatted and free from vulnerabilities such as **buffer overflow** or **encoding attacks**.

## Layer 7: Application Layer

The **application layer** interfaces directly with end-user applications and provides services such as email, file transfer, and web browsing. Protocols like **HTTP**, **FTP**, and **SMTP** operate at this layer.

Given its proximity to users, the application layer is a prime target for attacks such as **SQL injection**, **cross-site scripting (XSS)**, and **buffer overflow** exploits. Penetration testers commonly assess web applications for these types of vulnerabilities using tools like **OWASP ZAP** and **Acunetix**, which automate vulnerability scans and highlight areas where secure coding practices are lacking.

# Tools for OSI Layer Analysis

Penetration testers need a diverse set of tools to evaluate each layer of the OSI model. Here are some essential tools used to assess vulnerabilities across various layers:

*Physical Layer Analysis Tools*

- **Oscilloscopes**: Measure signal quality and strength in physical media.

- **Cable testers**: Identify and resolve issues in physical connections, such as damaged or miswired cables.

*Data Link Layer Tools*

- **Wireshark**: A powerful packet analysis tool that allows testers to capture and analyze live network traffic, identifying issues like ARP spoofing.

- **ARP Spoofing Detection Tools**: Tools like **XArp** can detect ARP spoofing attacks in real-time.

*Network Layer Tools*

- **Nmap**: A widely used network scanning tool that helps map network topologies, identify active hosts, and assess open ports.

- **Traceroute**: Tracks the path data packets take across a network, helping penetration testers understand network routing.

*Transport Layer Tools*

- **Netcat**: A versatile tool that enables testers to open connections, send data, and test ports for vulnerabilities.

- **Hping**: Simulates various types of network traffic to test firewall configurations and network responses.

### Session Layer Tools

- **Cain & Abel**: Used for session hijacking and cracking encrypted passwords. It helps penetration testers analyze session management protocols.

### Presentation Layer Tools

- **Hex editors**: Tools like **HxD** allow testers to inspect and modify raw data to uncover potential data encoding vulnerabilities.

### Application Layer Tools

- **OWASP ZAP**: A tool for scanning web applications for common vulnerabilities like SQL injection and XSS.

- **Acunetix**: A comprehensive web vulnerability scanner designed to detect application layer weaknesses.

# Cross-Layer Communication and Its Implications

The layers of the OSI model don't function in isolation—they continuously interact to facilitate complete communication between systems. Each layer relies on the services provided by the layer directly below it while offering services to the layer above. Penetration testers must understand how these interdependencies can introduce vulnerabilities.

For instance, a penetration tester exploiting a vulnerability at the application layer (Layer 7) could disrupt functions at the network layer (Layer 3), such as routing or addressing, demonstrating how interconnected the layers are. Manipulating one layer often leads to cascading effects across the entire communication stack.

Cross-layer vulnerabilities are critical to identify because they can offer attackers multiple entry points or allow them to chain attacks across several layers simultaneously.

# Real-Life Applications of the OSI Model in Penetration Testing

Penetration testers often apply the OSI model when simulating attacks and uncovering vulnerabilities. Below are extended case studies that show how testers exploit weaknesses at different OSI layers to identify security gaps.

### *Case Study 1: Man-in-the-Middle Attack (Data Link Layer)*

A **Man-in-the-Middle (MITM) attack** occurs when an attacker intercepts and possibly alters communication between two parties. At the **data link layer**, attackers exploit weaknesses in the way devices communicate over local networks by manipulating ARP tables or redirecting traffic.

In this scenario, a penetration tester uses tools like **Ettercap** or **BetterCAP** to simulate an MITM attack on a target network. These tools allow testers to intercept and manipulate traffic flowing between devices by tricking devices into thinking the attacker's machine is the legitimate gateway (ARP poisoning).

- **Steps**: The tester first scans the network using **nmap** to identify active hosts. Once the hosts are identified, the attacker uses **Ettercap** to poison the ARP cache of the target device and the gateway, effectively positioning themselves between the two.

- **Result**: The penetration tester can now eavesdrop on communications, potentially capturing sensitive information such as login credentials, or even altering the data in transit. This highlights weak points in encryption or traffic filtering that the organization needs to address.

This attack emphasizes the need for robust encryption and network segmentation at the data link layer to prevent unauthorized access.

### *Case Study 2: Distributed Denial-of-Service (DDoS) Attack Simulation (Network & Transport Layers)*

A **Distributed Denial-of-Service (DDoS) attack** aims to overwhelm a target network or service with massive amounts of traffic, effectively taking it offline or disrupting its normal operations. These attacks operate at both the **network layer** and **transport layer**, where data is routed and connections are managed.

In this case, penetration testers simulate a DDoS attack using tools like **LOIC (Low Orbit Ion Cannon)** or **hping** to flood the target system with requests. These tools allow testers to simulate different types of traffic and observe how the target handles high volumes of malicious data.

- **Steps**: The tester first assesses the target's defenses by running a network scan with **nmap** to detect open ports and services. They then use **hping** to generate a large volume of SYN requests or UDP packets directed at the target's network.

- **Result**: If the system lacks proper rate-limiting or traffic filtering, the target may become overwhelmed, leading to slowdowns or outages. This helps organizations understand their vulnerability to DDoS attacks and take measures such as implementing **rate-limiting**, **load balancing**, and **firewall rules** to mitigate the risk.

This scenario demonstrates how critical it is to have robust defenses in place to protect against large-scale traffic surges at the network and transport layers.

### Case Study 3: Cross-Layer Attack Simulation

A **cross-layer attack simulation** focuses on exploiting vulnerabilities that exist across multiple OSI layers, demonstrating how one weakness can affect the entire communication stack. These attacks are particularly dangerous because they exploit the dependencies between layers, making them harder to detect and mitigate.

In this case, penetration testers target a web application by exploiting vulnerabilities in both the **application layer** (Layer 7) and **transport layer** (Layer 4). The tester first performs a SQL injection attack at the application layer using a tool like **SQLMap**, and then escalates the attack by manipulating session tokens to hijack a user's session at the transport layer.

- Steps:

    1. The tester identifies a vulnerable input field on the target website using **OWASP ZAP**. After confirming the vulnerability, they run **SQLMap** to perform a SQL injection attack, gaining access to the backend database.

2. Once database access is obtained, the tester captures session tokens used for user authentication by exploiting weak session management practices. They then use tools like **Burp Suite** to manipulate or replay session tokens, successfully hijacking user sessions.

- **Result**: This attack exposes weaknesses in the web application's input validation (application layer) and session management (transport layer), demonstrating the interdependency between these layers. The organization needs to enforce stronger session management controls and implement input validation to prevent such attacks.

This case study shows how vulnerabilities across different layers can be chained together to create more sophisticated and impactful attacks.

# Networking Sniffers and Protocol Analyzers

Understanding and utilizing **network sniffers** and **protocol analyzers** are essential skills for penetration testers aiming to elevate their expertise in network security. These tools enable the in-depth monitoring and analysis of network traffic, helping testers identify vulnerabilities, understand traffic behavior, and gain critical insights into the network's underlying architecture. Mastering these tools can significantly enhance the effectiveness of penetration tests and uncover hidden security risks.

## What Are Network Sniffers?

**Network sniffers**, or **packet sniffers**, are specialized tools designed to capture, monitor, and analyze data packets traveling through a network. By intercepting these packets in real time, sniffers give penetration testers a microscopic view of network operations, including communication between devices, network protocols in use, and data exchanges.

Network sniffers are invaluable for detecting potential security issues, such as unauthorized access attempts, unencrypted sensitive information, and unusual traffic patterns. By examining these packets, testers can better understand how data flows through the network and identify areas where security may be lacking.

**Example in Practice**: In a corporate environment, IT departments use sniffers like **Wireshark** to monitor internal network traffic. For instance, if an employee's device is sending large amounts of data to an unfamiliar external IP address, the IT team can use Wireshark to investigate this activity in detail. They can then take corrective action to prevent potential data breaches or malicious activities, such as halting data exfiltration or blocking unauthorized access.

## Popular Protocol Analyzers

While sniffers focus on capturing network packets, **protocol analyzers** interpret and analyze the contents of these packets to understand how specific protocols behave. One of the most prominent protocol analyzers is **Wireshark**, which provides comprehensive traffic analysis for various protocols.

Other widely used tools include:

- **Fiddler**: A powerful web debugging tool that captures HTTP/HTTPS traffic, allowing testers to inspect, modify, and manipulate web requests.

- **Tcpdump**: A command-line packet analyzer that captures and displays network packets, making it ideal for low-level packet analysis and network troubleshooting.

- **Tshark**: A command-line counterpart to Wireshark, providing similar functionality in environments where a graphical interface is impractical.

Each of these tools has unique strengths, making them valuable assets for different stages of penetration testing.

## Strategies for Effective Sniffing

Maximizing the capabilities of network sniffers requires strategic placement and configuration. To optimize data collection and traffic analysis, penetration testers and network administrators can apply the following strategies:

1. **Position Sniffers Near Critical Servers**: Place sniffers close to high-value targets (e.g., web servers or databases) to capture vital traffic and detect anomalies in real-time.

2. **Set Filters for Specific Protocols**: Configure filters for protocols such as HTTP, DNS, or SSL/TLS, allowing you to focus on traffic relevant to your testing objectives while reducing noise from unrelated packets.

3. **Set Up Automated Alerts**: Implement systems that trigger alerts when the sniffer detects suspicious traffic patterns, such as large outbound data transfers or unauthorized login attempts.

4. **Leverage AI-Based Anomaly Detection**: Use AI-powered tools to analyze traffic patterns over time, learning "normal" behavior and flagging deviations that might indicate malicious activity.

5. **Utilize Port Mirroring**: Configure switches to mirror traffic from one port to the sniffer, ensuring that all packets passing through critical network segments are captured for analysis.

6. **Employ Next-Generation Firewalls**: Use firewalls with deep packet inspection (DPI) to block or flag potentially malicious packets before they can interact with critical systems.

7. **Monitor Wireless Network Traffic**: Use wireless sniffers to analyze Wi-Fi traffic, detect rogue access points, and identify vulnerabilities specific to wireless protocols (e.g., WPA2 cracking).

8. **Perform Regular Packet Analysis**: Schedule routine packet captures to identify trends, monitor network performance, and detect vulnerabilities over time.

9. **Use a Dedicated Management Interface**: Separate network management traffic from user traffic to ensure that sensitive management data is not exposed to potential sniffing attempts.

10. **Conduct Continuous Training for Staff**: Regularly train network staff on the latest sniffing techniques and mitigation strategies, ensuring they stay informed of emerging threats.

These strategies help ensure comprehensive network traffic analysis while mitigating the risk of data breaches and improving overall network security.

## Application in Penetration Testing

Network sniffers and protocol analyzers play a critical role in various stages of penetration testing, from reconnaissance to post-exploitation.

### *Reconnaissance Phase:*

During the initial reconnaissance phase, network sniffers provide invaluable information about the network layout by capturing traffic between devices, identifying active hosts, and detecting open ports. By analyzing the captured data, penetration testers can map the network and identify key targets for further exploration.

- **Example**: A penetration tester can use **Tcpdump** to capture traffic between devices and gather information about the network's IP range, services, and open ports. This information helps testers understand the structure of the network and assess which areas are most vulnerable to attack.

### *Scanning Phase:*

In the scanning phase, sniffers help testers monitor how their activities are being detected. By capturing traffic during scans, testers can determine whether **Intrusion Detection Systems (IDS)** are triggering alerts based on their activities.

- **Example**: A tester can run **Nmap** scans on the network while using **Wireshark** to analyze the traffic for signs that the scans are triggering IDS rules. This allows the tester to adjust their scanning techniques to avoid detection.

### *Exploitation Phase:*

During the exploitation phase, protocol analyzers help penetration testers verify that their attacks are successful. Whether conducting a **Man-in-the-Middle (MITM)** attack or injecting malicious payloads, these tools allow testers to observe whether the payloads are being delivered as intended and whether the attack has achieved its desired outcome.

- **Example**: After injecting a malicious payload using **Metasploit**, the tester uses **Wireshark** to monitor the communication between the compromised host and the attacker's machine, confirming whether the payload has been successfully executed.

## *Post-Exploitation Phase:*

In the post-exploitation phase, sniffers are crucial for monitoring data exfiltration methods. Penetration testers can capture outgoing traffic to ensure that sensitive data is being exfiltrated undetected, simulating real-world attacks where attackers steal confidential data without triggering alerts.

- **Example**: A tester who gains access to a sensitive database could use **Fiddler** or **Wireshark** to capture and analyze outgoing data transfers, ensuring that the exfiltration process remains stealthy. This helps organizations improve their defenses against data leakage.

By using sniffers and analyzers strategically throughout the penetration testing process, testers can gain deeper insights into the network's behavior and pinpoint areas where security controls need to be tightened.

Next, in Chapter 3, we will explore advanced vulnerability assessment techniques that will take your penetration testing skills to the next level.

# CHAPTER 3

# Advanced Vulnerability Assessment Techniques

A 2023 study by a professor of mechanical engineering at the University of Maryland revealed that **cyberattacks occur every 39 seconds** on average across numerous systems worldwide (Cukier, n.d.). This alarming statistic underscores the urgency for thorough and advanced vulnerability assessments to safeguard networks and systems from relentless cyber threats.

In today's digital landscape, even minor oversights can lead to devastating security breaches. Organizations must adopt advanced vulnerability assessment techniques to identify and mitigate potential threats before they become full-scale attacks. By mastering these techniques, you can significantly reduce risks, protect critical assets, and fortify your organization's security posture.

In this chapter, we'll explore the **Nmap Scripting Engine (NSE)**, how NSE scripts work, customizing scans to identify specific vulnerabilities, and writing your own scripts to fit unique scenarios. By the end, you will be well-prepared to conduct thorough vulnerability assessments and understand the mechanics behind automated scans and custom vulnerability detection.

# Nmap Scripting Engine

The **Nmap Scripting Engine (NSE)** is a powerful tool that extends Nmap's capabilities beyond basic port scanning. It allows users to run scripts that automate various tasks, from network reconnaissance to detecting specific security vulnerabilities. The NSE enhances Nmap's flexibility, making it an indispensable tool for penetration testers and security professionals.

## Introduction to the NSE

One of Nmap's standout features is its ability to use and customize **NSE scripts**, written in the **Lua programming language**, to automate vulnerability detection and exploitation. These scripts can perform a wide range of functions, such as scanning for misconfigurations, identifying outdated software versions, and detecting common vulnerabilities.

Each script includes a well-defined structure consisting of:

1. **Comments**: To explain the script's functionality for easy readability.

2. **Code instructions**: To execute specific tasks.

3. **Output formatting**: For clear and user-friendly results.

This functionality provides penetration testers with unparalleled customization options, allowing them to tailor Nmap scans to their specific needs and automate tasks for faster, more thorough assessments.

For example, a single script might check for **SSL/TLS vulnerabilities**, while another detects **SQL injection points** in a web application. This level of customization makes NSE particularly valuable for penetration testers working in dynamic environments where adapting quickly to different networks and systems is essential.

## Customizing Scans for Specific Vulnerabilities

One of the most powerful features of the NSE is its ability to **customize scans** to focus on detecting specific vulnerabilities or misconfigurations. This capability allows penetration testers and network administrators to tailor their assessments based on known vulnerabilities relevant to their targets, significantly improving the efficiency and accuracy of their scans.

By leveraging NSE's automation features, repetitive tasks such as vulnerability detection and misconfiguration checks can be simplified, allowing security professionals to focus their efforts on analyzing results and developing effective mitigation strategies.

### Example: Detecting Specific CVEs

For instance, let's say you're tasked with identifying systems vulnerable to a particular **CVE (Common Vulnerability and Exposure)**. NSE scripts such as **vulscan** and **nmap-vulners** allow you to efficiently scan for these vulnerabilities across a network.

- **vulscan** queries local and remote CVE databases, providing a detailed report of potential issues associated with known vulnerabilities.

- **nmap-vulners** fetches real-time data from online vulnerability databases, ensuring the most up-to-date CVE information is considered during the scan.

This level of customization ensures that your scans are both **thorough and targeted**, reducing the risk of missing critical security gaps.

### Example: Detecting Misconfigurations

NSE also excels in identifying misconfigurations that could lead to security risks. For example, the **smb-vuln-cve-2017-7494** script checks for vulnerabilities in the **Server Message Block (SMB)** protocol, a commonly exploited service in Windows environments. Automated scans using scripts like this can ensure that network configurations follow best security practices, reducing the attack surface and preventing potential exploitation.

By integrating NSE into their regular security checks, organizations can automate these assessments, freeing up cybersecurity teams to focus on higher-priority tasks while continuously monitoring their network for new vulnerabilities.

## Commonly Used NSE Scripts for Detecting CVEs and Misconfigurations

The **NSE library** includes numerous scripts designed specifically to detect **CVE vulnerabilities** and **network misconfigurations**. Incorporating these scripts into your penetration testing workflow can significantly improve the depth and precision of your scans.

### *Vulscan*

**vulscan** is one of the most popular NSE scripts for **vulnerability detection**. It integrates with local CVE databases such as `scipvuldb.csv` and `cve.csv` to identify vulnerabilities in the services detected during an Nmap scan.

To use **vulscan**, you first need to clone its repository from GitHub and link it to your local Nmap scripts directory:

```
git clone https://github.com/scipag/vulscan scipag_vulscan
ln -s `pwd`/scipag_vulscan /usr/share/nmap/scripts/vulscan
```

Once installed, you can run a vulnerability scan with vulscan by specifying the script in your Nmap command:

```
nmap -sV --script=vulscan/vulscan.nse www.example.com
```

This command initiates a **version scan** to identify running services, then queries the local CVE databases to provide detailed information about known vulnerabilities associated with those services (Borges, 2020).

### *Nmap-Vulners*

Another highly useful script for vulnerability detection is **nmap-vulners**. This script connects to online CVE databases, allowing you to retrieve the most recent vulnerability data related to the services detected during a scan.

To install **nmap-vulners**, clone its repository and link it to your Nmap directory:

```
git clone https://github.com/vulnersCom/nmap-vulners.git
/usr/share/nmap/scripts/vulners
```

Once installed, you can use the script in your Nmap scan:

```
nmap -sV --script vulners <target>
```

The **nmap-vulners** script outputs a comprehensive list of vulnerabilities tied to the versions of the services it detects, allowing you to quickly identify and prioritize the necessary patches and security updates (Kime, 2022). This script is particularly useful when performing a network-wide audit of exposed services and their associated risks.

## Writing Custom Nmap Scripts

For advanced users, **writing custom Nmap scripts** allows for greater control and flexibility during penetration tests, enabling the scanning process to be tailored to specific requirements not covered by existing scripts. Nmap's Scripting Engine (NSE) leverages the **Lua programming language** for scripting, which is lightweight, efficient, and easy to learn.

Creating custom NSE scripts requires an understanding of Lua syntax and Nmap's internal scripting interface. Custom scripts can automate tasks such as network reconnaissance, vulnerability detection, and even exploitation, making them invaluable for penetration testers who need specialized functionality.

Here's a basic template to illustrate the structure of a simple NSE script:

```
    description = [[
A sample script to demonstrate custom Nmap scripting.
]]

-- Import necessary libraries
local nmap = require "nmap"
local shortport = require "shortport"
```

```
-- Define the action function
action = function(host, port)
    local result = "Host: " .. host.ip .. " Port: " .. port.number .. "\n"
    return result
end


-- Register the script with Nmap
portrule = shortport.port_or_service(80, "http")
```

This simple script captures and prints the **IP address** and **port number** of HTTP services (port 80). You can expand it to perform more sophisticated tasks, such as checking for specific vulnerabilities, handling errors, and formatting the output for easy interpretation.

## Real-World Scenarios Demonstrating Nmap Script Applications

## Custom Script Applications in Real-World Scenarios

Custom NSE scripts are incredibly useful for real-world penetration testing scenarios. They allow testers to automate processes, conduct highly specific vulnerability scans, and target precise weaknesses in a network.

### Scenario 1: Auditing Public-Facing Servers

Consider a company preparing for a major product launch. To ensure its public-facing servers are secure, a penetration tester may use customized NSE scripts to identify vulnerabilities in the web applications hosted on these servers.

Using scripts such as **http-sherlock** and **http-csrf**, the tester can quickly check for common web vulnerabilities like **cross-site request forgery (CSRF)** and **shellshock exploits**.

Example commands:

```
nmap -sV --script http-sherlock,www.example.com
nmap -sV --script http-csrf,www.example.com
```

These commands will identify potential weaknesses in the web application, allowing the company to patch vulnerabilities before the product launch. Automating these scans with custom scripts ensures that no critical security flaws are overlooked, and remediation can be applied efficiently.

# Exploiting HTTP Vulnerabilities

HTTP vulnerabilities present a wide range of security risks, from unauthorized access to full system compromise. Penetration testers must be familiar with common HTTP weaknesses and how they can be exploited to assess the security posture of web applications.

## *Prevalent HTTP Vulnerabilities*

1. **Directory Traversal**: Attackers manipulate file paths to access sensitive directories and files outside the permitted scope. This often involves inserting patterns like . . / to move up the directory tree.

   o **Example**: If a web application allows file access through a URL such as http://example.com/view?file=report.pdf, an attacker could manipulate the request to access sensitive files by altering the URL to something like http://example.com/view?file=../../etc/passwd.

2. **Insecure Cookies**: Cookies that are not configured with security attributes like **HttpOnly** and **Secure** can expose session data, leading to **cross-site scripting (XSS)** or session hijacking.

   o **HttpOnly** prevents client-side scripts from accessing cookies, mitigating XSS risks.

   o **Secure** ensures that cookies are transmitted only over encrypted HTTPS connections.

3. **Improper Input Validation**: Web applications that fail to validate and sanitize user inputs are vulnerable to injection attacks, such as **SQL injection** or **command injection**. Attackers exploit these flaws by injecting malicious code into input fields, leading to unauthorized database access or command execution.

   o  **SQL Injection Example**: Injecting code such as `' OR '1'='1'` into a vulnerable login form could bypass authentication and reveal sensitive data from the database.

## Step-By-Step Exploits and Practical Exercises

Practical exercises are essential for hands-on experience in exploiting specific vulnerabilities and evaluating web application security.

### *Exploiting Directory Traversal*

1. **Identify Input Fields**: Use tools like **Burp Suite** to intercept HTTP requests and locate fields that accept file paths.

2. **Modify the File Path**: Insert traversal patterns ( . . / ) into the file path parameter to attempt accessing unauthorized files.

   Example request:

```
GET /view?file=../../../../../etc/passwd HTTP/1.1
Host: example.com
```

**Analyze the Response**: If successful, the web server will return sensitive files like /etc/passwd, indicating a directory traversal vulnerability.

### *Manipulating Insecure Cookies*

1. **Capture Cookies**: Use **OWASP ZAP** or browser extensions like **EditThisCookie** to capture session cookies from a web application.

2. **Modify Cookie Values**: Change the cookie's value to see if the server properly validates session data.

   Example:

   o  Intercept a session cookie and modify its value to impersonate another user.

    o   If the server does not validate cookies properly, you may gain unauthorized access to another user's account.

### *Performing SQL Injection*

1. **Identify Vulnerable Input Fields**: Enter characters like `'` or `--` into form fields and observe the server's response.

2. **Inject SQL Commands**: Use **Burp Suite** to intercept the request, then modify the input to include a malicious SQL query.

   Example input:

```
input: ' OR '1'='1' --
```

3. **Analyze the Response**: If successful, the application may return sensitive data or allow you to bypass authentication.

### *Cross-Site Scripting*

1. **Inject JavaScript Code**: Use **Burp Suite** to modify input fields by injecting JavaScript code.

   Example:

```
<input type="text" name="username"
value="<script>alert('XSS')</script>">
```

2. **Observe Execution**: If the injected script is executed in the browser, the web application is vulnerable to XSS attacks.

## Analyzing Real-Life Exploitation Scenarios

Understanding real-world vulnerabilities through case studies provides valuable lessons for cybersecurity professionals. These examples illustrate how vulnerabilities were exploited and what remediation strategies were applied.

### *Case Study 1: Equifax Data Breach (2017)*

The **Equifax breach** occurred due to an unpatched vulnerability in **Apache Struts** (CVE-2017-5638), which allowed attackers to execute arbitrary code remotely. This incident underscores the critical importance of **patch management** and timely updates for web applications, especially when dealing with publicly known vulnerabilities.

### *Case Study 2: Yahoo Security Breach (2013–2014)*

Attackers exploited weak session management and improperly handled cookies, forging authentication tokens to gain unauthorized access to Yahoo's internal systems. This breach highlights the necessity of secure cookie attributes (e.g., HttpOnly, Secure) and robust session management practices to prevent session hijacking.

### *Case Study 3: Path Traversal in NASA Servers (2018)*

Path traversal vulnerabilities in several NASA servers allowed attackers to access sensitive internal documents and applications. Proper input validation and regular security assessments could have prevented the exploitation of this vulnerability.

## Using Metasploit Framework

**Metasploit** is a powerful and versatile tool designed to identify and exploit vulnerabilities in computer systems. It is indispensable for security professionals and penetration testers, simplifying complex cybersecurity tasks such as vulnerability assessments, exploitation, and post-exploitation processes. The **Metasploit Framework** (MSF) helps security experts model real-world attack scenarios, providing critical insights into system weaknesses and security threats before they can be exploited by malicious actors (Kennedy et al., 2011).

Metasploit is widely regarded as one of the most effective tools in the arsenal of ethical hackers due to its comprehensive suite of features, which include a vast library of pre-built exploits, payloads, encoders, and auxiliary modules. These features enable penetration testers to systematically evaluate systems, simulate attacks, and ensure that vulnerabilities are identified and remediated in a timely manner.

## Getting Started with Metasploit

To get the most out of Metasploit, it's essential to understand its core components: the **Framework** and the **Console**. The **Metasploit Framework** is the engine behind the tool, containing a wide range of pre-built modules designed for different stages of a penetration test, including **exploits**, **payloads**, **scanners**, and **auxiliary functions**. These modules can be combined and customized to suit specific testing scenarios.

The **Metasploit Console** is the primary interface through which users interact with the Framework. It provides a command-line interface (CLI) that simplifies complex tasks, such as searching for exploits, configuring payloads, and launching attacks. The Console is highly intuitive, making it accessible for both novice and experienced users alike.

## Launching an Assessment

To launch a vulnerability assessment using Metasploit, follow these steps:

1. **Download and Install the Framework**: Start by downloading and installing Metasploit on your system. The installation process is straightforward, and the framework is available for most platforms, including Linux, macOS, and Windows.

**Start the Console**: Once installed, initiate the Metasploit Console by running the following command from your terminal:

```
msfconsole
```

2. **Search for Exploits**: Metasploit's extensive library of exploits is one of its primary strengths. To search for an exploit related to a specific platform or vulnerability, you can use the `search` command. For example, to find Windows-based exploits, you would run:

```
search type:exploit platform:windows
```

3. **Select and Configure an Exploit**: After identifying a suitable exploit, use the `use` command to load it into the Console:

```
use exploit/windows/smb/ms17_010_eternalblue
```

4. You will then need to configure the exploit by setting parameters such as the target IP address and any specific payload preferences using commands like `set RHOST` for the target host and `set PAYLOAD` for the attack vector.

5. **Execute the Exploit**: Once the exploit and payload are configured, you can launch the attack using the `run` or `exploit` command. Upon successful exploitation, the payload is delivered to the target, granting the attacker control over the system.

## A Need for Configuration

Once a suitable exploit has been identified, launching it through Metasploit requires configuring various settings, including the target's IP address and specific payload preferences. Commands such as use, set RHOST, and run facilitate the seamless execution of these exploits.

A payload is delivered upon successful exploitation, granting control over the compromised system. Payloads vary widely, from simple shell access to sophisticated Meterpreter sessions that provide advanced functionalities.

In addition to prebuilt exploits, Metasploit allows users to create custom auxiliary modules tailored to specific circumstances. Auxiliary modules enhance assessments by providing additional functions like scanning, reconnaissance, or DoS attacks without directly exploiting vulnerabilities.

Writing a custom auxiliary module involves defining it in Ruby and utilizing Metasploit's APIs to integrate smoothly with the Framework. For instance, a custom module could be designed to perform rapid port scans, identifying open ports that traditional scanners might miss.

## Understanding Exploits, Payloads, and Auxiliary Modules

Metasploit divides its functionality into several components, each serving a unique purpose in the penetration testing workflow:

- **Exploits**: These are scripts that leverage specific vulnerabilities in a system. Exploits are the primary tools used to gain unauthorized access to a target.

- **Payloads**: Payloads are the actions carried out upon successful exploitation. They can range from opening a shell to running complex scripts such as **Meterpreter** sessions, which allow advanced post-exploitation functionality like file system manipulation and privilege escalation.

- **Auxiliary Modules**: Auxiliary modules are used for tasks other than exploitation, such as scanning, reconnaissance, or denial-of-service (DoS) attacks. For example, an auxiliary module may be used to conduct port scans or brute force login attempts on a network.

Metasploit's **extensibility** allows users to customize these components or even write new modules in Ruby, adapting the tool to specific requirements.

## Creating and Customizing Auxiliary Modules

While Metasploit comes pre-packaged with a wide array of auxiliary modules, users may need to create custom modules to perform specific tasks. Writing a custom auxiliary module involves defining the module in Ruby and using Metasploit's API to integrate it into the Framework.

For instance, a custom auxiliary module could be written to perform rapid port scanning on a network. This module would allow you to identify open ports that may be missed by traditional scanners, giving you deeper insight into the target's attack surface. Writing custom modules enables testers to extend Metasploit's capabilities to meet unique testing environments and challenges.

## Combining Metasploit with Other Tools

While Metasploit is a powerful tool on its own, it truly shines when integrated with other cybersecurity tools. Combining **Metasploit** with tools like **Nmap** and **Burp Suite** enhances the effectiveness of vulnerability assessments by offering expanded scanning capabilities and more comprehensive exploitation.

**Nmap**: Nmap is ideal for network discovery and security auditing. You can import **Nmap** results directly into Metasploit, streamlining the process of correlating identified vulnerabilities with available exploits. For example, after scanning a network with Nmap, you can import the XML data into Metasploit using the `db_import` command:

```
db_import /path/to/nmap_results.xml
```

- This allows you to quickly map discovered services to exploits within Metasploit.

- **Burp Suite**: For web application testing, **Burp Suite** pairs well with Metasploit, providing comprehensive security analysis of web interfaces. After identifying vulnerabilities like SQL injection or cross-site scripting (XSS) with Burp Suite, you can use Metasploit to craft and deliver payloads, allowing you to probe deeper into the target system.

By combining the strengths of these tools, penetration testers can perform more **thorough assessments**, gaining better insight into vulnerabilities across the network.

## Setting Up a Testing Environment

To master the Metasploit Framework, hands-on experience is key. Setting up **lab environments** with intentionally vulnerable machines is an excellent way to practice Metasploit's capabilities in a controlled, risk-free setting. Platforms like **VulnHub**, **Hack The Box**, and **TryHackMe** provide virtual machines that mimic real-world systems with known vulnerabilities, allowing you to simulate attack scenarios.

- **VulnHub**: Offers downloadable virtual machines designed to be vulnerable to specific exploits. You can use Metasploit to attack these machines and develop your skills.

- **Hack The Box**: A popular platform that allows users to participate in capture-the-flag (CTF) challenges, testing their skills against real-world scenarios.

- **TryHackMe**: Provides a gamified approach to penetration testing, offering tutorials and challenges for all skill levels.

Simulating these attack scenarios in lab environments builds proficiency and confidence, ensuring you are well-prepared for real-world operations.

## Staying Updated and Engaging with the Community

The cybersecurity landscape is constantly evolving, and so is Metasploit. New exploits and modules are continuously added to the Framework by both developers and the security community. Staying updated with these developments is critical to maintaining a cutting-edge skill set.

- **Community Contributions**: The open-source nature of Metasploit means that new features and modules are regularly contributed by the global community. Engaging with forums, blogs, and official documentation helps users stay informed about the latest vulnerabilities, exploits, and best practices.

- **Continuous Development**: The Metasploit development team releases frequent updates, ensuring the tool remains relevant against emerging threats. Regularly updating your Metasploit installation ensures access to the latest features and security patches.

## Overcoming the Learning Curve

While **Metasploit** offers immense value, its depth and versatility can make it overwhelming for beginners. However, a wealth of resources, including tutorials, video guides, and comprehensive documentation, is available to ease the learning process.

- **Tutorials**: Step-by-step guides walk users through common tasks, such as launching exploits, configuring payloads, and performing reconnaissance.

- **Video Guides**: Many platforms offer video-based walkthroughs that demonstrate how to use Metasploit in real-world scenarios.

- **Documentation**: Metasploit's official documentation provides a comprehensive reference for all commands, modules, and features, making it an invaluable resource for mastering the tool.

By starting with basic commands and gradually advancing to more complex operations, users can steadily build their knowledge and confidence.

# Securing Systems With GNU Privacy Guard

In today's digital landscape, where data breaches and unauthorized access are constant threats, **GNU Privacy Guard (GPG)** plays a vital role in ensuring the confidentiality and integrity of sensitive information. GPG is a powerful, open-source encryption tool that helps protect data from unauthorized access by transforming it into an unreadable format, making it a fundamental asset for anyone looking to secure their communications.

## Why Data Protection Matters

As we continue to store and transmit personal, financial, and professional data online, the risk of exposure to cyberattacks grows significantly. Without proper encryption, unauthorized individuals can intercept and exploit sensitive information such as emails, contracts, or personal identification. GPG addresses this concern by providing robust encryption that ensures only authorized recipients can access the data, making it a trusted solution for enhancing digital privacy.

## What Is Encryption?

To fully appreciate how GPG protects your data, it's important to understand the concept of **encryption**.

**Encryption** is the process of converting readable data, or plaintext, into an unreadable format, known as ciphertext. This transformation ensures that only someone with the correct decryption key can convert the ciphertext back into plaintext. Encryption is a foundational technology in modern cybersecurity, and it plays a critical role in protecting everything from personal emails to financial transactions.

For example, if you send a message that reads, "Meet me at the park at 3 p.m.," encryption would scramble it into a random string of characters, like "7f8g9d5k2h3l." Without the correct decryption key, the message would remain indecipherable to anyone who intercepts it.

## How GPG Works

At the heart of GPG's encryption system is a **public-key cryptography** model, which involves two types of keys: a **public key** and a **private key**. This is known as **asymmetric encryption** because the encryption and decryption processes use different keys.

- **Public Key**: This key can be shared with anyone and is used to encrypt data.

- **Private Key**: This key is kept secret by the owner and is used to decrypt data encrypted with the corresponding public key.

Here's how GPG works in practice:

1. If someone wants to send you a secure message, they use your **public key** to encrypt the message.

2. Once encrypted, the message becomes unreadable to anyone except the holder of the corresponding **private key**.

3. You, as the private key holder, can then use your **private key** to decrypt and read the message.

This system ensures that only the intended recipient, who possesses the private key, can unlock the message, even if it is intercepted during transmission. For example, if you want to send an encrypted email, you would first obtain the recipient's public key, encrypt the message with that key, and send it securely.

## Setting Up GPG

Setting up **GPG** is a straightforward process that involves the following steps:

1. **Install GPG**: Most modern operating systems (Linux, macOS, and Windows) offer GPG as a downloadable program. You can install it via a package manager (e.g., `apt` for Ubuntu, `brew` for macOS) or download it from the GPG website.

**Linux:**

```
sudo apt-get install gnupg
```

**macOS:**

```
brew install gnupg
```

**Windows**: Download GPG from the official GnuPG website.

1. **Generate Your Key Pair**: After installation, the next step is to generate your **key pair**—this includes both your **public** and **private** keys. You will be prompted to provide basic information, such as your name and email address.

To generate the key pair, run the following command:

```
gpg --gen-key
```

Follow the prompts to create a secure key pair. GPG will generate a **public key** that you can share with others and a **private key** that you must keep secure.

2. **Distribute Your Public Key**: Once your key pair is created, you can share your public key with anyone you want to communicate with securely. You can also upload it to a **public key server** so that it's easily accessible to anyone who needs it.

To export and share your public key, use:

```
gpg --export -a "Your Name" > publickey.asc
```

Send this file via email or upload it to a key server for public access.

3. **Keep Your Private Key Secure**: Your private key is crucial for decrypting messages and should never be shared. Protect it with a strong passphrase and store it securely. If someone gains access to your private key, they could decrypt any messages sent to you.

## Why Use GPG?

There are several key advantages to using GPG for encryption:

1. **Data Privacy and Security**: GPG ensures that your sensitive communications remain confidential. Even if someone intercepts an encrypted email, file, or message, they won't be able to read it without the corresponding private key. This makes GPG an excellent tool for securing emails, financial documents, and personal data.

2. **Authentication and Integrity**: In addition to encryption, GPG also allows you to **digitally sign** your messages. This verifies that the message came from you and has not been altered during transmission. The recipient can use your public key to validate your signature and ensure the authenticity of the message.

To sign a message, use:

```
gpg --sign message.txt
```

This adds a digital signature that proves the message's origin and integrity.

3. **End-to-End Encryption**: GPG ensures end-to-end encryption, meaning the message remains encrypted from the moment it is sent until it is decrypted by the recipient. This is particularly important for industries where data security is critical, such as **finance**, **healthcare**, and **government**.

## Practical Example: Sending Encrypted Emails

Let's consider a practical example of sending an encrypted email using GPG:

1. **Obtain the Recipient's Public Key**: Before you send an encrypted email, you need to have the recipient's public key. This can be obtained directly from the recipient or downloaded from a public key server.

2. **Encrypt the Email**: Once you have the public key, use GPG to encrypt the email. For instance, if you want to encrypt a file called `email.txt`, you would run:

```
gpg --encrypt --recipient recipient@example.com email.txt
```

3. **Send the Encrypted Email**: After encrypting the email, send the encrypted file to the recipient. Only they will be able to decrypt it using their private key.

**Decrypting the Email**: When the recipient receives the encrypted email, they can use their private key to decrypt it:

```
gpg --decrypt email.txt.gpg
```

This process ensures that the email remains secure throughout its journey, from sender to recipient.

In the next chapter, we will delve into exploit development and custom payloads, focusing on how vulnerabilities are exploited to gain unauthorized access.

# CHAPTER 4

# Exploit Development and Custom Payloads

In the field of cybersecurity, understanding how to develop exploits and create custom payloads is a critical skill. This chapter will introduce basic techniques for building buffer overflow exploits, writing shellcode, and tailoring them for real-world scenarios. Mastering these skills is essential for both offensive security (penetration testing) and defensive strategies, as it helps identify and mitigate vulnerabilities before they are exploited by malicious actors.

## Why Exploit Development Matters

Exploit development is crucial for uncovering weaknesses in systems before they can be exploited. By learning how vulnerabilities are found and how malicious payloads are crafted, security professionals can not only prevent attacks but also create more secure software.

For example, a **database poisoning attack** occurs when an attacker gains unauthorized access to a database, often due to weaknesses in a web application or poorly secured entry points. Once inside, the attacker can corrupt data or inject malicious inputs, compromising the integrity of the system.

### Case Study: The 2016 Panastar Attack

In 2016, the online retailer Zalando was targeted by attackers who exploited vulnerabilities in the company's review submission system. The attackers injected fake reviews, which misled consumers and manipulated product ratings. This is a classic example of a database poisoning attack, demonstrating the importance of secure coding practices and vulnerability assessments.

# Writing Buffer Overflow Exploits

**Buffer overflows** are one of the most common and significant vulnerabilities in software development. A buffer overflow occurs when a program attempts to store more data in a buffer (a fixed-size storage location) than it can hold, resulting in the corruption of adjacent memory. This overflow can potentially allow an attacker to execute arbitrary code, leading to full system compromise.

### How Buffer Overflows Work

A buffer overflow occurs when input data exceeds the storage capacity of a buffer, causing data to "spill over" into adjacent memory spaces. If attackers can manipulate this overflow, they can gain control of the program's execution flow, often leading to code execution vulnerabilities.

- **Real-World Example**: The infamous **Morris Worm**, one of the first widespread Internet worms, leveraged buffer overflow vulnerabilities to propagate across networks, causing significant damage.

### Steps to Write a Buffer Overflow Exploit

1. **Identifying Vulnerabilities**: The first step in crafting a buffer overflow exploit is finding vulnerable code. In languages like C and C++, functions such as `strcpy`, `scanf`, and `gets` are common culprits because they fail to perform bounds checking on input data. Vulnerabilities often arise when user inputs are not validated, leading to potential overflow.

2. **Analyzing the Code**: A typical vulnerable code might look like this:

```
void vulnerable_function(char *user_input) {

    char buffer[50];

    strcpy(buffer, user_input); // Vulnerable: no bounds checking

}
```

If the user_input exceeds 50 characters, it will overflow into adjacent memory, potentially leading to the execution of arbitrary code.

3. **Tools for Buffer Overflow Exploits**: To exploit such vulnerabilities, security testers often use tools like the **GNU Debugger (GDB)**. GDB allows testers to inspect program execution, set breakpoints, and observe memory behavior during testing.

For example, using GDB, you can trace how an overflow affects the program's control flow:

```
gdb ./vulnerable_program

run $(python -c 'print("A"*60)')
```

4. **Disabling Protections for Testing**: Modern systems often have security protections like **stack canaries** and **Address Space Layout Randomization (ASLR)** that make exploiting overflows harder. For testing and development purposes, these can be disabled to simulate real-world conditions where protections might be absent:

   o Disable stack protection: `-fno-stack-protector`

   o Disable ASLR: `echo 0 > /proc/sys/kernel/randomize_va_space`

5. **Crafting the Exploit**: Once you identify the vulnerability, the next step is to craft an input that will trigger the buffer overflow. This involves creating patterns of characters to analyze how memory is overwritten, then fine-tuning the input to control program execution.

Example: Use a tool like **pattern_create** (part of the Metasploit framework) to generate a unique string that helps determine the exact offset of the overflow:

```
/usr/share/metasploit-framework/tools/exploit/pattern_create.rb -l
100
```

6. **Debugging and Fine-Tuning**: After triggering the buffer overflow, use tools like **GDB** to examine the memory layout, CPU registers, and stack behavior to refine your exploit. Commands like `info registers` (to check CPU register contents) and `x/x $esp` (to examine the stack pointer) provide valuable insights for debugging.

# Crafting Shellcode

**Shellcode** is the sequence of machine instructions that are executed after a vulnerability is exploited. The name comes from its original purpose of opening a command shell on the target system. Writing effective shellcode is an essential skill for penetration testers, as it serves as the payload for many exploits.

### What is Shellcode?

Shellcode is written in low-level assembly language specific to the target architecture (e.g., x86, x86-64, ARM). It is designed to be small, self-contained, and executable, often fitting within tight memory constraints imposed by the buffer being overflowed.

When a vulnerability is exploited (such as a buffer overflow), the shellcode is injected into the program's memory and executed, allowing the attacker to control the system or perform specific actions (e.g., opening a shell, creating a backdoor).

### How to Write Simple Shellcode

1. **Understanding Assembly**: Before writing shellcode, you need to be comfortable with **assembly language**, which directly communicates with the processor. For example, on x86 architecture, you will work with instructions like `mov`, `xor`, `jmp`, and `call`, manipulating CPU registers and memory.

   **Example: Writing Shellcode to Spawn a Shell** Here's a simple shellcode that spawns a shell:

   ```
   xor eax, eax        ; clear EAX

   push eax            ; null-terminate string

   push 0x68732f2f     ; push //sh

   push 0x6e69622f     ; push /bin

   mov ebx, esp        ; set EBX to the address of the string

   push eax            ; null-terminate argv

   push ebx            ; push pointer to "/bin//sh"
   ```

```
mov ecx, esp          ; set ECX to argv

xor edx, edx          ; set EDX to 0 (no envp)

mov al, 0xb           ; syscall number for execve

int 0x80              ; trigger interrupt to make syscall
```

This shellcode directly invokes the execve system call to spawn a /bin/sh shell, giving the attacker command-line access to the target.

3. **Setting Up Your Development Environment**: Use assemblers like **NASM** or **yasm** to write and compile shellcode. For example, on Linux, you can install NASM and compile the shellcode with:

```bash
Copy code
nasm -f elf32 shellcode.asm

ld -m elf_i386 -o shellcode shellcode.o
```

4. **Testing Shellcode**: It's crucial to test shellcode in a safe environment. Virtual machines or controlled lab environments are ideal for testing without risking real-world systems.

## Testing and Debugging Exploits

Testing your exploit involves extensive debugging to ensure it behaves as expected. Tools like **GDB** or **Immunity Debugger** (on Windows) are invaluable for monitoring the execution of your exploit, fine-tuning payloads, and observing system behavior.

- Use GDB commands such as break main to set breakpoints and run to execute the program under controlled conditions. As the exploit progresses, you can use info registers to inspect CPU register values, helping you adjust your shellcode as necessary.

### *Writing the Shellcode*

Start writing shellcode by creating a simple assembly file. Once you have written the shellcode, you need to compile it.

After compiling, run the shellcode within a controlled environment, preferably on a virtual machine, to avoid harming your primary system. This environment allows you to test your code safely. You can check for execution by observing if a new shell opens up.

### *Encoding Shellcode*

Common encoding methods include XOR encoding, Base64 encoding, and using polymorphic engines to create diverse variants of the same shellcode.

| Encoding Method | Overview | Example |
|---|---|---|
| XOR encoding | Using the XOR operation, a simple encryption method involves combining each data byte with a byte from a key. This can obscure the data but is relatively easy to break. | Original text: "Hello"<br><br>Key: "key"<br><br>Encoded:<br><br>\x1b\x0e\x01\x01\x0b<br><br>(resulting byte sequence) |
| Base64 encoding | A binary-to-text encoding scheme that encodes binary data into an ASCII string format using 64 different characters. This is commonly used in data transmission and storage. | Original text: "Hello"<br><br>Encoded: "SGVsbG8=" |
| Polymorphism | A technique that allows a program or a payload to change its form and appearance each time it is executed, making it harder for detection and analysis. | A malware that encrypts its payload using different algorithms each time it runs, resulting in a unique binary each time while maintaining the same functionality. |

### Making Your Shellcode Smaller

Ultimately, writing shellcode requires practice, patience, and continued learning. As you become more familiar with writing and deploying shellcode, you will find many resources to deepen your understanding. Try building upon your knowledge with hands-on projects, and explore various assembly languages beyond just x86.

Here, we outline a step-by-step methodology, emphasizing the importance of the execution context and recommended tools.

1. **Identifying vulnerable points:** Determine where to inject the shellcode in the target application. This could involve exploiting a buffer overflow or using return-oriented programming techniques.

2. **Creating exploit payloads:** Construct payloads incorporating no-operation (NOP) instructions, shellcodes, and necessary pointers to redirect the program's execution flow. An NOP slide increases the chances that execution will hit the shellcode, regardless of slight address variances.

3. **Using tools:** Tools like Metasploit, Pwntools, and Immunity Debugger are invaluable. They help automate creating and deploying payloads, debugging, and analyzing the target application's response.

# Evading Antivirus Detection

To develop effective exploits that bypass security measures, understanding the mechanics of **antivirus detection** is crucial. Antivirus software typically relies on two primary methods for identifying malicious code: **signature-based scanning** and **heuristic analysis**. Each method has its strengths and limitations, and modern malware often incorporates techniques to evade detection by either or both methods.

## Signature-Based Scanning

Signature-based scanning works by comparing files to a database of known malware **signatures**. If the antivirus finds a match, the file is flagged as malicious. While this method is effective against known threats, it has limitations:

- **Limited to Known Threats**: It can't detect new or modified malware until signatures are updated.

- **Easily Evaded by Polymorphic Malware**: Malware that changes its code with each infection can bypass signature detection.

## Heuristic Methods

On the other hand, heuristic methods analyze the behavior and structure of files to detect suspicious activities. These methods use predefined rules and algorithms to flag files exhibiting behaviors common among malware, such as attempts to modify system files or network traffic patterns that resemble botnet communications.

### *Signature-Based or Heuristic?*

Heuristic analysis is more flexible than signature-based methods, but advanced malware can still get around it. This type of malware can imitate normal behavior or use new attack methods not covered by current rules.

Here's a table that showcases their unique features:

| Signature-Based Detection | Heuristic Detection |
|---|---|
| **Unique aspect:** Relies on an extensive database of known malware signatures; quick to detect known threats. | **Unique aspect:** More adaptable to new or unknown threats; evaluates risky behavior making evasion harder. |
| **Example:** Identifies specific ransomware by recognizing its unique code signature. | **Example:** Flags new executables as suspicious due to modifying system files, even if not previously identified. |

## Using Evasion Techniques

For penetration testers, mastering evasion techniques is essential to enhancing the effectiveness of payloads and bypassing antivirus detection. A common and straightforward method is **encoding**, where payloads are transformed into alternate formats to avoid detection. However, more advanced techniques, such as **polymorphism** and **metamorphism**, offer deeper methods of evasion.

### *Polymorphism and Metamorphism*

**Polymorphic** and **metamorphic** code techniques are sophisticated methods for evading antivirus detection.

- **Polymorphic code** alters its appearance with every execution by changing its encryption while retaining the same functionality. This can generate a unique signature each time, making it harder for signature-based detection to catch.

- **Metamorphic code** takes it a step further by completely rewriting itself each time it runs, ensuring that even advanced detection systems find it difficult to recognize the malware across different executions. While these techniques demand a deep understanding of programming and malware creation, they significantly increase the likelihood of avoiding detection.

### *Practical Implementation*

Hands-on practice is vital for developing evasive payloads effectively. Start by generating a basic payload using tools like **msfvenom**. Once the initial, unmodified payload is ready, test it against antivirus scanners, such as **VirusTotal**, to assess its initial detection rate.

From here, systematically modify the payload to reduce its detectability. This can include:

- Altering the code structure

- Applying polymorphic techniques to change the payload's encryption each time it runs

- Integrating metamorphic engines that rewrite the payload with each execution

Each modification should be tested against multiple antivirus engines to measure effectiveness. For instance, a practical exercise might involve modifying the size of a **Metasploit payload** and recompiling it, introducing subtle changes that reduce detection rates.

### Testing Evasion Strategies

Testing your evasion techniques is just as important as creating them. Set up a controlled lab environment using **virtual machines (VMs)** running various operating systems and antivirus software. Isolating these VMs from production networks ensures you can safely test without risking unintended breaches.

Track the results of each change to analyze how they impact the payload's performance and detectability. By setting goals for acceptable detection rates, you can refine your approach, continually adjusting until the payload achieves the desired level of stealth.

# Systems Hardening

Systems hardening is a crucial practice in cybersecurity. Its main goal is to reduce and eliminate security risks by making it more difficult for attackers to find vulnerabilities in a system. Businesses and individuals can protect their data and assets from potential threats by working to harden a system.

## Why Is Systems Hardening Important?

**Systems hardening** is another critical aspect of cybersecurity, aiming to reduce vulnerabilities and make systems more resilient to attacks. The goal is to minimize the potential attack surface by addressing weak points that can be exploited by attackers.

### Why Systems Hardening Is Essential

In today's interconnected world, every device and system connected to the internet is at risk. These risks include malware infections, unauthorized access attempts, and accidental exposure of sensitive data. For organizations, the consequences of a security breach—such as financial loss, reputational damage, or legal implications—can be severe. Therefore, systems hardening is not just a best practice but a necessity.

## *Steps to Harden Your Systems*

1. **Understand Your System**: The first step in hardening a system is fully understanding its architecture and components. This includes knowing what hardware, software, operating systems, and network devices are in use. Identifying vulnerable areas, such as outdated software or weak configurations, helps prioritize what needs to be hardened first.

2. **Apply Security Patches**: One of the simplest yet most effective methods of system hardening is applying security patches. Software vendors frequently release updates to fix vulnerabilities, so keeping systems up to date is essential. For example, promptly applying patches to a widely used web application can significantly reduce the risk of attack.

3. **Minimize Software Installation**: The more software installed, the larger the attack surface. Limit software to only what is necessary. For example, if a program is only used during specific times of the year, uninstall it when it's not needed to reduce potential vulnerabilities.

4. **Configure Security Settings**: Most systems come with default security settings that are not always optimal. Review and configure these settings to enhance security. For example, changing default passwords to strong, unique ones and enabling properly configured firewalls are simple but effective steps.

In the next chapter, we will delve into **web application penetration testing**, where the concepts of securing and testing systems come together to identify vulnerabilities in online environments.

# CHAPTER 5

# Web Application Penetration Testing

Web application penetration testing is a critical process that involves various techniques to identify and exploit vulnerabilities within web applications. Ethical hackers and cybersecurity professionals use these methods to assess the security posture of applications, helping to uncover flaws that malicious actors could exploit. By conducting thorough penetration tests, organizations can ensure that their web applications remain secure for end users and protect sensitive data.

## Understanding Web Application Security

One common technique in web security is the use of **token generation**. For instance, when a user logs in to a web application, a unique **Cross-Site Request Forgery (CSRF)** token is generated and stored in the user's session or a secure cookie. This token should be unpredictable to prevent attackers from guessing it and executing unauthorized actions.

Implementing **token validation middleware** strengthens an application's defense by ensuring that all requests performing sensitive actions (such as changing passwords or making payments) are legitimate. By verifying the CSRF token, the server can confirm that the request originated from the authenticated user, preventing attackers from exploiting these actions via CSRF attacks.

In this chapter, we will explore CSRF and other web application vulnerabilities, such as **SQL injection**, and methods to identify and mitigate them to enhance the security of your web applications.

# Structured Query Language Injection Attacks

**SQL injection** is one of the most prevalent attack vectors targeting database-driven web applications. This technique exploits vulnerabilities in insecure database queries, allowing attackers to manipulate or retrieve sensitive data from the backend database. SQL injection can lead to unauthorized access, the exposure of user credentials, financial records, and other confidential information.

## How to Identify SQL Attacks

One common approach is to observe error messages generated by the web application. These errors can inadvertently reveal clues about the underlying database structure and potential injection points.

For example, if you put a single quote (') in a form field and it causes an error in the database, the input is treated as part of an SQL command. Another way to test the application is by looking at how it reacts to different inputs. By trying out different special characters and combinations, testers can see how the application handles and filters the input, and find any weaknesses.

Consider a more advanced SQL injection technique: It involves retrieving specific data from the database. Attackers can use UNION-based injection to merge results from multiple queries.

For instance, consider an application querying for user details:

```
SELECT name, email FROM users WHERE id = 1;
```

An attacker could modify the id parameter to execute an additional query:

```
id= 1 UNION SELECT credit_card_number, expiration_date FROM
credit_cards;
```

This union query fetches and displays data from the credit_cards table alongside the original query results. Attackers can thus access a wealth of confidential information through carefully constructed injections.

Mitigating SQL injection vulnerabilities requires robust defensive measures. One of the most effective techniques is using prepared statements (parameterized queries). Prepared statements separate SQL code from data inputs, ensuring user inputs cannot alter the query's structure. Here's an example using prepared statements in PHP:

```php
$stmt = $pdo->prepare('SELECT * FROM users WHERE username =
:username AND password = :password');
$stmt->execute(['username' => $username, 'password' => $password]);
```

In this approach, placeholders (:username, :password) are used, and actual data values are bound to these placeholders before execution. This prevents input from modifying the query syntax, effectively neutralizing SQL injection threats.

### Input Validation

Input validation is another critical defense strategy. Applications should rigorously validate all user inputs, adhering to strict length, type, format, and content constraints. By filtering out potentially harmful characters and sequences, developers can significantly reduce the risk of injection attacks.

Implementing allow lists (accepting only well-defined, expected input) rather than blocklists (blocking known bad input) ensures more comprehensive protection.

Imagine a web application with a login form where users input their username and password. When the form is submitted, the application constructs an SQL query to check if the credentials are valid, like this:

```sql
SELECT * FROM users WHERE username = 'input_username' AND password =
'input_password';
```

If a malicious user inputs the following for the username:

```
' OR '1'='1
```

and for the password:

```
' OR '1'='1
```

The resulting SQL query becomes:

```
SELECT * FROM users WHERE username = " OR '1'='1' AND password = "
OR '1'='1';
```

Since the condition '1'='1' is always true, this query would return all users, potentially allowing the attacker to bypass the login and gain unauthorized access.

### *Error Handling*

Error handling also plays a pivotal role in security. Developers should ensure that detailed error messages are never exposed to end users. Instead, generic error messages should be displayed, while detailed logs are maintained internally for debugging purposes. This approach minimizes the risk of revealing helpful information to potential attackers.

One common example of an SQL injection attack involving error handling occurs when a web application reveals specific database error messages to users.

For instance, consider a web application that includes a search feature. When a user submits a search query, the application constructs an SQL query like this:

```
SELECT * FROM products WHERE product_id = 'input_product_id';
```

If a malicious user inputs the following for the product ID:

```
1' AND 1=CONVERT(int, (SELECT @@version)) --
```

The resulting query might look like:

```
SELECT * FROM products WHERE product_id = '1' AND 1=CONVERT(int,
(SELECT @@version)) --';
```

If the application is poorly designed and uses error handling that provides detailed SQL error messages, it might reveal the database version, such as:

```
Incorrect syntax near '1'.
```

This information enables the attacker to gain insight into the database system, which can be exploited for further attacks. To mitigate such vulnerabilities, it's essential to implement error handling that does not disclose specific database error messages to the users.

# Cross-Site Scripting (XSS)

**Cross-Site Scripting (XSS)**, a prevalent and dangerous web security vulnerability, allows attackers to inject malicious scripts into webpages viewed by unsuspecting users. XSS exploits weaknesses in a web application's input validation process, leading to the execution of malicious code in a victim's browser. Understanding XSS is critical, as it involves not only knowing its various types but also recognizing the impact it can have on both users and web applications.

## Overview of Different Classes of XSS Vulnerabilities

XSS vulnerabilities fall into three primary categories: stored, reflected, and Document Object Model (DOM)-based XSS.

| Class | Overview | Examples |
|---|---|---|
| Stored XSS | Malicious script is permanently stored on a server (e.g., in a database) and is served to users when they access the affected page. | A forum post containing a malicious JavaScript payload that executes when other users view the post. |
| Reflected XSS | Malicious script is reflected off a web server, typically via URL parameters. The script is executed immediately, often when a user clicks a link. | A search result page that includes user input in the results; if the input is a malicious script, it executes without sanitization. |

| DOM-based XSS | The vulnerability exists in the client-side code (JavaScript) that modifies the DOM. It does not require a server response to execute the malicious script. | A single-page application that retrieves user input from the URL and directly inserts it into the HTML, allowing execution of a script from the URL without validation. |
| --- | --- | --- |

## Tools and Techniques for Identifying XSS in Web Applications

Identifying **Cross-Site Scripting (XSS)** vulnerabilities requires a combination of both manual and automated approaches. Web developers and penetration testers can utilize browser developer tools to inspect and manipulate the Document Object Model (DOM) in real time, injecting malicious scripts into input fields to observe how the web application processes them.

For a more thorough analysis, **automated tools** available in penetration testing distributions like Kali Linux provide powerful features for detecting XSS vulnerabilities. These tools can crawl entire web applications, identify injection points, and report potential security risks. A widely used tool, **Burp Suite**, offers an active scanning feature that automatically probes for XSS vulnerabilities, highlighting areas where malicious scripts might be inserted and executed.

Beyond traditional scanners, advanced tools like **XSStrike** employ intelligent fuzzing techniques specifically designed for XSS detection. XSStrike tests various payloads and analyzes responses to identify exploitable flaws, allowing penetration testers to validate XSS vectors efficiently and assess their impact.

## Manipulation of User Sessions and Data Through XSS

XSS vulnerabilities pose a serious threat because they allow attackers to manipulate user sessions and data. One of the most damaging outcomes is **session hijacking**, where an attacker uses a malicious script to steal session cookies—small pieces of data that keep users logged into their accounts.

For example, an attacker might inject a script that captures a user's session ID from their cookies and sends it to the attacker's server. The attacker can then use this session ID to impersonate the user and gain unauthorized access to their account, effectively taking control of the victim's session.

Another significant consequence of XSS is the ability to **inject malicious scripts** into webpages viewed by unsuspecting users. Attackers can craft scripts to perform harmful actions such as:

- **Redirecting users to phishing sites.**

- **Loading keyloggers** to steal sensitive data like login credentials.

- **Modifying webpage content** to deceive users or trick them into taking unintended actions.

In more severe cases, injected scripts can even disable security mechanisms within the application, leading to further vulnerabilities.

## Best Practices for Developers to Prevent XSS Vulnerabilities

To protect web applications from XSS attacks, developers must adhere to several best practices throughout the development lifecycle. Implementing these measures ensures the integrity and security of web applications and safeguards users from exploitation.

### 1. Output Encoding

One of the most effective strategies to prevent XSS is **output encoding**. Before rendering user-generated content or any untrusted data in the browser, it is critical to encode this data properly. This involves converting special characters, such as < and >, into their HTML entity equivalents (e.g., &lt; and &gt;). By doing this, even if an attacker injects malicious scripts, they will be displayed as plain text rather than executed as code.

Developers can leverage libraries or frameworks that handle output encoding automatically. Modern frameworks like **React** and **Angular** offer built-in methods to ensure dynamic content is handled safely, dramatically reducing the risk of XSS vulnerabilities.

### 2. Content Security Policy (CSP)

Implementing a **Content Security Policy (CSP)** is another robust defense mechanism against XSS attacks. A CSP defines which content sources (e.g., scripts, stylesheets) are considered trusted and blocks everything else. For example, a CSP can restrict JavaScript execution to only scripts loaded from a specific domain, reducing the likelihood of malicious scripts being executed.

To implement a CSP, developers can configure an HTTP header on their web server that instructs browsers on how to handle content from different sources. It is essential to review and update CSP settings regularly to ensure they provide adequate protection without breaking legitimate application functionality.

### 3. Avoiding Inline JavaScript

Using **inline JavaScript**—JavaScript written directly within the HTML markup—introduces unnecessary risks as it increases the chances of XSS vulnerabilities. A more secure approach is to separate JavaScript into external files, which can then be linked to the HTML page. This practice enhances code organization and facilitates security measures like CSP, which can block inline scripts by default.

By avoiding inline JavaScript and using external scripts, developers can better manage their codebase and reduce the risk of executing untrusted or malicious code, resulting in cleaner and more secure web applications.

# Automated Tools

Automated tools are essential for streamlining the web application penetration testing process, making it more efficient and comprehensive. Several powerful tools, available in Kali Linux, can quickly and accurately identify vulnerabilities, saving time while ensuring thorough assessments. Among the most widely used tools are **Burp Suite** and **OWASP ZAP**, each with unique strengths suited to different testing needs. Selecting the appropriate tool for specific tasks is crucial to maximize efficiency and results.

## 1. Burp Suite

**Burp Suite** is highly regarded for its extensive features tailored specifically for vulnerability assessments and penetration testing. It offers robust capabilities, including intercepting HTTP requests and responses, scanning for vulnerabilities, and supporting manual testing.

One of Burp Suite's standout features is its ability to detect **token entropy and randomness**, which is vital for cryptographic analysis and evaluating the security of session cookies (Joseph, 2023).

Additionally, Burp Suite allows users to perform **text or regex searches** within HTTP requests and server responses, providing flexible options for in-depth analysis.

Burp's **active scanning** capability can uncover a wide range of vulnerabilities, from **SQL injection** to **cross-site scripting (XSS)**, making it a versatile tool for penetration testers. Its integrated manual testing functionalities, such as **Repeater** and **Intruder**, allow testers to fine-tune and exploit vulnerabilities uncovered during automated scans.

## 2. OWASP ZAP

In contrast, **OWASP ZAP** is an open-source tool that excels in **API integration** and automation, making it an ideal choice for **DevOps** and **DevSecOps** environments. ZAP's robust **API support** allows it to integrate seamlessly into **continuous integration and continuous development (CI/CD)** pipelines, offering a significant advantage over Burp Suite for developers who need to incorporate security checks into their development workflows.

While ZAP may lack some native capabilities found in Burp Suite, such as token entropy detection and advanced request searching (Joseph, 2023), it offers extensive functionality through various extensions. ZAP's **ease of use** and **community-driven development** make it a strong choice for both beginners and experienced professionals.

Additionally, ZAP's **spidering** feature efficiently maps web applications by crawling accessible endpoints, and its **active scanning** capability identifies common vulnerabilities, such as insecure configurations and missing security headers.

## Effective Use of Burp Suite and OWASP ZAP

To harness the full potential of these tools, proper configuration is key.

- **For Burp Suite**, start by setting up the proxy to intercept traffic between the browser and the web application. This configuration allows you to inspect, modify, and analyze HTTP requests and responses in real time. Ensure **SSL/TLS interception** is enabled to handle encrypted traffic, giving you complete visibility of the application's behavior. Once configured, Burp's **passive and active scanners** can be fine-tuned to focus on specific vulnerabilities, providing a detailed analysis of potential threats.

- **For OWASP ZAP**, begin by setting up the local proxy and ensuring SSL certificates are correctly installed in the browser to capture all traffic. Use ZAP's spidering functionality to explore the entire web application, identifying all endpoints. Enable both **active** and **passive scanning** to uncover weaknesses, and adjust the scan settings to align with your testing goals. ZAP's **API integration** allows it to be integrated into CI/CD pipelines, ensuring continuous monitoring and rapid detection of new vulnerabilities as the application evolves.

# Combining Automation and Manual Testing

While automated tools like Burp Suite and OWASP ZAP are excellent for quickly identifying common vulnerabilities, their true power lies in their ability to complement **manual testing**. Automated scans efficiently detect potential issues such as SQL injection points or missing security headers, but manual verification and exploitation are often necessary to confirm and fully understand these vulnerabilities.

For example, an automated scan might highlight a vulnerable input field susceptible to **SQL injection**. A penetration tester can then manually craft tailored payloads to test whether sensitive data can be extracted, validating the vulnerability and assessing its real impact. In Burp Suite, features like **Repeater** and **Intruder** allow for manual testing, while in OWASP ZAP, testers can leverage custom scripts and fine-tune attacks to explore more complex vulnerabilities.

Manual testing is particularly critical for identifying vulnerabilities that automated tools may overlook, such as **business logic flaws** or issues related to unique application behaviors. These flaws often require human intuition and experience to detect and exploit, as they may not fit the patterns that automated scanners are designed to identify.

### Balancing Automation and Manual Testing

While automated tools significantly speed up the identification of common security issues, they can also generate **false positives**—flagging vulnerabilities that don't exist. Conversely, they may miss more subtle, nuanced issues that require human insight. For this reason, relying solely on automated tools is insufficient for a thorough penetration test. Combining the efficiency of automated scans with the depth of manual testing ensures a comprehensive assessment of the application's security.

By integrating both approaches, penetration testers can provide a detailed and accurate evaluation, uncovering critical vulnerabilities that automated tools might miss and confirming the real impact of potential threats.

In the next chapter, we'll delve into advanced topics such as **reverse engineering** and **malware analysis**, providing a deeper understanding of how to analyze and protect against complex threats.

# CHAPTER 6

# Reverse Engineering and Malware Analysis

In October 2017, the **Reaper botnet**, also known as "IoT Reaper," gained notoriety for its ability to exploit multiple vulnerabilities in Internet of Things (IoT) devices. Its decentralized structure and advanced capabilities made it a significant cybersecurity threat. Fortunately, the combined efforts of Cisco's **Talos Intelligence Group** and other independent researchers helped neutralize the threat. Their approach? Reverse engineering the malware to understand its inner workings and dismantling it from within.

This chapter delves into the essential techniques of **reverse engineering** and **malware analysis**—two critical skills for cybersecurity professionals. By breaking down malicious software, experts can uncover how it operates, what damage it can cause, and how to defend against it. Let's explore both **static** and **dynamic** analysis methods to help you protect systems from advanced threats.

## Static Analysis Techniques

**Static analysis** refers to examining malware without executing it, offering an in-depth understanding of its structure and functionality. Here are some of the primary techniques used in static analysis:

### 1. File Type Identification

The first step in malware analysis is identifying the file type. Knowing the file type helps determine which tools and methodologies are appropriate for the analysis.

For example:

- If the malware is an **executable file** (e.g., `.exe`), tools like **CFF Explorer** or **PE Studio** can be used to analyze the file's internal structure.

- For **script-based or document malware**, such as those embedded in **Word documents** or **PDFs**, tools like **OfficeMalScanner** are more suitable.

Correctly identifying the file type ensures that analysts apply the most effective tools and avoid misleading assumptions.

## 2. Header Examination

Another critical component of static analysis is examining **Portable Executable (PE) headers**, which contain metadata about the file, such as code sections, libraries, and required resources.

For example:

- **PEview** or **Dependency Walker** can provide a detailed overview of the PE structure, revealing key indicators of compromise (IOCs).

- Unusual timestamps, suspicious imports, or modified entry points may indicate that the file has been tampered with or is behaving maliciously.

By scrutinizing these details, analysts can uncover the malware's intent and potential attack vectors (Baker, 2023).

## 3. String Extraction

**String extraction** is another powerful technique. It involves pulling readable characters from the malware's binary file, which can provide valuable clues about its functionality.

These strings might include:

- **URLs** or **IP addresses** related to the malware's command-and-control (C2) server.

- **Registry keys**, **file paths**, or **function names** that point to its targeted systems.

Tools like **Strings by Sysinternals** or **BinText** can help extract and analyze these strings, offering insights into the malware's purpose. For instance, if you find strings referencing certain system files or network addresses, you can form hypotheses about how the malware operates.

### 4. Control Flow Graphs (CFG)

**Control Flow Graphs (CFGs)** map out the malware's execution flow, showing how different parts of the program are linked. Visualizing the paths taken during execution can help analysts predict the malware's behavior without running it.

CFGs can reveal:

- **Obfuscated code** sections designed to hide the malware's real intentions.

- **Redundant paths** meant to confuse or delay analysis, allowing attackers to evade detection.

Tools like **IDA Pro** can help generate CFGs, providing a clearer picture of the malware's execution logic.

# Dynamic Analysis Methods

**Dynamic analysis** involves running the malware in a controlled environment to observe its behavior in real time. This method is essential for understanding how malware interacts with a system and what damage it can cause.

Here are the key dynamic analysis techniques:

### 1. System Monitoring

Monitoring system activities such as file system changes, registry modifications, and network communications provides invaluable insight into how malware interacts with its host system.

- **File system monitoring** tracks any attempts to create, delete, or modify files, which can indicate data theft or malicious activities.

- **Registry monitoring** helps identify persistent malware by tracking changes to registry keys in Windows systems. Malicious programs often modify the registry to maintain persistence or alter system settings.

- **Network monitoring** reveals how the infected machine communicates with external servers, often exposing how it sends stolen data or receives commands from its C2 server.

Tools like **Process Monitor** and **Wireshark** can be used to capture and analyze these activities in real-time.

### 2. Debugging

**Debugging** is an essential technique for deep analysis of the malware's code. By using debuggers, security professionals can step through the malware's execution, line by line, to uncover hidden functions, conditional behaviors, and payloads.

- **OllyDbg** or **WinDbg** are popular debuggers that provide granular control over the execution flow.

- By setting **breakpoints** at specific code locations, analysts can pause the malware's execution to inspect memory, registers, and variables.

This method helps reveal obfuscated routines or **anti-debugging techniques** that malware authors often employ to prevent analysis.

## Combining Static and Dynamic Analysis

In practice, static and dynamic analysis techniques complement each other. For example:

- **Static analysis** provides a high-level understanding of the malware's structure and capabilities without the risk of execution.

- **Dynamic analysis** confirms suspicions and uncovers the malware's real-world behavior by observing how it interacts with its environment.

Together, these methods offer a comprehensive view of how malware operates, allowing analysts to craft defenses or build patches to prevent future exploitation.

## Sandboxing

**Sandboxing** is a fundamental technique in malware analysis, providing a controlled and isolated environment to safely execute and observe malicious code without risking harm to the host machine or network. By running malware in a virtualized or containerized setup that mimics a normal operating system, analysts can closely monitor its behavior while ensuring that any destructive actions remain confined within the sandbox.

As **Firdiyanto (2023)** explains, sandboxing facilitates comprehensive behavior analysis, enabling security professionals to observe various system interactions, including network communications, file modifications, and registry changes. Even if the malware attempts to spread or perform harmful activities, the sandbox keeps these actions contained, safeguarding the analyst's primary system and network.

### *Evasion Techniques and Detection*

Some sophisticated malware is designed to detect whether it is being run in a sandbox environment and may alter its behavior to evade detection. For example, the malware might check for virtual machine (VM) markers, such as specific hardware configurations or the presence of monitoring tools. If detected, the malware may go dormant, delay execution, or act benignly.

Understanding and mitigating these evasion techniques is critical for effective sandboxing. By configuring the sandbox to closely mimic real-world environments, including installing common applications and mimicking typical user activity, analysts can coax the malware into revealing its true behavior. Refining sandbox configurations and adjusting parameters such as system resources and network activity helps improve detection capabilities.

### *Dynamic Analysis in a Sandbox*

Dynamic analysis in a sandbox complements static analysis by allowing analysts to observe the malware's real-time interactions with the system. While static analysis examines the malware's code without executing it, dynamic analysis reveals how the malware behaves when it runs, offering deeper insights into its functionality.

One key advantage of sandboxing is the ability to **capture network traffic** during the malware's execution. This helps identify communication with **command-and-control (C2)** servers, **data exfiltration attempts**, or **lateral movement** within a network. Monitoring outgoing and incoming traffic can reveal malicious activities, such as attempts to send sensitive information (e.g., keystrokes, screenshots) to remote servers. This information is crucial for incident response teams to develop effective countermeasures.

### *Tools for Monitoring System Activities*

To thoroughly analyze malware within a sandbox, analysts use a range of tools to monitor system activities in real-time:

- **Process Monitor (ProcMon)**: A powerful file monitoring tool from Sysinternals, **ProcMon** allows analysts to track file system changes, registry modifications, and process creations as they occur. It also offers customizable filters to focus on specific events, making it easier to pinpoint malware-related activities.

- **Regshot**: A registry monitoring tool that takes snapshots of the registry before and after malware execution, allowing analysts to detect which registry keys were altered by the malware. This helps identify persistence mechanisms or system configuration changes that the malware uses to stay active.

- **Wireshark**: A network protocol analyzer that captures and inspects network traffic, providing insights into any communication between the infected system and external servers. This tool helps identify potential C2 communications or malicious data transmissions.

### *Setting Up a Virtual Machine for Sandboxing*

Virtual machines (VMs) provide an ideal platform for creating isolated environments where malware can be analyzed without risking damage to the host system. Proper configuration is essential to ensure the VM closely resembles a standard user environment, making the malware believe it is running on a real system.

- **Install commonly used applications** and **regular system updates** to create a realistic environment.

- **Maintain typical user privileges** to mimic everyday user behavior, as this can elicit more authentic malware behavior.

- **Snapshots and rollbacks** are crucial for efficient testing. Snapshots allow analysts to capture the VM's state at a specific point in time, making it easy to revert to a clean state if the malware causes significant damage. This saves time and enables repeat tests under the same conditions to compare results.

# Hybrid Analysis: Combining Static and Dynamic Techniques

**Hybrid analysis** merges the benefits of both static and dynamic analysis, offering a more comprehensive understanding of malware behavior. This approach allows analysts to detect vulnerabilities and behaviors that might be missed by using only one method.

- **Static analysis** provides a deep understanding of the malware's structure, while **dynamic analysis** reveals its real-time behavior.

- After observing suspicious activities during dynamic analysis, static tools can be used to dissect **memory dumps** or other system artifacts, helping uncover additional indicators of compromise (IOCs).

This combined approach ensures a more robust and thorough malware analysis, providing insights that enhance both detection and mitigation strategies (Baker, 2023).

### *The Advantage of Hybrid Analysis*

Hybrid analysis is particularly useful for uncovering malware that employs sophisticated evasion tactics or hides critical payloads. For instance, after dynamic analysis reveals unusual behavior or communication patterns, static analysis can dissect these interactions in more detail, allowing analysts to identify hidden code, backdoors, or encryption routines.

By leveraging the strengths of both methods, hybrid analysis provides a fuller picture of the malware's behavior, ultimately leading to more effective defenses against future attacks.

# Social Engineering Attacks

Have you heard of the "Bait and Switch" attack? It's a form of cyberattack and an advanced one, too.

In this scenario, an attacker posed as a delivery person and gained access to the office using a legitimate-looking company uniform and identification badge.

The attacker had prearranged with an insider to deliver what appeared to be a new piece of office equipment that the target company was expecting.

Once inside the building, the attacker took advantage of the pretext, engaging employees in casual conversation and establishing rapport. While performing the "delivery," they subtly looked around to gather information about the office's layout and security measures.

Here are more social engineering attacks:

| Attack type | Brief overview | Examples |
|---|---|---|
| Phishing | An attacker sends emails that appear to be from trusted sources, tricking users into providing sensitive information. | Fake bank alerts requesting account verification. |
| Pretexting | The attacker creates a fabricated scenario to steal personal information or gain access. | Posing as tech support to gain access to a company's network. |
| Tailgating | An attacker follows an authorized person into a restricted area. | Sneaking into a secure building behind an employee. |
| Spear phishing | Targeted phishing is aimed at specific individuals or organizations to steal sensitive data. | Personalized emails that contain details about the recipient. |

| | | |
|---|---|---|
| Vishing | Voice phishing, where attackers use phone calls to trick victims into revealing personal information. | A caller pretending to be from a bank asking for account details. |
| Quizzing | The attacker uses seemingly innocent questions to gather personal information. | Asking a person about their favorite pet to gain password hints. |
| Watering hole attack | The attacker infects websites the target frequents, allowing malware to spread unknowingly. | Compromising a site frequented by employees of a particular organization. |
| Impersonation | The attacker pretends to be someone else, often in a position of authority, to manipulate the target. | Someone posing as a company executive requesting sensitive information. |

# Deobfuscating Malicious Code

Malware authors often employ a variety of **obfuscation techniques** to conceal their code's true purpose, making it difficult for analysts to understand and mitigate the threats posed by the malicious software. The goal of these techniques is to hinder analysis by security researchers and evade detection from automated scanning tools.

### Identifying Common Obfuscation Techniques

Obfuscation techniques are designed to hide the malicious intent of the code and make reverse engineering more challenging. Some of the most common methods include **XOR encoding** and **string encryption**. Understanding these techniques is crucial for deobfuscating and revealing the underlying malicious functionality.

### XOR Encoding

**XOR encoding** is a straightforward but highly effective technique often used in data encoding and encryption. XOR stands for **"exclusive OR"**, a logical operation that compares two binary bits. The result is 1 (true) if the bits are different and 0 (false) if they are the same.

In malware, XOR encoding is used to scramble data, making it look unintelligible until it's decoded. Here's a simplified explanation:

1. **The XOR Operation**: At its core, XOR compares two bits:

   o 1 XOR 0 = 1

   o 0 XOR 1 = 1

   o 1 XOR 1 = 0

   o 0 XOR 0 = 0

2. **Data and Key**: The process starts with the **original data** (e.g., a piece of malware or sensitive information) and a **key** (a sequence of bits). The XOR operation is applied between the data and the key, producing encoded output.

3. **Reversibility**: XOR encoding is **reversible**—by applying the same XOR operation again with the same key, you can decode the data back to its original form.

For example, if your original data is `"malicious"`, applying XOR encoding with a key scrambles the data, making it unreadable. To reverse the process and recover the original string, XOR the scrambled data with the same key again.

Although XOR encoding is relatively simple, it's still effective at hiding data, particularly when combined with other techniques or a sufficiently complex key. However, it's also a common technique, and automated tools can often detect and decode XOR-encoded malware.

### *String Encryption*

**String encryption** is another obfuscation method that conceals readable text (such as API calls, file paths, or domain names) within a program. This makes it harder for antivirus programs and static analysis tools to recognize suspicious strings within the code.

A widely used algorithm for string encryption is **RC4**, a stream cipher that encrypts data by combining it with a keystream generated from a variable-length key. This results in an encrypted output that is almost impossible to understand without knowing the decryption key.

- **RC4 Encryption Process:**

  o RC4 generates a keystream based on the encryption key.

  o The plaintext (original string) is XOR'd with the keystream, producing an encrypted version of the string.

  o The result is a string of random-looking characters that masks the original data.

For instance, the word "malware" might be transformed into a series of unreadable characters like Kj28!zX1#, making it nearly impossible to identify without decrypting the string first.

This technique allows malware to hide its intent, including API calls or function names, which are key indicators for security tools. Without proper decryption, analysts and security tools will struggle to understand the full scope of the malware's functionality.

*Tools for Deobfuscation*

Deobfuscating malicious code often requires specialized tools that can reverse the obfuscation process, allowing analysts to view and interpret the hidden functionality.

Here are key tools used in the deobfuscation process:

- **Decompiler**: A decompiler translates binary executables back into high-level source code, which provides a more understandable view of the malware's logic and behavior. While decompilers don't always generate perfect source code, they can offer valuable insights into what the code is trying to accomplish.

  o **Example**: **Ghidra** is a widely used open-source decompiler that helps security analysts reverse-engineer malicious binaries by generating human-readable code from executables.

- **Disassembler**: Disassemblers convert binary machine code into low-level assembly instructions. Although this process doesn't recover the original high-level programming code, it can still reveal how the malware interacts with the system at the hardware level, showing the actual operations being carried out by the CPU.

  o **Example**: **IDA Pro** is one of the most powerful disassemblers available, offering deep insights into malware by translating its binary instructions into assembly code for closer inspection.

Using these tools, analysts can reconstruct the original behavior of the malware and uncover hidden instructions. This is crucial for developing effective countermeasures and enhancing overall cybersecurity defenses.

Here are the tools you should consider using:

| Decompilers | Disassemblers |
|---|---|
| Ghidra | IDA Pro |
| Uncompyle6 | Radare2 |
| JEB Decompiler | Binary Ninja |
| RetDec | Hopper |
| Dedaub | OllyDbg |

## Tailored Malware Analysis Tools

When dealing with complex malware, specialized tools like **Mandiant's FLOSS** and **CAPA** play a crucial role in deobfuscation. These tools are designed to emulate deobfuscation routines, revealing hidden strings, embedded functionality, and malware behavior that would otherwise remain obscured.

Effectively utilizing these tools can significantly streamline the reverse engineering process, making it easier for analysts to dissect malicious code. However, choosing the right tool depends on the **complexity of the malware** and the **specific obfuscation techniques** being used. Combining multiple tools often enhances the accuracy and depth of the analysis, ensuring no important details are overlooked.

## Manual vs. Automated Deobfuscation

Deobfuscation can be approached through either manual methods or automated tools, each offering distinct advantages and limitations:

### *Manual Deobfuscation*

Manual deobfuscation relies heavily on the analyst's expertise. It involves manually decoding obfuscated code by analyzing patterns, understanding encryption algorithms, and writing custom scripts to reverse-engineer the malware.

- **Precision**: This method offers greater control over the deobfuscation process, making it particularly useful for highly complex or heavily obfuscated malware.

- **Time-Consuming**: The downside is that it is labor-intensive and time-consuming, especially when dealing with advanced malware that uses sophisticated obfuscation techniques.

For instance, when faced with XOR encryption or multi-layered string obfuscation, an experienced analyst can write scripts to reverse these techniques step by step, providing deeper insights into the malware's structure.

### *Automated Deobfuscation*

Automated tools quickly decode obfuscated code without requiring extensive manual intervention. Tools like **UNPACME** can automatically unpack and deobfuscate packed malware samples, significantly speeding up the analysis process.

- **Efficiency**: Automated deobfuscation is ideal for straightforward or less complex malware, enabling analysts to rapidly assess malicious code and gain a general understanding of its behavior.

- **Limitations**: However, these tools may struggle with more complex or novel obfuscation techniques, which can result in missed details or incomplete deobfuscation.

For example, malware that employs unique or custom obfuscation methods may bypass automated detection or unpacking, requiring manual intervention to fully reverse-engineer the code.

## Combining Manual and Automated Deobfuscation

The effectiveness of manual versus automated deobfuscation often depends on the **analyst's familiarity** with the obfuscation methods and the **complexity of the malware**. In many cases, combining both approaches yields the best results.

- **Manual methods** allow for precise control and a deeper understanding of the malware, particularly when dealing with custom or advanced obfuscation.

- **Automated tools** can handle the more routine aspects of deobfuscation, quickly identifying common obfuscation patterns and significantly reducing the time spent on analysis.

By leveraging the strengths of both approaches, analysts can maximize the efficiency and accuracy of their deobfuscation efforts.

## Extracting Functionality Through Focused Analysis

In malware analysis, focusing on **specific modules** or functions within the obfuscated code can lead to more targeted and effective examination. This strategy involves isolating critical components of the malware, such as sections that interact with system APIs or perform suspicious activities, which often contain the most important functionality.

### Techniques for Focused Analysis:

1. **Function Identification**: Identifying and isolating functions that interact with system-level APIs or execute potentially malicious tasks allows analysts to concentrate on the most significant parts of the malware. Tools like **IDA Pro** help map out function calls, interactions, and behavior, making it easier to trace the malware's logic and understand its objectives.

2. **Code Segment Evaluation**: Breaking down large, complex malware into smaller segments and analyzing these sections individually simplifies the deobfuscation process. This modular approach is particularly helpful for understanding malware that uses multiple layers of obfuscation or complex control flows, as it allows for incremental analysis.

In the next chapter, we'll dive into the tactics used by **Advanced Persistent Threats (APTs)**, exploring how they infiltrate and maintain long-term access to targeted networks.

# CHAPTER 7

# Advanced Persistent Threats Tactics

Cozy Bear, also known as **APT29**, is a highly sophisticated Russian cyber espionage group linked to the Russian Foreign Intelligence Service (SVR). Their activities underscore the growing threat posed by state-sponsored cyber espionage, targeting governments, critical infrastructure, and major corporations. The operations of groups like Cozy Bear exemplify the advanced tactics used in cyber warfare, raising serious concerns about national security and the integrity of global cyber defenses.

In this chapter, we will dive into the **tactics** and **methodologies** employed by groups like Cozy Bear, with a focus on understanding their attack strategies, lifecycle, and the defenses necessary to mitigate such threats. By gaining insights into these tactics, you can better prepare your cyber defenses against nation-state actors and other advanced adversaries.

## Understanding the Advanced Persistent Threat (APT) Lifecycle

An **Advanced Persistent Threat (APT)** attack is one of the most challenging and sophisticated forms of cyber assault. Unlike quick, opportunistic attacks, APTs are carefully orchestrated, long-term operations aimed at infiltrating a target's network, remaining undetected, and extracting valuable information or causing significant disruption. These attacks often persist for months, if not years, allowing the attacker continuous access to a compromised system.

Understanding the **APT lifecycle** is critical in recognizing the phases of an attack and deploying countermeasures at each stage.

### *Phases of an APT Attack*

The lifecycle of an APT typically unfolds through the following phases:

1. **Reconnaissance**: In this phase, attackers focus on gathering intelligence about their target. Using techniques such as **open-source intelligence (OSINT)** and **social engineering**, they learn about the organization's infrastructure, key personnel, and potential vulnerabilities. Attackers may also use scanning tools to map the target's network and identify weak points.

2. **Infiltration**: Armed with intelligence from the reconnaissance phase, attackers exploit vulnerabilities to gain access. Common techniques include **spear-phishing emails** containing malicious attachments or links, exploiting unpatched software, and leveraging stolen or compromised credentials.

3. **Establishing a Foothold**: Once inside the network, attackers install **backdoors** or malware that allows them to maintain access, even if initial vulnerabilities are patched. They use **custom malware** and **remote administration tools (RATs)** to solidify their presence and ensure persistence.

4. **Lateral Movement**: Attackers extend their control over the network by moving laterally, often using **credential harvesting** and exploiting **trust relationships** between systems. This allows them to escalate privileges, access sensitive data, and increase their hold over the environment.

5. **Data Exfiltration and Persistence**: The ultimate goal of APTs is usually to extract valuable data—whether that's intellectual property, classified information, or personal data. Attackers use **encrypted channels** or stealth techniques to avoid detection. They may also employ multiple persistence mechanisms to ensure continued access to the compromised system, even if some aspects of the attack are uncovered.

## Common Attack Vectors

APTs rely on several key attack vectors to gain access and achieve their objectives. Understanding these pathways is essential for building robust defenses.

### *Exploiting Software Vulnerabilities*

Attackers frequently target unpatched or outdated software to gain access. Software bugs, whether in **operating systems**, **applications**, or **middleware**, provide openings that hackers can exploit to infiltrate a system. Timely installation of security patches is critical in mitigating this risk. Vulnerabilities such as the **EternalBlue exploit** used in the WannaCry ransomware attack demonstrate how dangerous unpatched systems can be.

### *Supply Chain Attacks*

In **supply chain attacks**, hackers infiltrate less secure third-party suppliers or service providers to gain access to the ultimate target. By compromising vendors or subcontractors with weaker security protocols, attackers can infiltrate larger, more secure organizations upstream. The **SolarWinds attack**, where attackers compromised a widely used IT management software to breach major companies and government agencies, exemplifies the far-reaching impact of supply chain vulnerabilities.

## Indicators of Compromise (IOCs)

**Indicators of Compromise (IOCs)** are forensic markers that signal a potential security breach. Identifying IOCs quickly can help organizations respond before an attack escalates. Key IOCs include:

- **Unusual network traffic**: A sudden spike in outbound traffic could indicate **data exfiltration**. Monitoring network traffic for anomalies is essential for spotting early signs of a breach.

- **Unrecognized processes**: Unknown processes running on a system may be linked to malware. Regular audits of system processes help to detect rogue software.

- **Modified files or protocols**: Unexpected changes to system files or protocol behaviors could indicate tampering or unauthorized access.

- **Failed login attempts**: A surge in failed login attempts might point to a **brute-force attack** aimed at stealing credentials.

## Real-World Case Studies of APT Attacks

Real-world examples illustrate how APT attacks unfold and the consequences they bring.

- **SolarWinds Attack (2020)**: This infamous supply chain attack was orchestrated by **Cozy Bear (APT29)**. By embedding malicious code into the widely used SolarWinds Orion software, attackers gained access to multiple U.S. government agencies and Fortune 500 companies. The attack remained undetected for months, demonstrating the sophistication of APT strategies.

- **Hafnium Attack (2021)**: This Chinese state-sponsored group exploited vulnerabilities in **Microsoft Exchange Server**, allowing them to access sensitive emails and exfiltrate data from defense contractors, research institutions, and government entities. The attackers used zero-day vulnerabilities to gain entry and quickly spread across compromised networks.

- **APT41**: A versatile Chinese group known for targeting industries ranging from healthcare to finance. Their activities included stealing **intellectual property**, conducting **financial fraud**, and exploiting software vulnerabilities. In 2020, the U.S. Department of Justice indicted several members of APT41, highlighting the international reach and complexity of their operations.

# Guidelines for Defense Against APTs

Defending against APTs requires a **multi-layered defense strategy**, often referred to as **defense in depth**. This approach employs multiple layers of security measures, making it difficult for attackers to penetrate and compromise systems.

1. **Timely Patch Management**: Regularly apply security patches to address known vulnerabilities. This practice helps mitigate exploitation attempts targeting outdated software.

2. **Network Segmentation**: Isolating critical systems through **network segmentation** reduces lateral movement, making it harder for attackers to gain access to sensitive areas.

3. **Behavioral Monitoring and Threat Detection**: Implement **behavioral monitoring tools** that analyze user and system behavior. These tools can detect anomalies that might indicate an APT in progress.

4. **Zero-Trust Architecture**: Adopting a **zero-trust** approach, where every request for access is authenticated and verified, reduces the risk of unauthorized access.

5. **Regular Penetration Testing**: Frequent **penetration testing** simulates APT tactics, allowing organizations to identify weaknesses before real attackers exploit them.

## Gaining and Maintaining Persistence

APT actors are known for their resilience and creativity, often employing a range of sophisticated techniques to ensure long-term access to compromised networks. Their goal is not just to infiltrate a system but to maintain a **stealthy presence** for extended periods, allowing them to continue their operations undetected. These persistence methods ensure that even if parts of their attack are uncovered or removed, they can still regain access and continue their malicious activities.

Here are some of the most effective methods used to gain and maintain access:

## Credential Dumping and Reuse

One of the critical stages in an APT attack is **credential dumping**, where attackers extract login credentials from compromised systems. By obtaining usernames and passwords, attackers can deepen their access across the network. Tools like **Mimikatz** are often employed to harvest credentials directly from memory, capturing **plaintext usernames and passwords**.

Attackers target various operating system components, including the **Security Account Manager (SAM)** database on Windows systems and the **/etc/passwd** and **/etc/shadow** files on Linux. They also exploit cached domain credentials and mine **Local Security Authority Subsystem Service (LSASS)** memory for valuable login data.

Once credentials are harvested, they are reused to move laterally across the network, impersonating legitimate users to evade detection. This technique allows attackers to escalate privileges and compromise other connected systems or networks, further expanding their reach.

To defend against **credential dumping**, organizations should:

- Implement **multifactor authentication (MFA)** to minimize reliance on static passwords.

- Restrict **administrative privileges** and use separate accounts for standard and elevated tasks.

- Regularly **monitor and refresh credentials** and reduce the lifetime of cached credentials.

## Command and Control (C2) Setup

Establishing a **Command and Control (C2) infrastructure** is essential for APT actors to sustain their operations within a network. C2 channels enable attackers to send commands, retrieve data, and coordinate further attacks—all while maintaining a low profile.

APT actors often leverage legitimate external services, such as social media platforms or cloud services, as part of their C2 channels, making the traffic appear benign. More covertly, attackers use techniques like **DNS tunneling** or **HTTPS-based C2 communications** to blend their traffic with normal web activity, making detection difficult.

To combat C2 setups, organizations should:

- Use **network traffic analysis** tools to spot unusual communication patterns.

- Enforce **strict firewall rules** to control outgoing traffic.

- Deploy **sandboxing technologies** to isolate suspicious processes and analyze them in a controlled environment.

- Regularly engage in **threat hunting** exercises to identify C2 traffic indicators before attackers can act.

## Evading Detection Mechanisms

APT actors are highly skilled in evasion tactics, utilizing multiple methods to remain undetected while they execute their objectives. These techniques are designed to bypass security tools and conceal their presence within the network.

### *Disabling Security Tools*

One of the first steps APT actors take is disabling security tools such as firewalls, antivirus software, and intrusion detection systems (IDS). By doing this, attackers neutralize defenses that would otherwise alert security teams to their presence. For example, if an attacker disables antivirus software on a target system, they can freely introduce malware without triggering alarms.

To defend against this, organizations should:

- Regularly check the operational status of security tools.

- Ensure **automatic updates and maintenance** of security software.

- Implement **application whitelisting** to prevent unauthorized changes to critical systems.

### *Altering Logs*

Attackers often manipulate or delete system logs to cover their tracks. Logs are crucial for forensic analysis, providing a record of system activities. By altering or erasing these logs, attackers make it difficult for security teams to reconstruct their activities and trace the breach.

To protect logs from tampering:

- Implement **logging practices** that create regular backups.

- Use **immutable logs** stored in secure, tamper-evident environments.

- Deploy tools that generate alerts for unusual log modifications or deletions.

### *Using Encryption to Conceal Malicious Traffic*

Encryption is frequently used by APT actors to hide their malicious activities. By encrypting communication between compromised systems and external C2 servers, attackers make it harder for security tools to analyze the content and detect suspicious behavior. For instance, exfiltrating sensitive data over an encrypted channel can make the activity invisible to intrusion detection systems (IDS).

Organizations should:

- Implement **network monitoring solutions** that detect anomalies in encrypted traffic patterns.

- Deploy **TLS inspection** tools to analyze encrypted traffic for potential threats.

### *Custom Malware*

APT actors often develop **custom malware** specifically designed to evade detection. Unlike off-the-shelf malware that antivirus solutions are trained to detect, custom malware can slip through standard defenses. Attackers may use **polymorphic malware**, which changes its code with every execution, making it difficult for traditional security solutions to detect and flag.

## Data Exfiltration Strategies

One of the primary goals of APT actors is to **exfiltrate sensitive data** from the target network without being detected. To achieve this, they employ various sophisticated techniques that enable them to remove valuable information discreetly.

### *Common Exfiltration Techniques*

- **Direct Transfer**: Attackers may use standard protocols like FTP or SCP to move data directly to an external server. Although straightforward, this method can be detected if traffic is monitored carefully.

- **Tunneling and Encapsulation**: Attackers often encapsulate stolen data within legitimate-looking traffic, using protocols like SSH, VPNs, or DNS tunneling to avoid detection.

- **Cloud Services**: Using cloud storage services like **Dropbox**, **Google Drive**, or **AWS S3**, attackers upload stolen data while blending with normal cloud activity. Since many organizations rely on cloud services, this method can easily evade detection.

- **Removable Media**: In some cases, attackers may use **USB drives** or other removable media to exfiltrate data, especially in environments where network monitoring is strong but physical security is lax.

- **Email Attachments**: Attackers may email stolen data as encrypted attachments to external addresses, bypassing traditional **Data Loss Prevention (DLP)** systems.

### *Stealthy Data Exfiltration Methods*

- **Encryption and Compression**: Attackers often compress and encrypt data before exfiltration, speeding up transfers and concealing the content. Commonly used utilities include **Lz77** for compression and **AES** for encryption.

- **Steganography**: By embedding data within innocuous-looking files like images or audio files, attackers can hide stolen data using tools like **LSB-Steganography**.

- **Living off the Land**: Attackers often use built-in system tools like **PowerShell** or **native Linux commands** to avoid introducing new, detectable elements to the system. This method allows them to carry out malicious activities without raising red flags.

## Target Selection for Exfiltration

Advanced Persistent Threats (APTs) are patient and methodical, carefully planning their actions to maximize the impact of their operations. One of the most critical aspects of an APT attack is the selection of target data for exfiltration. APT actors don't rush; instead, they meticulously analyze the network to determine which data is most valuable and aligns with their objectives. Understanding this process provides insights into how APTs operate and why they choose specific data over others.

## Value of Data to APTs

APTs first evaluate the data within a compromised network to identify valuable information such as **trade secrets**, **customer details**, or **sensitive financial records**. The value of data is often tied to its **monetary potential**, **strategic leverage**, or **usefulness for future attacks**.

For example, stealing proprietary research from a pharmaceutical company can provide financial gains through corporate espionage, while compromising sensitive customer data can be used for identity theft or sold on the dark web. APTs prioritize data that offers the highest return on investment, whether it's for financial gain, competitive advantage, or long-term espionage.

## Relevance to Objectives

Beyond data value, APTs focus on **relevance** to their specific objectives. Each APT operation has distinct goals, whether it's **espionage**, **financial theft**, or **disruption of critical services**. The data selected for extraction directly supports these goals.

For instance, if the objective is **corporate espionage**, attackers may target sensitive intellectual property or executive communication. If the aim is **disruption**, extracting operational documents or details that enable unauthorized access to key systems might be prioritized. By aligning their data selection with their goals, APTs ensure that their actions have the maximum possible impact.

## Factors Influencing Prioritization

Several key factors influence how APTs prioritize data for exfiltration. These factors demonstrate the **thoroughness** and **strategic foresight** that make APTs so dangerous.

- **Ease of Access**: Data that is easier to obtain, such as **unencrypted files** or **poorly protected databases**, is often the first target. APTs exploit vulnerabilities in network defenses, looking for weak points where they can access high-value data quickly and discreetly.

- **High-Impact Outcomes**: Data that has the potential to cause **significant damage** or **leverage future attacks** is prioritized. For example, stealing government contract details may enable APTs to **undermine national security** or **disrupt public services**.

- **Data Longevity**: APTs prefer data with a **longer shelf life**—information that remains valuable over time. **Historical financial data** or **previous contracts** may provide valuable insights for months or years, as opposed to data that becomes obsolete quickly.

## Observing Patterns in Data Usage

APTs don't just randomly extract data; they meticulously observe **patterns in data usage** and **access rights**. By monitoring how data is used within the organization, they can identify high-value targets, such as documents frequently accessed by executives or files related to **strategic planning**.

For example, if a specific document is repeatedly accessed by a senior executive, it likely contains crucial information about the company's long-term strategy. APTs will prioritize extracting this document over less frequently accessed files. Additionally, any unusual behavior, such as an employee suddenly accessing sensitive files, might indicate compromised credentials, which APTs will exploit for further data extraction.

## Timing of Data Extraction

The **timing** of data exfiltration is a strategic decision in an APT attack. APTs often choose to extract data when defenses are at their lowest, such as during **weekends**, **holidays**, or **system maintenance windows**, when there is less personnel actively monitoring systems.

They may also conduct **layered extractions**, initially extracting less critical data to establish a foothold within the network and build trust with the system before moving on to high-value, sensitive data. This patience and calculated timing are hallmarks of APT methodology, reflecting their ability to adapt and minimize detection.

## Utilizing Technology for Data Selection

Modern APTs increasingly use **advanced technology** to enhance their data selection process. Tools that leverage **machine learning (ML)** and **automation** help APTs quickly analyze vast amounts of data and identify **high-value targets** based on access patterns and historical behaviors.

By employing ML algorithms, APTs can detect trends in data access, pinpoint valuable information, and prioritize extraction based on **past usage** and **security configurations**. For example, if ML tools reveal that certain files are accessed before key meetings, those files might contain important operational details or strategies, making them prime targets.

## Preventive Measures for Data Loss

Understanding how APTs select and exfiltrate data allows organizations to better protect themselves. One of the major threats organizations face is **data exfiltration**, where sensitive information is transferred from a network without permission. Implementing **preventive measures** is critical for mitigating the risks posed by APTs.

### 1. Establishing a Comprehensive Security Policy

A robust **security policy** is the foundation of effective data protection. Organizations must outline **access controls**, **data classification** procedures, and **incident response plans** to safeguard sensitive information. Regular **audits** and **employee training** ensure compliance and raise awareness of potential threats.

### 2. Using Data Loss Prevention (DLP) Tools

**DLP tools** are essential for monitoring and preventing unauthorized data transfers. These tools can detect, block, and report suspicious activity, ensuring that sensitive information remains protected, even when accessed remotely. For example, DLP solutions can prevent sensitive documents from being uploaded to external sites or emailed to unauthorized recipients.

### 3. Employing Encryption Techniques

Encryption protects data by making it unreadable to unauthorized users. Organizations should implement **encryption** for data **at rest** and **in transit**, ensuring that even if attackers gain access, the information remains useless without the decryption key.

### 4. Restricting USB and External Device Usage

Limiting or disabling the use of **USB drives** and other external storage devices can reduce the risk of data exfiltration through physical means. Organizations can implement policies that block the use of unauthorized devices, ensuring that sensitive data isn't easily removed from the network.

### 5. Responding to Incidents Swiftly

Organizations must have a well-defined **incident response plan** to quickly address any breaches. Early detection and swift containment are key to minimizing the damage caused by data exfiltration. Regularly **testing** and **updating** the incident response plan ensures that it remains effective in a crisis.

# CHAPTER 8

# Wireless Network Penetration Testing

Wireless network penetration testing is an indispensable skill for cybersecurity professionals, as wireless networks remain a prime target for attackers with malicious intent. Without mastering this skill, organizations and individuals alike are vulnerable to various forms of wireless cyberattacks.

A notorious example is the **Evil Twin attack**. In this scenario, an attacker sets up a rogue wireless access point that mimics a legitimate one. Unsuspecting users may inadvertently connect to this malicious network, thinking it's a safe connection. Once connected, their sensitive information—such as passwords, emails, and credit card details—can be intercepted by the attacker, leading to identity theft or unauthorized financial transactions.

This type of attack highlights the inherent vulnerabilities in wireless networks and underscores the need for robust wireless security measures. In this chapter, I will guide you through the essentials of wireless network penetration testing, equipping you with the knowledge to uncover and mitigate these vulnerabilities before they can be exploited.

## Breaking WPA/WPA2 Security Protocols

Understanding the inner workings of WPA (Wi-Fi Protected Access) and WPA2 encryption protocols is fundamental for effective wireless network penetration testing. These security standards were developed to protect wireless communications, but they are not foolproof. Both WPA and

WPA2 have weaknesses that, when leveraged properly, can grant unauthorized access to the network.

### *What Is WPA/WPA2?*

WPA and WPA2 are security protocols developed to secure wireless networks, with WPA being introduced as a stopgap measure to address the severe flaws of its predecessor, Wired Equivalent Privacy (WEP). WPA used **Temporal Key Integrity Protocol (TKIP)** to enhance encryption, but WPA2 eventually replaced it with **Advanced Encryption Standard (AES)** for stronger, more secure encryption.

However, despite their widespread adoption, WPA and WPA2 have vulnerabilities that can be exploited. For example, one common weakness in WPA2 networks is the use of **weak passphrases**, which are prone to brute-force attacks. In these attacks, an adversary systematically tries different password combinations until the correct one is found.

Another significant vulnerability is the **Key Reinstallation Attack (KRACK)**. This exploit targets the WPA2 four-way handshake process, allowing an attacker within range of the network to manipulate cryptographic handshake messages. By exploiting this flaw, the attacker can reuse encryption keys, decrypt traffic, and even inject malicious packets into the victim's communication stream.

As a penetration tester, understanding how these weaknesses operate and how they can be exploited is essential for conducting a thorough assessment of a wireless network's security.

## WPA Handshake Capture Techniques

Capturing the **four-way handshake** is a pivotal step in cracking WPA/WPA2 passwords. The handshake occurs when a client device attempts to connect to a Wi-Fi network and both the client and the access point verify that they have the correct credentials. By intercepting this handshake, attackers can try to crack the WPA or WPA2 passphrase using brute-force or dictionary attacks.

Popular tools like **Aircrack-ng** and **Wireshark** are commonly used to capture these handshakes. However, it's important to stress that penetration testers should only attempt such actions in environments where they have explicit permission to conduct these tests.

Timing is another critical factor. To capture a handshake, the client must be actively reconnecting to the network, which means you'll need to either wait for the client to reconnect naturally or force the reconnection yourself through techniques such as **deauthentication attacks**.

Here's a step-by-step process to capture WPA/WPA2 handshakes:

| Step | Description | Purpose |
| --- | --- | --- |
| Selecting the target network | Identify the WPA-/WPA2-protected network you want to test. | This step ensures you are targeting the correct network for testing. |
| Monitoring Mode | Use a compatible network adapter capable of monitoring mode to eavesdrop on all wireless packets. | Enables sniffing of wireless traffic, essential for capturing data. |
| Deauthentication attack | Perform a deauthentication attack using tools like Aireplay-ng to force a re-handshake between the client and the access point. | This step interrupts the connection, prompting the client to reconnect and allowing for handshake capture. |
| Capturing the handshake | Once the client reconnects, capture the handshake using Airodump-ng. | The handshake is crucial for cracking the WPA/WPA2 password. |

### Cracking WPA/WPA2 Handshakes

After successfully capturing the WPA/WPA2 handshake, the next challenge is to crack it to gain unauthorized access to the network. Several techniques are commonly employed to crack handshakes, each with varying degrees of effectiveness depending on the complexity of the network's password and the resources available.

### Brute-Force Attacks

Brute-force attacks are one of the most straightforward methods of cracking a password. This approach involves systematically trying every possible combination of characters until the correct password is found. The process starts with simple combinations and gradually includes more complex ones involving numbers, symbols, and uppercase and lowercase letters.

While brute-force attacks are reliable and guaranteed to succeed if given enough time and resources, they can be incredibly time-consuming, especially if the target password is long and complex. The amount of time required to crack a password grows exponentially with its length and complexity.

For example, cracking a simple six-character password may take minutes, while an eight-character password with mixed case, numbers, and symbols could take days or longer. This method, while exhaustive, highlights the importance of strong, complex passwords as a primary defense mechanism.

### Dictionary Attacks

Unlike brute-force attacks, dictionary attacks focus on efficiency by leveraging a precompiled list of common or known passwords. The idea is to try each password from the list against the captured handshake, hoping that the target has used one of the passwords in the dictionary.

Dictionary attacks exploit the human tendency to choose simple, easily memorable passwords such as "password123" or "qwerty." These attacks are much faster than brute-force methods because they eliminate the need to test all possible character combinations, focusing instead on commonly used passwords.

However, their effectiveness depends on the strength of the target's password. If the password is not included in the dictionary or is sufficiently complex, the attack will fail. This reinforces the importance of using unique, random, and complex passwords to mitigate this type of attack.

### Rainbow Tables

Rainbow tables are precomputed tables that map password hashes to their original plaintext passwords. When a password is entered into a system, it is often hashed (converted into a fixed-length string of characters) before being stored. Rainbow tables work by reversing this process, allowing an attacker to quickly retrieve the original password from its hash without needing to compute it in real-time.

For example, if an attacker captures a hashed password from a WPA/WPA2 handshake, they can consult a rainbow table to find the original password corresponding to that hash. This method is faster than brute-force or dictionary attacks because it relies on precomputed data.

However, rainbow tables have limitations. They are less effective against **salted hashes**, a security measure that adds random data to passwords before hashing them, making the use of precomputed tables ineffective. Additionally, rainbow tables can take up significant storage space, as they need to contain many possible hash-to-password mappings.

| Attack Type | Method | Strengths and Weaknesses |
|---|---|---|
| **Brute-force attack** | Tries every possible character combination | It is guaranteed to find the password eventually, but it can be very slow for long and complex passwords. |
| **Rainbow table** | Uses precomputed hash tables | This method allows for quick retrieval of passwords from the table, but it doesn't work well with salted hashes and the tables can take up a lot of space. |
| **Dictionary attack** | Attempts passwords from a predefined list | It is quick for breaking weak passwords and more efficient than brute force for common passwords, but it is limited to known words and won't work on strong, complex passwords. |

## Mitigation Strategies

While understanding how to crack WPA/WPA2 networks is important for penetration testers, it is equally vital to recognize and implement mitigation strategies that reduce the effectiveness of these attacks. By addressing the weaknesses in network security, organizations and individuals can better protect their wireless networks from unauthorized access.

| Security Measure | Description | Examples |
|---|---|---|
| Complex passwords | Use long, complex passwords with a combination of uppercase, lowercase letters, numbers, and symbols. This makes brute-force and dictionary attacks less feasible. | Example: `G7$kLp9#qW2!` |
| Regular firmware updates | Keep routers and other networking devices updated with the latest security patches to address known vulnerabilities. | Update router firmware regularly. |
| Additional security layers | Use virtual private networks (VPNs) or other encryption tools to add layers of protection, even if the WPA/WPA2 protocol is compromised. | VPN services like NordVPN or ExpressVPN |
| Segment networks | Split the network into smaller segments (e.g., guest and main networks) to limit the scope of an attack if one segment is compromised. | Create separate guest networks. |
| Use IDS | Implement intrusion detection systems (IDS) to monitor wireless network traffic and alert administrators to suspicious activities. | IDS tools like Snort or Cisco IDS |

# Rogue Access Points Attacks

A **rogue access point (rogue AP)** is a wireless access point that is added to an organization's network without the knowledge or authorization of the network administrator. These unauthorized devices can be introduced either unintentionally by employees or maliciously by attackers to intercept or manipulate network traffic.

Understanding rogue APs is critical for cybersecurity professionals. These devices mimic legitimate access points but lack the proper security configurations of authorized network components, making them vulnerable to exploitation and posing serious risks. Attackers commonly set up rogue APs in public places or in close proximity to targeted organizations, hoping to lure unsuspecting users into connecting. Once connected, the attacker can intercept sensitive data, launch phishing attacks, or distribute malware.

For example, employees might connect personal routers to the corporate network, unknowingly creating a weak point that malicious actors can exploit. Once a rogue AP is in place, attackers can easily manipulate or steal sensitive data.

### *How to Set up a Rogue AP*

Using tools like **AirBase-ng** (part of the **Aircrack-ng** suite), setting up a rogue AP is a relatively straightforward process. Below are the steps to create a rogue AP:

1. **Install the necessary tools**: Ensure you have **Kali Linux** and the **Aircrack-ng** suite installed. Always keep your repositories updated for the latest versions.

2. **Identify your wireless interface**: Run the command `airmon-ng` to list available wireless interfaces. Use `airmon-ng start wlan0` (replace `wlan0` with your interface name) to start monitoring mode.

3. **Start the rogue AP**: Set up an open network, for example, by simulating an SSID like "Free Wi-Fi."

4. **Configure routing and IP forwarding**: Enable IP forwarding using the command `echo 1 > /proc/sys/net/ipv4/ip_forward` to allow the rogue AP to route traffic.

5. **Provide DHCP service**: Use **dnsmasq** to assign IP addresses to devices connecting to the rogue AP, ensuring they can communicate with the internet or internal network.

### *Common Misconfigurations*

While setting up a rogue AP, several common mistakes can occur, such as:

- **Unsecured backend connection**: Failing to secure the network link behind the rogue AP can make it easy for security tools to detect it.

- **Improper network isolation**: Not isolating the rogue network from the legitimate network can expose sensitive data or create a backdoor into the main network.

Ethical considerations must always be prioritized, ensuring that rogue AP setups are used solely for authorized penetration testing and never for malicious purposes.

### *Exploiting Data with Traffic Sniffing*

Once a rogue AP is set up, it becomes a powerful tool for **traffic sniffing**. By capturing and analyzing the data flowing through the rogue AP, penetration testers or attackers can intercept sensitive information, such as login credentials or email contents. Tools like **Wireshark** allow you to capture packets and analyze network traffic in real time.

For instance, passwords transmitted over **HTTP** can be easily captured in plaintext, whereas **HTTPS** encrypts traffic, making it more secure unless the attacker performs additional steps, such as **SSL stripping**, to downgrade the connection.

The consequences of data exploitation vary, ranging from unauthorized account access to full identity theft. Assessing the impact of intercepted data helps determine the vulnerability's severity and the necessary preventive measures.

### *Preventing Rogue AP Attacks*

Mitigating the threat of rogue APs involves several strategic actions:

- **Network segmentation**: Dividing the network into smaller segments using **VLANs** ensures that unauthorized access to one segment doesn't compromise the entire network.

- **Logging and auditing**: Implement advanced logging mechanisms to track suspicious activity related to rogue APs. Keeping detailed logs can aid in forensic analysis if a rogue AP is detected.

# Bluetooth and IoT Device Targeting

The security of **Bluetooth** and **IoT (Internet of Things)** devices is a growing concern, as they have become ubiquitous in modern life. While these technologies offer great convenience, they also introduce specific security risks that require careful evaluation and mitigation.

### *Bluetooth Vulnerabilities Overview*

Bluetooth technology, commonly used in smartphones, laptops, and IoT devices, has several vulnerabilities that attackers can exploit.

One of the primary issues is the **insecure pairing process**. When devices pair, they exchange keys that, if not properly secured, can be intercepted. Additionally, older versions of Bluetooth are vulnerable to **legacy protocol attacks**, making them easier targets for exploitation.

Here are two common Bluetooth attacks:

| Feature | Bluejacking | Bluesnarfing |
|---------|-------------|--------------|
| Definition | Sending unsolicited messages via Bluetooth to nearby devices. | Gaining unauthorized access to data on a Bluetooth-enabled device. |
| Purpose | Used mainly for pranks or sending anonymous messages. | Used to steal data like contacts, calendars, and messages. |
| Security | Generally harmless but invasive. | Considered malicious and a significant security threat. |
| Target | Bluetooth-enabled devices in proximity. | Same as Bluejacking, but with intent to access data. |
| Consent | No consent needed from the recipient. | No consent needed; done stealthily |

## *Exploiting IoT Vulnerabilities*

The rapid expansion of IoT devices has created new opportunities for cybercriminals. IoT devices often have inconsistent security practices, making them attractive targets.

- **Weak passwords**: Many IoT devices come with default usernames and passwords, such as "admin" and "password123," which users often forget to change. Attackers can easily exploit these weak credentials using automated tools to scan for vulnerable devices.

- **Unpatched firmware**: Manufacturers frequently release firmware updates to address security flaws. However, many users neglect to update their devices, leaving them vulnerable to known exploits.

For instance, failing to apply an available patch for a security flaw can allow cybercriminals to gain unauthorized access to an IoT device before the user even knows a problem exists.

## Bluetooth and IoT Penetration Testing Methodologies

Penetration testing for Bluetooth and IoT devices requires a structured approach. The following steps outline the methodologies used in a typical penetration test:

1. **Information Gathering**: Collect data on the target devices, including the make, model, and firmware version, to identify known vulnerabilities.

2. **Risk Assessment**: Evaluate the potential impact of each exploit and prioritize vulnerabilities based on their severity.

3. **Social Engineering**: Exploit human factors, such as tricking users into pairing their devices or revealing sensitive information.

Penetration tests on IoT devices, such as smart thermostats, can reveal flaws in their communication protocols, while tests on medical IoT devices might uncover vulnerabilities that threaten patient safety.

Documenting all findings during a penetration test is essential to developing effective mitigation strategies.

## Securing Bluetooth and IoT Devices

Securing Bluetooth and IoT devices requires a multi-pronged approach, including regular software updates and strong authentication mechanisms. Here are some effective strategies:

| Attribute | MFA | Behavioral Authentication | Public Key Infrastructure |
|---|---|---|---|
| Description | Requires multiple verification factors for access. | Monitors user behavior patterns for verification. | Uses digital certificates for authentication. |
| Strengths | Increases security by needing more than one check. | Adapts to user behavior, enhancing security. | Provides a high level of trust and security. |
| Weaknesses | Can be inconvenient for users. | May produce false positives. | Complex to implement. |

Encouraging manufacturers to implement these practices and educating users about updating devices and using strong, unique passwords can greatly enhance Bluetooth and IoT security.

In the next chapter, we'll explore **post-exploitation strategies**, focusing on what steps to take after gaining access to a system.

# CHAPTER 9

# Post-Exploitation Strategies

Organizations, on average, take around 272 days to identify and contain a data breach (Kosinski, 2024). This extended timeline underscores the challenges of responding to breaches and highlights the critical importance of robust post-exploitation strategies.

A high-profile example of this is the **23andMe data breach** of 2023, where hackers accessed and leaked sensitive genetic data, emails, and personal information related to users' genetic relatives. This breach, like many others, was part of a broader trend of targeting customer data for identity theft, fraud, or more sophisticated attacks. The event emphasized the importance of having a comprehensive plan for responding to data breaches, particularly for organizations handling personal data.

In this chapter, we will explore **post-exploitation techniques** used to maintain access, escalate privileges, persist in the compromised environment, extract valuable data, and eliminate traces of unauthorized activity. These skills are vital for penetration testers and ethical hackers seeking to enhance their knowledge and technical capabilities in managing post-breach scenarios effectively.

## Privilege Escalation Techniques

One of the key objectives of post-exploitation is to achieve higher levels of access within compromised systems. **Privilege escalation** is essential for enhancing control over a target network and unlocking more advanced exploitation opportunities.

The first step involves identifying weak points within the system, such as misconfigurations or outdated software. Common vulnerabilities can range from incorrect file permissions to unpatched security flaws, providing an avenue for attackers to exploit.

### Exploiting SUID and SGID Binaries

A common approach to privilege escalation is through **Set User ID (SUID)** and **Set Group ID (SGID)** binaries. These binaries allow programs to run with the privileges of the file's owner or group, regardless of the executing user's permission level.

| Feature | SUID (Set User ID) | SGID (Set Group ID) |
| --- | --- | --- |
| **Definition** | Allows an executable file to be usable with the privileges of the file's owner. | Allows an executable file to be usable with the privileges of the file's group. |
| **Common usage** | Often used for programs that require elevated privileges to perform certain tasks (e.g., changing passwords). | Commonly used in shared directories to maintain group privileges when files are created. |
| **Exploitability** | Can be exploited to gain unauthorized elevated privileges if the program contains vulnerabilities (e.g., buffer overflows, poor input validation). | Can allow unauthorized elevated privileges if the program mismanages permissions or contains vulnerabilities. |
| **Example of risk** | If a SUID program is writable by the user, they can modify it to create a backdoor, granting themselves root access. | If an SGID program mismanages permissions, it can allow unauthorized users to execute sensitive actions. |
| **Mitigation** | Regularly audit SUID files, limit their usage, and ensure they are not executable by untrusted users. | Implement similar audits, restrict permissions, and utilize security tools to identify vulnerabilities. |

When misconfigured, these binaries can give attackers unintended elevated privileges. For instance, if a writable SUID binary is owned by root, an attacker could modify it to create a backdoor, granting themselves root access upon execution. Regular auditing and restricting the execution of SUID/SGID files to trusted users can help mitigate these risks.

### *Manipulating Environment Variables*

Another advanced privilege escalation technique involves **manipulating environment variables**. Environment variables are used by system processes and can be exploited to alter the behavior of privileged programs.

By changing the **PATH** environment variable, for example, attackers can trick a system into executing malicious scripts disguised as legitimate programs. Suppose an attacker creates a fake version of a common command (e.g., `ls` or `cp`) and places it in a directory they control. By modifying the PATH variable to prioritize that directory, any calls to those commands by a privileged program will execute the attacker's version.

Using automated scripts to manipulate environment variables and inject malicious commands further enhances the efficiency of this method.

### *Kernel Exploits*

**Kernel exploits** are among the most powerful tools in an attacker's arsenal. These exploits target vulnerabilities within the OS kernel, giving attackers full control over the compromised system. Such vulnerabilities may arise from **buffer overflows**, **race conditions**, or logic flaws within the kernel.

Here are three notable real-world kernel exploits:

| Name of Kernel Exploit | Year It Happened | What Happened |
|---|---|---|
| Dirty (Copy-on-Write) COW | 2016 | This privilege escalation vulnerability in the Linux kernel allowed attackers to gain write access to read- |

| | | only memory, leading to unauthorized privilege escalation and potential full control of the system. |
|---|---|---|
| Blue Pill | 2006 | This exploit allowed attackers to create a virtual machine that could run unnoticed under the host OS, enabling complete control over the system and evading detection by security software. |
| Meltdown | 2018 | This critical vulnerability in modern processors allowed unauthorized access to sensitive data in memory, exposing numerous systems to potential data breaches and requiring hardware and software updates to mitigate risks. |

Kernel exploits are particularly dangerous because they target the core of the operating system. Once successful, they provide unrestricted access, enabling attackers to bypass security mechanisms, modify system settings, and steal sensitive data. Mitigating kernel exploits requires applying patches and updates regularly and using technologies like kernel-level protection.

# Maintaining Undetected Persistence

Maintaining persistent, undetected access to target systems is a critical component of post-exploitation strategies. This involves using advanced remote access tools and techniques that blend into normal network traffic to avoid raising alarms. Successful post-exploitation relies on both the selection of appropriate tools and the careful management of backdoors to ensure ongoing control.

### Use Solutions

To maintain covert access, it's crucial to employ remote access solutions that are designed for stealth and evade detection. Below are some widely used tools that offer discreet remote access:

- **Cobalt Strike's Beacon**: Beacon is part of the **Cobalt Strike** penetration testing toolkit. It allows remote control of compromised systems by mimicking normal network traffic patterns, making it difficult to detect. Beacon supports a wide range of post-exploitation tasks, including command execution, file transfers, and data exfiltration while operating quietly within the network.

- **Meterpreter**: A payload within the **Metasploit Framework, Meterpreter** provides an interactive shell and allows for deep system control, including privilege escalation, file system manipulation, and network scanning. Its stealth features, like running in memory without creating disk artifacts, help attackers maintain a low profile and evade detection tools.

- **NanoCore**: A feature-rich **Remote Access Trojan (RAT)** designed for stealthy system control. NanoCore enables keylogging, screenshot capture, and remote command execution, all while remaining concealed from many antivirus solutions. Its minimal resource footprint and evasion capabilities make it effective for maintaining long-term access.

- **QuasarRAT**: An open-source RAT that provides discreet remote access to compromised systems. **QuasarRAT** is popular for its lightweight design, offering functions like file management, keylogging, and remote command execution, while minimizing the risk of detection by blending into regular network traffic.

- **Empire**: An open-source post-exploitation framework that leverages **PowerShell** and **Python** agents for stealthy operation. **Empire** enables remote access, data exfiltration, and further exploitation tasks while flying under the radar of traditional security defenses. Its modular design allows for scripting and automation, enhancing its flexibility and stealth.

## Creating Persistent Backdoors

A **backdoor** is a hidden method used to bypass regular authentication processes and gain unauthorized access to a system. Attackers or penetration testers create backdoors as part of post-exploitation to ensure they can regain access even after system reboots or security patches.

Backdoors can be created in several ways:

- **Modifying startup scripts** to re-execute malicious payloads every time the system boots.

- **Embedding backdoors in legitimate services** so that they are overlooked by administrators.

- **Creating new user accounts with hidden privileges** to allow future logins without raising suspicion.

- **Modifying existing system binaries** or adding new scheduled tasks to execute backdoor programs at specified intervals.

Here are some backdoor-creation techniques and step-by-step guides:

| Technique | Description | Step-By-Step Guide |
|---|---|---|
| **Malware** | Malware is malicious software that creates a backdoor. | Step 1: Install the malware on the target system.<br><br>Step 2: It can be hidden in legitimate software to avoid detection. |
| **Exploits** | Exploits take advantage of vulnerabilities in the system. | Step 1: Identify weaknesses in the software.<br><br>Step 2: Use an exploit tool to gain access to the system. |
| **Remote access** | Remote access involves using tools that are hidden. | Step 1: Install a remote access tool on the target system.<br><br>Step 2: Access the system from another location using this tool. |
| **Hardcoded passwords** | Hardcoded passwords are included in applications. | Step 1: Analyze the software to find hardcoded credentials.<br><br>Step 2: Use these credentials to access the system. |

| Rootkits | Rootkits are tools that hide the existence of other software. | Step 1: Install a rootkit to conceal malicious activities. Step 2: Maintain control over the system without detection. |
|---|---|---|

## Run Tasks on Schedule

Maintaining persistence through scheduled tasks is another effective strategy. Scheduled tasks can automatically execute at predefined intervals, ensuring your presence on the system even after reboots.

For instance, a system administrator sets up a scheduled task to run a security script every night at 2 a.m. This script ensures that any unauthorized changes to the system are detected and logged, thereby maintaining a secure environment.

## Name a Task Properly

Understand naming conventions. When we talk about naming conventions, we are really looking at the way we systematically name things. Naming conventions are essential in various fields, from programming to cybersecurity. They help people understand the purpose of a file or process just by looking at its name.

For instance, naming a task something like "WindowsUpdateCheck" can easily blend in with routine maintenance activities. Configure the task to run during periods when the system is least monitored, such as late at night or early morning.

Here are naming conventions that you can follow:

| Naming Convention | Explanation | Example |
|---|---|---|
| CamelCase | Words are concatenated without spaces, with each word starting with a capital letter (except for the first word). | myVariableName |

| PascalCase | Similar to CamelCase, but every word, including the first, starts with a capital letter. | MyVariableName |
| --- | --- | --- |
| Snake_case | Words are separated by underscores, with all letters in lowercase. | my_variable_name |
| Kebab-case | Words are separated by hyphens, with all letters in lowercase. | my-variable-name |
| UPPERCASE | All letters are capitalized, often used for constants or macros. | MY_CONSTANT |

## Manipulate Logs

Log manipulation is important in keeping unauthorized access concealed. Logs are often the first place security analysts look when investigating suspicious activity. Therefore, learning to manipulate logs can help obscure traces of your presence.

Here are the different log manipulation techniques you can use:

| Technique | Description | Specific Tools | Significance |
| --- | --- | --- | --- |
| **Log cleaners** | Software that automatically removes or alters log entries. | CCleaner, LogCleaner | Helps attackers hide their activities from monitoring systems. |
| **Log spoofing** | Creating false log entries to mislead investigators. | πLogger, LogSpoof | Confuses forensic analysis and can delay incident response. |
| **Log redirection** | Sending logs to a remote server or storage location. | Syslog-ng, Fluentd | Makes it difficult for defenders to track activities directly. |

| **Scripted manipulation** | Using scripts to automate the modification of logs. | Bash, PowerShell scripts | Enables quick changes to multiple logs simultaneously, increasing efficiency for evasion. |
|---|---|---|---|
| **Anonymization tools** | Tools that alter logs to protect user identities. | LogMasher, AnonLog | Can be misused by attackers to obscure their identity while conducting malicious activities. |

# Data Mining Strategies

Efficient data extraction from compromised systems is vital for understanding attack methods, identifying vulnerabilities, and improving future defenses. Following a streamlined and structured process ensures a swift and thorough response to security incidents. Here's a detailed guide for post-breach data extraction and handling:

## 1. Assess the Situation

Begin by confirming the breach through careful monitoring of logs and alerts. Determine the scope of the compromise—identify which systems and data have been affected, the entry points, and potential ongoing threats. This initial assessment sets the stage for a focused and effective response.

## 2. Establish a Response Team

Assemble a cross-functional response team including representatives from IT, legal, compliance, and public relations (PR). Clearly define the roles and responsibilities of each team member, ensuring efficient communication and task delegation during the crisis. The team should be prepared to handle both technical containment and external communication.

## 3. Contain the Breach

Once the breach is confirmed, prioritize containment to limit further damage. Isolate affected systems from the network, disable compromised accounts, and immediately change passwords and credentials. Ensure that any additional vulnerabilities are patched or mitigated to prevent lateral movement by attackers.

### 4. Implement Digital Forensics

Deploy digital forensic tools to collect and preserve evidence from affected systems. Analyze system logs, configuration files, memory snapshots, and network traffic to understand the extent of the breach. This step is critical for tracing the attackers' actions and gathering evidence for future legal or regulatory actions.

### 5. Extract Relevant Data

Focus on collecting essential data, such as user activity logs, compromised databases, and system configurations. Prioritize data that will reveal the attackers' methods and the damage done. Ensure compliance with relevant legal and regulatory requirements when handling and storing the extracted data, especially if it involves personally identifiable information (PII).

### 6. Document All Actions

Maintain a meticulous record of every action taken during the response. This should include timestamps, individuals involved, systems accessed, and data extracted. Documenting these actions is crucial for transparency, legal compliance, and post-breach review.

### 7. Analyze the Extracted Data

Thoroughly analyze the data to uncover the attackers' methods, vulnerabilities, and potential attack vectors. Leverage data mining and anomaly detection techniques to identify patterns, trends, or suspicious activities. This analysis will guide remediation efforts and future defensive strategies.

### 8. Communicate Findings

Communicate the breach findings clearly and transparently to stakeholders, including management, affected customers, and regulatory bodies. Provide a clear overview of what was compromised, the impact of the breach, and the steps taken to mitigate risks. Address customer concerns with honest, timely updates and provide guidance on any actions they should take.

## 9. Review and Strengthen Security

Conduct a post-breach security review to determine the root cause of the breach. Based on this review, implement stronger security protocols, patch vulnerabilities, and update software across the organization. Regularly conduct security audits and penetration tests to proactively identify potential weaknesses. Employee training should also be enhanced to prevent social engineering attacks and improve overall security awareness.

## 10. Monitor for Future Threats

Post-breach monitoring is essential to ensure the attackers do not attempt to regain access. Set up enhanced system monitoring with real-time alerts for any suspicious activity. Continuously update security policies and incident response plans to address new and emerging threats.

## Use Secure Data Exfiltration

To ensure the security of sensitive data during exfiltration, it is essential to first assess the nature and importance of the data being transferred. This evaluation involves categorizing the data based on its sensitivity—whether it is customer information, financial records, intellectual property, or proprietary business data. Understanding the type and context of the data helps organizations implement the most suitable security measures for its protection. Once the sensitivity and criticality of the data have been established, different strategies can be employed to safeguard it throughout the exfiltration process.

### Encryption for Secure Exfiltration

Encryption is a fundamental technique for ensuring data security during transfer. It works by converting data into an unreadable format that can only be deciphered by individuals with the appropriate decryption key. To achieve optimal encryption, organizations should adopt robust encryption algorithms such as **AES (Advanced Encryption Standard)** or **RSA (Rivest-Shamir-Adleman)**. These widely recognized encryption methods provide strong defense against unauthorized access during the exfiltration of sensitive data.

For secure data handling, encrypted data should only be accessible to trusted individuals. Decryption keys must be stored securely and shared selectively. Even if the encrypted data is intercepted, it will remain unusable without the corresponding decryption key. Additionally, organizations should regularly rotate their encryption keys and closely monitor their usage to prevent unauthorized access or compromise.

## Custom Encryption Algorithms

For highly sensitive or mission-critical data, standard encryption methods may not always suffice, especially in unique operational environments. In such cases, **custom encryption algorithms** can be designed to offer tailored security solutions. These custom algorithms often involve creating specific key generation methods and data manipulation techniques that align with the organization's specific security requirements.

### Steps for Developing Custom Encryption Algorithms:

1. **Define Security Requirements**: Identify the specific data to be protected and the threats it faces. For instance, a financial institution might require custom encryption to better safeguard customer transactions from highly targeted attacks.

2. **Select the Encryption Type**:

    o **Symmetric Encryption**: Uses a single key for both encryption and decryption. This method is faster and efficient for large data transfers.

    o **Asymmetric Encryption**: Employs two keys—public and private—which simplifies secure key distribution and mitigates the risk of key exposure.

3. **Design the Algorithm**: Create unique logic for encrypting and decrypting data, which could involve advanced mathematical functions or direct binary manipulation to enhance security.

4. **Implement the Algorithm**: Write the code using programming languages such as **Python**, **Java**, or **C++**, ensuring that the algorithm is both efficient and secure.

5. **Test and Validate**: Rigorously test the algorithm under various scenarios to ensure it performs as intended, provides robust security, and is resilient to known attacks.

*Network Pattern Analysis for Detection Avoidance*

In both ethical penetration testing and cyberattacks, **network pattern analysis** plays a key role in avoiding detection during data exfiltration. By analyzing network traffic patterns, such as peak usage times and typical traffic volumes, attackers can time their data transfers to coincide with normal network activity, making them harder to detect. On the defensive side, network administrators can use traffic analysis to detect irregularities that signal potential exfiltration attempts.

**Advanced Data Exfiltration Techniques:**

1. **DNS Tunneling**: This technique hides data within DNS queries and responses by encoding information inside DNS requests, often using port 53. Since DNS traffic is generally trusted, this method can bypass traditional security defenses.

   o **Example**: An attacker uses DNS tunneling to exfiltrate sensitive data from a corporate network by embedding the data in DNS packets that appear normal.

2. **HTTPS Traffic Masquerading**: Attackers can disguise malicious traffic as legitimate HTTPS traffic using encrypted channels, making it difficult for firewalls or intrusion detection systems (IDS) to differentiate between legitimate and malicious activity.

   o **Example**: A cybercriminal sends malicious commands to a compromised system via HTTPS, blending the malicious traffic with regular web traffic to evade detection.

3. **Traffic and Flow Analysis**: Monitoring network traffic and flow records helps security teams detect anomalies or irregular patterns that may indicate data exfiltration. This method focuses on observing unusual traffic behaviors, such as spikes in outbound data.

   o **Example**: A network administrator notices an unusual surge in outbound data transfers, which could indicate sensitive data being exfiltrated by an attacker.

4. **Intrusion Detection Systems (IDS)**: IDS solutions monitor network traffic for suspicious behavior or breaches of security policies. By setting alerts for unusual activity, such as abnormal login attempts or unexpected data transfers, IDS can help detect and prevent potential exfiltration.

o **Example**: An IDS flags repeated failed login attempts on a secure server, indicating a possible brute-force attack aimed at stealing credentials for future exfiltration efforts.

## Preventive Measures for Secure Exfiltration

To protect against data breaches and ensure secure exfiltration, organizations should adopt a layered defense strategy that combines encryption, monitoring, and strict access controls.

1. **Implement Strong Encryption**: Always encrypt sensitive data before transferring it. Use robust encryption standards like AES-256 and ensure the keys are well-protected and rotated periodically.

2. **Utilize Data Loss Prevention (DLP) Tools**: DLP tools monitor and restrict unauthorized data transfers. These systems can block or flag suspicious data exfiltration attempts based on predefined policies, providing real-time protection.

3. **Monitor Network Traffic Continuously**: Set up real-time monitoring and anomaly detection systems that flag irregular traffic patterns. This helps identify potential data breaches or exfiltration efforts early.

4. **Restrict the Use of External Devices**: Limiting or disabling the use of external storage devices such as USB drives minimizes the risk of data being exfiltrated via physical means.

5. **Use Multi-Factor Authentication (MFA)**: Implement MFA for accessing sensitive systems and networks, reducing the chances of compromised credentials leading to data exfiltration.

## Creating Custom Scripts for Data Extraction

Writing custom scripts for data extraction allows security professionals to tailor tools to fit specific operational needs. These scripts can be adapted for a wide range of tasks, making them indispensable in various penetration testing and data management scenarios. Popular scripting languages like **Python**, **PowerShell**, and **Bash** are widely used for crafting these scripts due to their flexibility and extensive libraries that simplify complex programming tasks.

### *Key Considerations When Writing Custom Scripts*

When developing custom scripts, it's crucial to account for the operating environment and any potential challenges that may arise. For example, scripting on **Windows** often requires leveraging **PowerShell**, a powerful tool for automating built-in system commands and workflows. In contrast, scripting on **Linux** might involve **Bash**, which can execute shell commands and streamline administrative tasks. A well-written custom script can automate crucial processes such as password collection, sensitive file searches, and network configuration checks.

However, custom scripts are not without limitations. **System permissions** and administrative rules may restrict script execution or limit access to specific files or resources. To mitigate these risks, it is essential to rigorously test custom scripts in a controlled environment, such as a virtual machine or sandbox, before deploying them in a live network. This ensures the script functions correctly and securely without causing unintended consequences.

### *Real-World Applications of Custom Scripts*

Real-life examples demonstrate the value of tailored scripts in cybersecurity. For instance, a security tester once developed a **Python script** that scanned a company's file system for documents containing sensitive keywords. The script not only identified files containing classified information but also encrypted them automatically, significantly reducing the risk of data leaks. This method ensured that only the necessary documents were shared, streamlining the data-handling process while enhancing security.

By writing custom scripts, testers can automate repetitive tasks, expedite data collection, and improve the accuracy of assessments. This approach also allows for scalability—scripts can be easily modified to accommodate new requirements or environments, making them versatile tools in any penetration tester's toolkit.

In **Chapter 10**, we'll explore real-world penetration testing scenarios where these techniques come to life. It's one thing to discuss strategies in theory, but applying them in practical settings is where the real excitement begins.

# CHAPTER 10

# Real-World Penetration Testing Scenarios

I n this final chapter, we'll delve into the practical application of penetration testing techniques within real-world environments. Applying the theoretical knowledge of cybersecurity in realistic scenarios is where penetration testers can truly hone their skills and gain meaningful insights into their effectiveness.

**Real-world penetration testing** is essential for transitioning from conceptual learning to actual defensive and offensive strategies in cybersecurity. These scenarios simulate genuine cyber threats, enabling ethical hackers and penetration testers to test systems under conditions that closely resemble real-world attacks.

### Case Study: HackerOne and Bug Bounty Programs

One notable platform that bridges theory with practice is **HackerOne**, a cybersecurity firm offering organizations a structured platform for real-world penetration testing, bug bounty programs, and vulnerability disclosure.

HackerOne's **bug bounty program** is particularly effective. It allows ethical hackers and security researchers to identify and report vulnerabilities on behalf of organizations. Participants are incentivized with financial rewards based on the severity and potential impact of the vulnerabilities they uncover. For example, critical vulnerabilities such as SQL injection or cross-site scripting (XSS) could result in payouts ranging from hundreds to thousands of dollars.

This collaborative approach to cybersecurity encourages continuous improvement in organizational defenses. Bug bounty platforms like HackerOne provide a structured environment for discovering, reporting, and resolving security issues. These programs not only reward ethical hackers but also help companies strengthen their cybersecurity frameworks, proving the real-world value of penetration testing.

# Building a Comprehensive Penetration Test Report

A well-documented **penetration test report** is a key deliverable in any security assessment. The report outlines the vulnerabilities discovered, their potential impact, and practical steps for remediation. A comprehensive and clear report transforms technical findings into actionable insights, bridging the gap between cybersecurity professionals and decision-makers.

### *Why Reporting Matters*

Penetration testing reports serve two primary purposes:

1. **Risk Communication**: They convey potential threats to stakeholders.

2. **Guidance**: They offer a roadmap for remediation, helping organizations prioritize security measures.

Here's a step-by-step guide on creating an effective penetration testing report:

### *Step 1: Clarify Objectives*

Before diving into the details, it's crucial to outline the objectives of the test. The report should clearly communicate the scope and goals of the assessment. This ensures that the results are contextualized and aligned with organizational priorities.

For example, if the goal of the test is to assess the strength of an organization's firewall against external attacks, this objective should be stated upfront.

### *Step 2: Structure the Report*

A well-structured report is easier to navigate, especially for non-technical stakeholders. A typical report structure includes:

1. **Executive Summary**: A high-level overview that condenses key findings into a one- or two-page summary. This section should be easy to digest, highlighting critical vulnerabilities and their potential impact on the organization.

   For instance, if the test uncovered a severe authentication flaw, the executive summary should emphasize how it compromises security and the necessary steps to address it.

2. **Detailed Analysis**: After the executive summary, the report should dive into more specific technical findings. This section should provide a deeper analysis of each vulnerability, explaining how it was discovered, how it can be exploited, and its overall risk level.

### *Step 3: Identify and Prioritize Vulnerabilities*

Clearly document each vulnerability, including its type, impact, and which systems or data it affects. Assign each vulnerability a **risk level** (e.g., low, medium, or high) based on its potential to cause damage and the likelihood of exploitation. Prioritizing vulnerabilities helps guide organizations in addressing the most critical issues first.

For example, a SQL injection vulnerability in a public-facing web application would typically rank as high-risk, given its potential to expose sensitive user data.

### *Step 4: Provide Remediation Recommendations*

For each identified weakness, offer detailed recommendations on how to remediate or mitigate the issue. Providing actionable solutions is essential for ensuring that organizations can effectively address their security gaps. Remediation strategies could include applying software patches, updating configurations, or enhancing access control mechanisms.

### *Step 5: Leverage Reporting Tools*

Automated tools play a significant role in enhancing report generation. These tools can analyze vast amounts of data, highlighting vulnerabilities and even suggesting initial remediation steps. Tools like **Nessus**, **OpenVAS**, or **Burp Suite** provide valuable insights into the severity of each issue, allowing testers to focus on critical vulnerabilities.

Combining automated reports with manual validation ensures accuracy and completeness, as automated tools may miss certain vulnerabilities or overestimate their impact

Here is a selection of tools that you can use:

| Serpico | Dradis | MagicTree |
|---|---|---|
| Open-source reporting tool for penetration testers. | Collaboration and reporting tool for managing and sharing findings. | Reporting tool focused on documentation and presentation of findings. |
| Customizable templates for creating and modifying report templates to fit specific needs. | Centralized information sharing to collect, store, and share findings in one platform. | User-friendly interface that simplifies the documentation process for testers. |
| Markdown support for easy formatting and organized presentations. | Integration with other tools to automatically import findings. | Findings organization to categorize and organize findings in a structured manner. |
| Automated findings to import data from various security tools to save time. | Custom report generation using customizable templates for tailored reports. | Customizable templates to create reports that match organizational or client preferences. |
| Collaboration for multiple users to contribute to reports. | Team collaboration allows for real-time teamwork and input. | Integration capabilities for importing findings from several security tools. |
| Output formats to generate reports in PDF and HTML formats. | Export options for saving reports as PDF and HTML. | Professional output to generate clear and professional reports. |

These tools save time by gathering and analyzing data automatically. In turn, this lets penetration testers focus on more complicated findings.

But, it's important to check and confirm the automated reports to make sure they're accurate and relevant since these tools can sometimes show false positives or miss important details.

### Step 6: Choose Effective Templates

Selecting the right template for your penetration testing report is crucial for maintaining clarity, professionalism, and consistency. A standardized template ensures all critical information is included, helping the report flow logically and making it easier for stakeholders to interpret the findings.

A well-structured template also promotes uniformity across reports, enhancing readability and comprehension. Standardized sections, such as summaries, methodologies, detailed findings, and remediation suggestions, ensure nothing important is left out.

### Tips for Choosing Effective Templates:

- **Include Standard Sections:** Ensure the template includes essential sections such as an executive summary, detailed findings, risk levels, remediation recommendations, and appendices. This comprehensive structure helps present key information in an organized manner.

- **Customization Options:** Opt for a template that allows flexibility for tailoring the report to specific engagements. This includes adding sections for scope, methodology, findings, and any client-specific branding elements.

- **Clarity and Readability:** Choose a template that prioritizes clear headings, well-organized sections, and a logical flow of information. Avoid overly complex designs that might distract from the report's main content. Simplicity enhances readability.

- **Incorporate Visual Elements:** Look for templates that allow the inclusion of visual aids like charts, graphs, and tables. Visuals can effectively convey complex data and trends, helping stakeholders quickly grasp important findings.

- **Audience-Specific Design:** Consider who will be reading the report—technical staff, management, or clients. Choose a template that matches the audience's level of technical expertise, ensuring the content is understandable and aligned with their needs.

## Step 7: Crafting Follow-Up Recommendations

After identifying vulnerabilities, it's vital to provide **clear and actionable follow-up recommendations**. Effective remediation guidance ensures that security flaws are addressed efficiently, helping organizations mitigate potential risks. Your recommendations should align with the organization's unique context and available resources.

For example, if outdated software caused a vulnerability, your recommendation could be to update to the latest version and implement a patch management system to prevent future issues.

### Best Practices for Crafting Follow-Up Recommendations:

- **Prioritize Findings:** Rank vulnerabilities by their severity and impact on the organization. This prioritization helps focus remediation efforts on the most critical issues, ensuring that resources are used effectively to mitigate high-risk vulnerabilities first.

- **Provide Specific Remediation Steps:** Avoid vague suggestions. Offer **concrete, actionable steps** that clearly outline what needs to be done. This reduces ambiguity, making it easier for technical teams to implement fixes.

- **Establish Realistic Timelines:** Recommend remediation timelines based on the vulnerability's risk level. Assigning deadlines creates urgency and ensures accountability, helping organizations stay on track with their security improvements.

- **Offer Additional Resources:** Include links to tools, guides, or best practices that can assist in remediation. Offering these resources empowers the organization to go beyond immediate fixes, fostering a proactive approach to security.

- **Promote Security Awareness Training:** Recommend ongoing security training and awareness programs for employees. Building a security-conscious culture helps reduce human error and equips staff with the knowledge to recognize and respond to potential threats.

# The Importance of Transparency

Effective follow-up after delivering the penetration test report is essential. Engaging with clients through transparent communication fosters a collaborative environment, allowing for clarification, addressing concerns, and offering further guidance. Regular communication builds trust and ensures that remediation efforts are aligned with the client's security objectives.

A lack of transparency can have serious repercussions, as demonstrated by the 2013–2014 **Yahoo data breach**. Although billions of user accounts were compromised, Yahoo delayed disclosing the breach until 2016, resulting in significant criticism and loss of trust. Prompt and open communication is critical in mitigating the impact of security incidents and maintaining strong client relationships.

# Executing a Complete Penetration Test Cycle

Mastering the entire penetration test process—from planning and execution to analysis and reporting—is essential for ethical hackers. This process involves thorough preparation, executing rigorous assessments, analyzing the findings, and providing actionable feedback to the client.

### Planning and Preparation

The initial stage of a penetration test involves careful planning and preparation. Clearly defining the **scope of the test** ensures the objectives align with the client's expectations, and all necessary areas are covered without exceeding authorized boundaries. This phase usually includes detailed discussions with the stakeholders to understand their concerns, security policies, and past incidents.

A well-known example of insufficient planning is the **2014 Sony Pictures cyberattack**, which resulted in massive data theft and significant reputational damage. The attack highlighted the importance of thorough planning in penetration testing. Proper planning not only helps identify vulnerabilities but also ensures that testing is conducted in a controlled, efficient manner.

## *Execution of Tests*

Once planning is complete, the **execution phase** begins. This is where various automated and manual testing techniques are applied to uncover vulnerabilities. While automated tools are useful for identifying common issues quickly, manual testing is critical for discovering more complex or subtle vulnerabilities that automated scans may miss.

Ethical hackers need to be adaptable during this phase. Real-world conditions often differ from initial plans, requiring adjustments in tactics. A key aspect of vulnerability exploitation is maintaining stealth—**minimizing detection by the target's security systems** ensures the test results are realistic and reflective of actual risks.

To avoid detection, ethical hackers may use VPNs, proxies, and **obfuscation techniques** to alter their digital footprint. Flexibility is key during test execution, as new findings often require real-time adjustments to the approach.

## Analysis and Review

After completing a penetration test, the next critical step is to thoroughly analyze and review the results. This phase is essential for assessing the risks identified, refining methodologies, and developing strategies for continuous improvement. Careful evaluation of the data collected allows you to gauge the severity and potential impact of each vulnerability found during the test.

Analyzing the results involves categorizing vulnerabilities based on their risk level and mapping potential exploitation paths. Comprehensive documentation detailing how each vulnerability was identified and exploited is vital. This serves as both proof of concept and a reference for other testers or developers, ensuring they understand the system's weaknesses and how to address them.

### *Key Areas to Focus on During Analysis:*

- **Authentication Mechanisms:** Test the strength of authentication methods, such as password policies, multi-factor authentication (MFA), and account lockout mechanisms, to ensure robust user verification processes.

- **User Permissions:** Evaluate user roles and permissions, verifying that the principle of least privilege is enforced and excessive permissions are not granted to any accounts.

- **Physical Security:** Assess physical access controls, surveillance systems, and environmental security measures protecting critical infrastructure to ensure a comprehensive defense.

A vital aspect of post-test analysis is the practice of continuous refinement. Post-test reviews help identify what worked well and highlight areas for improvement. By reflecting on the methodologies used and their effectiveness, testers can adapt and develop stronger approaches for future assessments, enhancing their overall skill set.

## The Importance of a Feedback Loop

Establishing a **feedback loop** is a crucial part of the penetration testing process. Regular communication with all stakeholders during and after the test helps clarify results and ensure everyone understands the implications of the findings.

*Entities to Gather Feedback From:*

| Entity | Example Feedback |
|---|---|
| Internal security team | This report provides insights into existing vulnerabilities and security gaps, recommendations for improving security policies, and lessons from previous penetration tests. |
| End users | There have been reports of unusual behavior, concerns about usability versus security measures, and suggestions for improving user awareness and training regarding potential threats. |

Incorporating feedback not only enhances future penetration tests but also contributes to strengthening the organization's overall security posture. Regular debriefing sessions and structured updates ensure ongoing collaboration and maintain transparency, fostering a continuous improvement environment.

# Evaluating Security Postures

Evaluating an organization's **security posture** is critical for identifying weaknesses, ensuring compliance, and improving risk management. This process also helps in building trust and adapting to emerging threats. Assessing security measures provides insights into how well systems protect company assets, reputation, and customer trust.

## *Methods for Evaluating Security Postures:*

- **Red Teaming:** Simulates real-world cyberattacks to test an organization's defenses. Google's Red Team, for example, regularly tests responses to cyber threats, refining its security measures.

- **Bug Bounty Programs:** External security researchers report vulnerabilities for rewards. Facebook's bug bounty program has been instrumental in identifying and fixing numerous security flaws.

- **Capture-the-Flag (CTF) Competitions:** These educational competitions enhance participants' cybersecurity skills through simulated challenges. The DEF CON CTF competition is one of the most prestigious, promoting skill-building in the cybersecurity community.

## Red Teaming

**Red teaming** involves simulating advanced attacks that mimic real-world threats. Teams are composed of skilled security professionals who use sophisticated techniques to challenge an organization's security systems. Red teaming exercises often reveal hidden vulnerabilities, helping to fortify defenses against future attacks.

| Team composition | Frequency | Outputs |
|---|---|---|
| Experienced security professionals | Scheduled intervals (e.g., quarterly) | Detailed reports highlighting vulnerabilities and improvement recommendations. |

## Bug Bounty Programs

**Bug bounty programs** invite external researchers to identify and report vulnerabilities in exchange for monetary rewards. These programs tap into a diverse pool of talent, enabling organizations to discover vulnerabilities that internal teams may overlook.

| Participant composition | Frequency | Outputs |
| --- | --- | --- |
| Security enthusiasts and professionals | Ongoing | Vulnerability reports, with payouts based on the severity of the findings. |

## Capture-the-Flag Competitions

**CTF competitions** provide an engaging platform for individuals to hone their cybersecurity skills. These events simulate real-world scenarios, enabling participants to solve security-related challenges in a competitive environment.

| Participant composition | Frequency | Outputs |
| --- | --- | --- |
| Beginners to experts in cybersecurity | Regularly hosted by organizations | Points-based rankings and skill-building opportunities. |

## Concluding Remarks

I hope this chapter has given you a comprehensive understanding of real-world penetration testing scenarios and methods. With the knowledge you've gained throughout this guide, you're well-equipped to apply these techniques effectively.

But before we wrap up, I've prepared a concluding message for you in the next chapter to highlight key takeaways and reinforce your learning.

# CONCLUSION

Did you know that companies employing ethical hackers are staying ahead in the cybersecurity race? These organizations tend to have more secure systems compared to those that don't, showcasing the invaluable role of ethical hacking in today's world.

As we conclude this journey through *Linux for Hackers*, I hope you've gained a wealth of knowledge and practical skills to enhance your ethical hacking capabilities. Each chapter in this book has been designed to provide you with the insights needed to navigate the complexities of modern cybersecurity.

## Key Takeaways

Understanding ethical hacking is a crucial step in protecting systems against cyber threats. By learning how to be a skilled ethical hacker, you not only strengthen your own expertise but also become a valuable asset to any organization, with growing opportunities in the field of cybersecurity.

### Why Ethical Hacking Matters

Ethical hacking takes a proactive approach to security. By identifying and addressing vulnerabilities before malicious actors can exploit them, organizations safeguard their networks, data, and reputation. For instance, conducting a penetration test that mimics a real-world attack allows you to uncover weaknesses that might otherwise go unnoticed, preventing costly security breaches.

## Getting Started With Ethical Hacking

If you're just starting out, all the concepts and techniques discussed in this book will serve as a solid foundation. Begin with mastering the basics of networks, systems, and operating environments. Explore additional resources, such as online courses, interactive labs, and certifications like CompTIA Security+ or Certified Ethical Hacker (CEH), which provide structured learning recognized by employers.

## Essential Tools for Ethical Hackers

As covered throughout this book, tools like **Wireshark**, **Metasploit**, and **Nmap** are indispensable for ethical hackers. Learning how to effectively use these tools will streamline your processes and enhance your ability to detect, analyze, and exploit vulnerabilities. Familiarizing yourself with these tools is one of the most practical steps toward becoming a proficient ethical hacker.

## Building Skills Through Practice

Practical experience is key to mastering ethical hacking. Setting up a home lab using virtual machines (VMs) allows you to simulate networks and environments where you can safely practice and refine your techniques. Platforms like **Hack The Box** and **TryHackMe** offer real-world challenges to apply your skills, while participating in **bug bounty programs** and **Capture-the-Flag (CTF) competitions** can further enhance your expertise in a competitive, hands-on setting.

## Keeping Up With Trends

Cybersecurity is constantly evolving, with new threats emerging regularly. Staying informed about these changes is crucial to maintaining effectiveness as an ethical hacker. Engage with cybersecurity blogs, attend webinars, and participate in online forums to stay current with the latest developments.

## Participating in Webinars and Conferences

Attending webinars and conferences is a great way to deepen your understanding of cybersecurity trends. These events often feature industry experts sharing insights into recent breaches and emerging attack techniques. Virtual attendance options now make it easier to participate in these discussions, giving you access to valuable knowledge from anywhere in the world.

# Time to Move Forward

Investing in advanced ethical hacking techniques opens doors to a wide range of career opportunities. From finance to healthcare, industries across the board are in need of skilled cybersecurity professionals. The demand for ethical hackers continues to grow, and by dedicating time to learning, practicing, and networking, you position yourself as a key player in the cybersecurity field.

## Real-World Application of Skills

Applying your skills in real-world settings solidifies your understanding. Consider volunteering with nonprofits or small businesses to assist with their cybersecurity needs. This not only provides practical experience but also expands your portfolio, making you a more competitive candidate in the job market.

## Certifications and Courses

Certifications such as **CompTIA Security+**, **Certified Ethical Hacker (CEH)**, and **Certified Information Systems Security Professional (CISSP)** provide structured pathways to enhance your expertise. These programs cover a wide range of topics, from the basics of cybersecurity to advanced hacking techniques, and are well-regarded by employers. Completing these certifications demonstrates your commitment to the field and can make you stand out in a competitive job market.

## A Parting Message

Thank you for embarking on this journey through advanced ethical hacking techniques. Your commitment to expanding your cybersecurity knowledge is commendable, and I trust the skills and insights gained from this book will serve you well in your future endeavors.

Stay vigilant, stay ethical, and above all, stay curious—the world of cybersecurity is vast, and it's waiting for your contributions.

# REFERENCES

*Advanced persistent threat: Attack stages, examples & mitigation.* (n.d.). HackerOne.
https://www.hackerone.com/knowledge-center/advanced-persistent-threats-attack-stages-
examples-and-mitigation

alphaSeclab. (2024). *All resource collection projects.* GitHub.
https://github.com/alphaSeclab/obfuscation-stuff/blob/master/Readme_en.md

*Analyzing BufferOverflow with GDB.* (n.d.). GeeksforGeeks.
https://www.geeksforgeeks.org/analyzing-bufferoverflow-with-gdb/

*Anatomy of an APT attack: Step by step approach.* (n.d.). Infosec.
https://www.infosecinstitute.com/resources/hacking/anatomy-of-an-apt-attack-step-by-
step-approach/

*AntiVirus evasion techniques.* (2024, July 3). Hive Pro. https://hivepro.com/blog/antivirus-
evasion-techniques/

Baker, K. (2023, April 17). *Malware analysis explained | Steps & examples.* CrowdStrike.
https://www.crowdstrike.com/cybersecurity-101/malware/malware-analysis/

Borges, E. (2020, May 26). How to detect CVEs using Nmap vulnerability scan scripts. *Security
Trails.* https://securitytrails.com/blog/nmap-vulnerability-scan

*BSAM: Bluetooth security assessment methodology.* (n.d.). Tarlogic.
https://www.tarlogic.com/bsam/

Buffer overflow attacks in C++: A hands-on guide. (2022, July 27). *Snyk.*
https://snyk.io/blog/buffer-overflow-attacks-in-c/

Cukier, M. (2007, February 9). *Study: Hackers attack every 39 seconds.* University of Maryland.
https://eng.umd.edu/news/story/study-hackers-attack-every-39-seconds

A deep dive into advanced persistent threats (APT). (n.d.). *ForeNova.*
https://www.forenova.com/blog/deep-dive-into-advanced-persistent-threats

Dhaameel. (2023, July 11). *The power and history of Kali Linux.* Medium.
https://dhaameel.medium.com/the-power-and-history-of-kali-linux-154f6fee8f3b

Dizdar, A. (2022, April 4). What is XSS? Impact, types, and prevention. *Bright Security.*
https://brightsec.com/blog/xss/

EC-Council. (2023, April 27). *How to use the Metasploit framework for penetration testing.*
Cybersecurity Exchange. https://www.eccouncil.org/cybersecurity-exchange/penetration-
testing/metasploit-framework-for-penetration-testing/

Firdiyanto, I. (2023, July 12). *Sandboxing in malware analysis.* Medium.
https://medium.com/@ilham.firdiyanto/cybersecurity101-sandboxing-in-malware-analysis-
ee4bc5382bce

Gibert, D., Mateu, C., & Planes, J. (2020, March). The rise of machine learning for detection and
classification of malware: Research developments, trends and challenges. *Journal of
Network and Computer Applications.* https://doi.org/10.1016/j.jnca.2019.102526

Gibert, D., Mateu, C., & Planes, J. (2020, March). The rise of machine learning for detection and
classification of malware: Research developments, trends and challenges. *Journal of
Network and Computer Applications.* https://doi.org/10.1016/j.jnca.2019.102526

Hacking the 3-way handshake: Exploiting vulnerabilities in WPA2. (2024, February 22). *Blue
Goat Cyber.* https://bluegoatcyber.com/blog/hacking-the-3-way-handshake-exploiting-
vulnerabilities-in-wpa2/

*How cybercriminals try to combat & bypass antivirus protection.* (2021, January 13). Kaspersky.
https://usa.kaspersky.com/resource-center/threats/combating-antivirus

How to protect against rogue access points on Wi-Fi. (n.d.). *Byos*. https://www.byos.io/blog/how-to-protect-against-rogue-access-points-on-wi-fi

IoT penetration testing explained. (2024, February). *Blue Goat Cyber*. https://bluegoatcyber.com/blog/iot-penetration-testing-explained/

Joseph, E. (2023, July 12). *Burp Suite vs OWASP ZAP: A comparison series*. Medium. https://medium.com/@Ekenejoseph/burp-suite-vs-owasp-zap-a-comparison-series-8e34162c42e6

*Kali Linux metapackages*. (n.d.). Kali Linux. https://www.kali.org/docs/general-use/metapackages/

Kennedy, D., O'Gorman, J., Kearns, D., & Aharoni, M. (2011, July 15). *Metasploit: The penetration tester's guide*. No Starch Press.

Kime, C. (2022, February 8). *Nmap vulnerability scanning made easy: Tutorial*. ESecurityPlanet. https://www.esecurityplanet.com/networks/nmap-vulnerability-scanning-made-easy/

Kosinski, M. (2024). *What is a data breach?* IBM. https://www.ibm.com/topics/data-breach

Lee, C. (2023, March 15). *25 top penetration testing tools for Kali Linux in 2023*. StationX. https://www.stationx.net/penetration-testing-tools-for-kali-linux/

More, T. (2023, October 31). *Malware forensics*. Medium. https://medium.com/@tanmaymore06/malware-forensics-d55bd6d08aad

Morgan, S. (2022, October 17). Cybercrime to cost the world 8 trillion annually in 2023. *Cybercrime Magazine*. https://cybersecurityventures.com/cybercrime-to-cost-the-world-8-trillion-annually-in-2023/

*Multiple nation-state threat actors exploit CVE-2022-47966 and CVE-2022-42475*. (2023, September 7). CISA. https://www.cisa.gov/news-events/cybersecurity-advisories/aa23-250a

Nagaraj, K. (2023, June 18). *The OSI model for cyber security: A comprehensive guide to securing network communications*. Medium. https://cyberw1ng.medium.com/the-osi-model-for-cyber-security-a-comprehensive-guide-to-securing-network-communications-b8b0170675dd

Network segmentation and how it can prevent ransomware. (2022, May 19). *Threat Intelligence.*
https://www.threatintelligence.com/blog/network-segmentation

Nur, Jamil, N., Yulisa Yusoff, & Laiha, M. (2024, January 1). A systematic literature review on advanced persistent threat behaviors and its detection strategy. *Journal of Cybersecurity.*
https://doi.org/10.1093/cybsec/tyad023

OS credential dumping. (n.d.). MITRE ATT&CK. https://attack.mitre.org/techniques/T1003/

*The OSI model: What is it?* (2024, August 8). SentinelOne.
https://www.sentinelone.com/cybersecurity-101/what-is-the-osi-model/

*Our most advanced penetration testing distribution, ever.* (2018, December 4). Kali.
https://www.kali.org/

Pastore, F. (2022, October 9). *Basic shellcode exploitation.* Medium.
https://2h3ph3rd.medium.com/basic-shellcode-exploitation-1e9ff274a194

*Rogue access point.* (n.d.). Zimperium. https://www.zimperium.com/glossary/rogue-access-point/

Semaphore. (2023, June 23). *Dynamic application security testing (DAST) tools are tools used to identify vulnerabilities in running applications. They operate by measuring an application's runtime inputs and outputs; testing the application's performance by sending it a range of inputs, including malicious input, SQL injection attacks, and cross-site scripting attacks. By doing so, they can identify vulnerabilities that may not be apparent during static analysis or code reviews.* Medium.
https://semaphoreci.medium.com/dynamic-application-security-testing-dast-tools-are-tools-used-to-identify-vulnerabilities-in-affe2fd9e3c1

*Stack shellcode.* (2018). Hacktricks. https://book.hacktricks.xyz/binary-exploitation/stack-overflow/stack-shellcode

*Testing directory traversal file include.* (n.d.). OWASP. https://owasp.org/www-project-web-security-testing-guide/v42/4-Web_Application_Security_Testing/05-Authorization_Testing/01-Testing_Directory_Traversal_File_Include

*Testing for cookies attributes.* (n.d.). OWASP. https://owasp.org/www-project-web-security-testing-guide/latest/4-Web_Application_Security_Testing/06-Session_Management_Testing/02-Testing_for_Cookies_Attributes

*Top 19 penetration testing tools.* (2024). Check Point Software. https://www.checkpoint.com/cyber-hub/cyber-security/what-is-penetration-testing/top-19-penetration-testing-tools/

What is behavioral biometrics? Use cases, types and benefits. (2023, February 28). *ASEE.* https://cybersecurity.asee.io/blog/what-is-behavioral-biometrics-authentication/

*What is cross-site scripting (XSS) and how to prevent it?* (n.d.). Portswigger. https://portswigger.net/web-security/cross-site-scripting

What is GPG? (2021, February 23). *Go Anywhere.* https://www.goanywhere.com/blog/what-is-gpg

*What is network segmentation?* (n.d.). Palo Alto Networks. https://www.paloaltonetworks.com/cyberpedia/what-is-network-segmentation

*What is the OSI model?* (2024, August 8). SentinelOne. https://www.sentinelone.com/cybersecurity-101/what-is-the-osi-model/

*The yasm modular assembler project.* (2024). Yasm. https://yasm.tortall.net/

Made in the USA
Monee, IL
29 December 2024

75500684R00227